# SURPRISED

## The Science & Art of Engagement

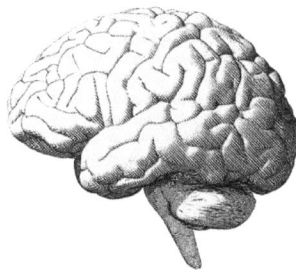

© 2023 Rich Carr, BcID
Published by Brain-centric, LLC

*For free bonuses, including ready-to-use templates, training, support, and other resources, visit* https://surprised.brain-centric.com

Hardback ISBN 979-8-9873359-5-6
Paperback ISBN 979-8-9873359-2-5
Audiobook ISBN 979-8-9873359-4-9
e-Book ISBN 979-8-9873359-6-3

Brain-centric, LLC.
14901 80th St E
Puyallup, WA 98372

Front Cover Design by Katarina Nešković
Back Cover Design by Joey Kwan
Interior Layout by Rich Carr

*Surprised: The Science & Art of Engagement* is available for bulk orders! Contact pfc@brain-centric.com for more information.

# Contents

3

# Everything we remember is shaped by Surprise.

**Surprise**: /sər͵prīz
**noun**
That abrupt moment of discovery, where what we think we know meets the unexpected twist of reality.

**Surprised**: /sər͵prīzd
**adj**
Experiencing the unforeseen, which sparks a mix of emotions and heightens awareness or reflection; often acting as a catalyst for renewed engagement or a shift in understanding.

**Surprisation**: /sər͵prīzāˈSHən/
**noun**
The act or process of strategically implementing unexpected feelings or reactions that enhance engagement, awareness, or inspire a shift in perspective, often resulting in deeper connections or insights.

# START

In a dimly lit and dilapidated apartment, a man sits alone, submerged in contemplation, burdened by profound sorrow. He rhythmically grinds his teeth, each grate mirroring the shadow of his troubled mind in this musky space. With a damp forehead cradled in his hand between an arthritic thumb and forefinger, the smoke of the flickering candle gasps for more fuel, and the hum of his dying refrigerator punctuates the background serving as a grim soundtrack to his reality.

When it seems his evening couldn't get any darker, the room suddenly erupts into a chorus of "Happy Birthday."

An old friend, someone he hadn't seen in years, unexpectedly walks in with a cake, his face glowing with joy. In that split second, the man's melancholy is pierced by a golden beam of Surprise, and the whole emotional landscape changes.

### Surprise: Engagement Amplified

I wrote SURPRISED: The Science & Art of Engagement with the core principle that Surprise is the catalyst transitioning individuals from passive observers to active participants. Surprise initiates engagement, sustains engagement, and elevates engagement. While there's a plethora of Surprise you can employ for various objectives, the endgame remains consistent: facilitating engagement. Whether executed with subtlety or grandeur, this transitory yet potent emotion amplifies your connection with others instantly.

Throughout the book, I'll guide you on leveraging Surprise for distinct purposes using specific instances. Given its universal applicability, examples span from business strategies to personal interactions, sales pitches to parenting moments, leadership scenarios to daily interactions. These diverse instances underscore the versatility and efficacy of strategically deployed Surprise. Envision yourself in these narratives and adapt them to enrich your personal and professional engagements. It's fun.

## An Emotion, A Bridge, A Connector

To truly grasp the transformative power of how emotions affect engagement and how Surprise facilitates that transition, ponder the following graphic metaphor, stretching out before you in a spectrum of colors and scenery.

Imagine standing before a broad panoramic landscape representing the whole of your emotional spectrum. On one end, there are deep, crimson valleys which symbolize emotions like sadness, anger, or fear. These valleys evoke the visceral feelings of stress, the heat of a fresh argument, or the boredom of another conference call. When you're fixated in these valleys, your brain feels trapped, a prisoner to its own thoughts, preventing genuine interaction or engagement with the world around. You can't see yourself out.

On the opposite side of this emotional landscape, imagine dazzling green summits representing the emotion of happiness and its nuanced shades of acceptance, trust, and enjoyment. Here, atop these peaks, your mind feels liberated and poised, completely open and ready to actively engage, connect, and respond to whatever comes at you.

Now, here's where the magic happens: Envision a golden-yellow bridge, symbolizing Surprise, that connects the valleys to the peaks. This isn't just any bridge; it's a transformative pathway possessing an undeniable, observable presence in our experiences. Like a cold splash of water on your face or the warmth of the sun on a winter's day as you emerge from the shadows, you travel this bridge, from the valley to the peaks, and your brain loves the trip. Much like discovering a shortcut during a mountain expedition or when that split-second a lightning strike reveals a visible path in the darkest of night, Surprise is that momentary brilliance that links the deep red valleys to the lofty green peaks facilitating your transition between the two.

That takes you from unengaged through every level of engagement, placing you in the dynamic intersection of attention, connection, and meaningful interaction. True engagement transcends surface-level interest, drawing the individual deeper, evoking emotions, curiosity, and delivers a genuine commitment to the subject or experience at hand. Shaped by Surprise, engagement is the product of moments that challenge, resonate, and spark a transformative shift in understanding or perspective. Surprise is the bridge between passive consumption and active participation.

This golden bridge of Surprise ensures that, no matter where you or your audience stand in the emotional landscape, there's always a way to cross over.

Surprise does so much more than offer pause from our emotional troughs; it accentuates those emerald peaks. When you stumble upon a piece of unexpected good news or witness an unprompted act of kindness, the joy you feel is not mere happiness — it's an intensified burst of elation. Surprise and its possibilities for you are boundless, profound, and teeming with applications for you to masterfully redefine the understanding of your audience.

At its core, this book elevates Surprisation to a masterful strategy carrying the power to create impact, shift perspectives, and kindle inspiration. This golden touch in communicating beckons, challenging you to braid it into narratives that resonate deeply and endure for effect.

When Surprise strikes, it's like a pause button for our brain, momentarily suspending our regular programming. This slight interruption isn't a glitch; it's a feature. It makes us receptive, open to new ideas and feelings. Think of it as the brain's refresh button, clearing away cognitive cobwebs and making space for new tabs of thoughts.

The Surprise in any communication is what is ultimately remembered. Embrace the art and science of this incredible emotion.

## The Superpower of Engagement

Picture yourself back when electric vehicles were intriguing novelties rather than the norm. If a passerby had mentioned, "Soon, electric trucks will be towing cargo across continents, and charging stations will outnumber gas pumps in many cities," might your eyebrows have shot up in disbelief? That's the gripping power of Surprise - the sledgehammer to complacency when a future vision stretches the elasticity of your comfort zone.

Fast-forward to the here and now, where artificial intelligence has shifted from science fiction to ubiquitous. Our daily routines are seamlessly entwined with prompt responses. Artificial intelligence navigates our commute, juggles our schedules, is the DJ of our preferred tunes, and even manipulates our home environments. The Surprise of yesterday is the banal normality of today.

But the echo of Surprise doesn't fade away. The Surprise is always remembered, as you'll soon learn.

As AI continues to evolve and shatter our expectations - from self-navigating care to algorithms that moonlight as artists, storytellers, and even medics with diagnostic precision - each breakthrough lands as a fresh Surprise, a hook that captures our attention and curiosity.

Reflect on it. How often have you been the herald of some AI novelty, stirring conversation amongst friends, family, or colleagues, playing with the possibilities at work, or musing over the future implications?

Behold the might of Surprise. It's more than an attention magnet. It's a thought catalyst, a communal journey of exploration and learning, a lesson that goes deep and is profoundly personal.

The one who experiences Surprise follows the breadcrumb trail of curiosity, engages in dialog, and evolves with the new normal. You're no longer a passive consumer of the story; you're a pivotal character.

Reflect momentarily on the tide of disruptive innovations that have shaped our world. Each groundbreaking shift wasn't just a headline in the news; it was a moment that halted your stride, demanded your attention, and resonated with an irresistible allure.

Remember that initial awe, the flurry of questions, the rush to share or discuss it with others? These aren't mere technological advancements; they're potent catalysts, inviting you to engage, adapt, and actively participate in the evolving narrative of progress. Whether it was the first time you tapped a touchscreen, spoke to a digital assistant, or took a ride in an electric vehicle, the essence remains unchanged: innovation doesn't just present a change—it beckons you to immerse yourself within it.

Surprise is a lightning strike of inspiration. The spark inflames curiosity, *stirs engagement*, and rockets us into the future. Each Surprising revelation transforms us from passive observers into active explorers in the thrilling expedition of discovery you want your audience to uncover.

With this book and the knowledge it provides, your influence escapes the boundaries of the typical and crafts lasting impressions that drive action you're looking for.

No matter your role—a parent shepherding a child's worldview, a salesperson persuading and influencing, a coach igniting motivation, or an educator cognitively sculpting minds—this book is your road map to engaging anybody, in anything, at any time.

Tailor a Surprise that seizes their attention to immerse their minds in a dance of engagement that transforms your facilitation into an unforgettable personal experience for them.

Because Surprise isn't limited to grand gestures or headline news, you'll be threading subtle deviations into the expectations of your audience that commands attention. It's about perceiving the heartbeat of anticipation and punctuating it with an unexpected twist that reverberates deep within. The connection transcends the fleeting moment, creating an indelible mark and fostering deep understanding.

Reading this book is an investment in self-improvement, refining your communication skills, and extending your sphere of influence. As you uncover these pages, you'll acquire the insights to mesmerize your audience, no matter who they are, where they are, and your message. This book enables you to capture the attention of one or engage the masses.

In your world, brimming with relentless information, the ability to communicate effectively and persuasively is a priceless asset. For those aspiring to make an impact, to persuade genuinely, and to influence with integrity, I implore you to invite Surprise to be your navigator in the complex terrain of impactful & persuasive communication of consequences.

As you uncover the potency of Surprise and learn to master it, you'll enhance your communication skills and revolutionize the essence of your engagements. By perfecting this art, you'll become more than a communicator. You'll become a riveting storyteller, a compelling influencer, and a potent change-maker.

Harness the power of Surprise. Let it breathe new life and engagement into your communications. Develop Surprise as your superpower. Because, frankly, that's precisely what it should be.

### Engagement Is The Game

The winding back roads of Washington state might seem like an odd place to start a conversation about engagement. But it was there, in a little roadside diner tucked between the curves of the Cascade mountains, that I stumbled upon a metaphor for something much more significant. I was calming a craving for a woodland drive and breakfast fare served on thick, white plates. I overheard an older couple at the next table as I sipped my excellent freshly-roasted coffee.

They were reminiscing about their first date, and the husband was laughing about how he'd surprised his wife by taking a wrong turn that led them to a magical overlook, a view that took their breath away. It was an unplanned, delightful accident. Yet, that Surprise twist led them to a moment of genuine connection, a bond that had lasted for decades.

That story reminded me of something quite extraordinary: the jack-in-the-box.

Now, stay with me here.

A child's toy, with its predictable melody, turns of the crank, and then - bam - a clown springs out. It's unexpected, powerful, and captivating. That sudden interruption of the repetitiveness triggers our curiosity and takes our engagement levels soaring. It's in this Surprise bridge that the heart of engagement is discovered.

Engagement is tossed around in business meetings or educational seminars as a destination, but it is much more than a noun. Treat engagement as a verb. It's a fundamental human dance of trust, intrigue, and relationship-building. It's as vital as the food and air we breathe, whether we are connecting with students, clients, children, or staff. It's a blend of art and science that finds its roots in the recesses of the human brain.

In "Brain-centric Design: The Surprising Neuroscience Behind Learning with Deep Understanding," Kieran O'Mahony, PhD., and I peeled back the layers of this fascinating concept, mapping out the road from simple awareness to profound comprehension. Throughout "SURPRISED: The Science & Art of Engagement" I will call out several engagement instruments from Brain-centric Design to ensure understanding and application here because it's a framework for life, a way of engaging with the world.

Let's deconstruct the layers, one by one, in a way that can be applied practically to your particular skill set.

### Engagement Has Layers

Engagement, the arrangement to do something, begins by 'making visible' via a simple acknowledgment of presence, the starting point of trust, when something suddenly becomes evident. It's like that first glance between two strangers across a room.

Next, we create a 'psychologically safe' environment where honesty and authenticity are cherished. It's like finding a confidante in a friend who allows you to be your true self.

Then, we move to 'emotional connection.' Here, the heartstrings are plucked, where empathy and compassion take center stage. It's the emotional resonance that turns acquaintances into friends.

The story grows more complex as we enter 'collaborative' territory, a symphony of different voices, a collective creation. It's the group project that leads to something more significant than the sum of its parts.

From there, we rise to 'generative' and 'contributive' engagement. Ideas are not just shared but actively cultivated and nourished. The brainstorming session leads to innovation, the contribution that adds a unique piece to the puzzle.

Finally, we reach the climax, the 'co-creative' engagement, where everyone paints on the same canvas and writes the same story. It's a masterpiece crafted by many hands, the orchestra playing in perfect harmony.

The magic in these layers and their profound potential is that each layer is predictable and manageable. When you know it's coming, when you know it is there, then you plan for it.

In the kitchen, the layers of engagement are easily evident.

**Making Visible** - By 'selecting the right ingredients,' an acknowledgment of the base flavor. It's like the first glance at a set of ingredients laid out on a kitchen counter.

**Psychologically Safe** - Next, the 'perfect setting' where the oven's temperature and cookware come into play. It's like having the right tools that let your culinary skills shine.

**Emotional Connection** - Then, we dive into 'mixing and blending.' Here, the flavors meld, and aromas start to emerge. It's the gentle stir that transforms individual items into a cohesive mixture.

**Collaborative** - The process gets intricate when we enter 'layering and texture,' combining different elements to give depth. Think of it as carefully layering a lasagna, ensuring each layer complements the other.

**Generative/Contributive** - We progress to 'seasoning and refining.' Here, spices aren't just sprinkled; they're thoughtfully added, bringing out the dish's essence. It's like the last-minute taste test that prompts a dash of salt or a squeeze of lemon.

**Co-Creative** - Finally, we arrive at the grand finale, the 'presentation and garnishing,' where everything comes together on the plate, telling a unified culinary story. It's the pièce de résistance, the dish served with flair and enjoyed with applause.

In our world filled with information overload, engagement has become the top currency. The ability to use that currency for understanding and application in your communications is what sets you apart, what makes you resonate in a world filled with noise.

Engagement takes planning and your understanding of what you want your audience to walk away with in the first place. We don't just engage, we engage for a purpose that can be measured.

Remember the jack-in-the-box next time you find yourself in a diner, classroom, or boardroom. At its core, this journey revolves around truly grasping a subject—feeling it resonate within you in such a way that you're not just aware, but profoundly connected. It's about harnessing the power of engagement, which is the captivating force that binds us, sparks our curiosity, and compels us to act. It's the difference between passive hearing and active listening. It's about mastering the art of cognitive communication, speaking not just to minds but to hearts and souls. For those bold enough to embrace this approach, to see the world through this transformative lens, the benefits are boundless. A vibrant, evolving world awaits.

Together, let's shape and own it.

# SURPRISED

## The Science

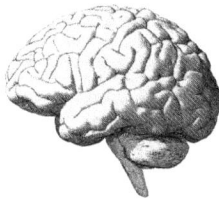

# SURPRISE. YOU WIN.

Easing into the vibrant space of Surprise is like unlocking a door in your mind that you never knew existed. Picture yourself on a regular day, managing your chores and tasks, chatting with the people you chat with, or just navigating your life's daily doings. With Surprise in your toolkit, every communication you have holds exciting potential, and each obstacle you face becomes an opportunity for personal triumph.

Grasping Surprise as an instrument for engaging your audience is your game-changer, turning the routine into magic in your hands. It's the key to breaking free from monotony and predictability. It means becoming the person in the room who can turn an ordinary presentation into an unforgettable one who can inspire and motivate effortlessly.

The benefits are immediate. People remember you. They're intrigued by your approach and captivated by your unpredictability. Opportunities find their way to you because you're not just another face in the crowd, but the one that made them look twice, think more profoundly and feel more.

Embracing Surprise is your ticket to a more vibrant, memorable, and impactful existence. If tangible results are what you seek, here's your goldmine:

**Enhanced Influence** - Harness Surprise to pierce through distractions, making you the beacon that lights up every room. Whether rallying your team, captivating students or crafting that unforgettable moment, Surprise supercharges your charisma and amplifies your influence.

**Deepened Connections** - It's more than just grabbing eyes—it's about forging heart-to-heart connections. Turn those brief chats into lifelong memories, deepening and enriching every relationship.

**Improved Adaptability** - Life throws curveballs. With Surprise knowledge, you don't just use it; you ride life's unpredictable waves with unmatched flair and grace.

**Unleashed Creativity** - Dive deep into Surprise, challenging the usual and fueling that fiery creativity. It's an open invitation to redraw boundaries and set your spirit free.

**Amplified Impact** - Turn the humdrum into the electric with Surprise in your toolkit. Be it a presentation, an event, a conversation with a coworker, or a lesson, sprinkle a bit of Surprise and watch your impact skyrocket.

You feel it. You unlock a renewed sense of awe, shake off old views, and fan the flames of endless curiosity. It's like pulling off tinted glasses and witnessing the world in vivid colors, where every moment brims with fresh excitement and intrigue.

To keep things simple and avoid diving too deep into scientific terms, I'll only include essential information to clarify the topic. Let's begin by setting the groundwork for what's ahead.

Surprise is a powerful tool for crafting stories, marketing products, shaking the status quo, and convincing others. Surprise's relationship with engagement is deeply rooted in neuroscience and psychological studies. Here are some compelling pieces of evidence:

**Neuroscientific Basis**: The brain's reward system releases dopamine in response to unpredictable stimuli. [1] Surprise serves as such an unexpected stimulus, leading to dopamine release, which is associated with pleasure, reward, and motivation. The more dopamine our brain releases, the more engaged and attentive we become.

**Enhanced Memory Retention**: Studies have shown that the amygdala, which processes emotions, can boost memory encoding and storage when stimulated by emotional events.[2] Because Surprise is an emotional response, surprising events or information can lead to better memory retention.

**Stimulating Curiosity**: Surprise naturally triggers curiosity, making individuals more likely to seek further information and remain engaged with the content.[3] It creates an information gap, which humans are naturally inclined to fill.

**Facilitating Change in Behavior**: Surprising stimuli can lead to reevaluating existing beliefs and understandings, prompting a shift in behavior or a change in perspective, essential for engagement in learning and development contexts.[4]

**Cognitive Engagement and Enhanced Attention**: Unexpected or surprising events cause individuals to pay more attention, increasing cognitive engagement.[5] This heightened attention ensures that the individual is more deeply engrossed in the task or information at hand.

As evidenced by these studies, incorporating Surprise can serve as a potent tool for boosting engagement across various domains, from education to marketing. When people are surprised, they're more attentive, curious, and motivated, ensuring more profound and lasting interactions with the content or experience presented to them.

This book is your expedition, your evolution. It's about mastering an art that elevates the mundane to the magical. And that's a craft worth diving into as we unfold in the chapters ahead.

Lastly, before we venture deeper into 'The Science' of this book, I'd like to pause for a moment. Picture this moment when I step out from behind the curtain, not as the book's author, but as a fellow traveler on the quest for understanding the science and art of engagement.

Why? Because I believe in the power of communication, of making knowledge accessible and understandable. By translating this dense scientific language into relatable metaphors and analogies, I aim to bring its magic to your fingertips, and yes, I'll be citing the original thinkers every step of the way.

# THE PUPPETEER & THE DIRECTOR

In the delicate dance between the known and the unexpected lies the true magic of life – the delightful interplay of science and art.

In a quaint village nestled between rolling hills, there was an old puppet theater. The puppeteer, a wise elder with silver hair, would make the characters come alive, enchanting the audience with tales of heroes, magic, and faraway places. They watched, knowing the strings that moved, yet captivated by the story unfolding.

This puppet theater is very similar to our minds.

The puppeteer? That is our brain skillfully orchestrating a play based on the whispers and tales it hears from the world outside. The strings are our senses, sending signals and feeding information to create the most enthralling act. Every rustle of leaves, opinion, the note of a distant song, a banner ad on a website, and the fragrance of blooming flowers get weaved into this grand performance. This show is our perception of reality – our brain's own crafted model of the world.

Every puppeteer orchestrates the play using the same instruments, but the elements that feed the narrative are different for each of us—every one.

The plot thickens: What happens when an uninvited character suddenly enters our personal stage? A door appears out of nowhere, exposing something incredible. A lighthouse in a stormy saga? This unexpected twist is the Surprise.

Such Surprises leave the puppeteer – our brain – momentarily stunned. It scrambles to understand how to incorporate this new player into the narrative. The strings quiver, the scene shifts, and the story takes a new direction. In this unexpected moment, our brain is furiously adjusting, reevaluating, and rewriting the script. The theater of our mind has to learn from this sudden turn of events, modify the tale, and realign the characters.

In our quaint village nestled between rolling hills, our puppeteer skillfully brings a world of characters to life, each with its own story.

If one were to peek behind the curtains of the learning science in cognitive neuroscience, this theater would become an apt metaphor for the intricate workings of the human mind. The puppeteer, you see, resembles the brain's robust neural network, an intricate weaving of billions of neurons, communicating and collaborating to give rise to our conscious experience[6].

The strings? Those represent our sensory pathways, each transmitting signals from the outside world, informing and guiding the puppeteer. For instance, when the wind rustles the leaves, auditory neurons in our brain fire in response to these auditory stimuli[7]. Every scent, sight, and sound is translated into electrochemical impulses, which our brain then weaves into the grand narrative of our perception[8].

Yet, despite the universality of our brain's structure and how it processes the incoming information, every narrative it crafts is unique, a symphony of personal experiences, memories, and learned responses.

Think of it: no two people will ever see, hear, or feel the exact same world.

But here lies the enigma: what happens when an unscripted event whacks your skull? When a mosquito flies up your nose or when your mobile phone suddenly goes dark? This intrusion is what we perceive as a 'surprise.' Neuroscientifically speaking, such events trigger a cascade of reactions, primarily in our brain's anterior cingulate cortex and the insular cortex, areas associated with unexpected outcomes and the processing of new information[9].

These surprises cause our brain to pause like our momentarily baffled puppeteer. This pause is the brain's way of reevaluating, determining whether the new information is a threat or an opportunity[10]. Then, like a masterful artist, it incorporates this Surprise into its ongoing story, reshaping the narrative, adjusting perceptions, and recalibrating predictions making the theater of our mind not a passive stage but a dynamic arena, constantly adapting, evolving, and rewriting its tales, influenced by the surprises life throws its way.

Another enigmatic figure watched from the shadows of this theater - the director. This director observed not just the puppeteer but the audience's reaction, every gasp, every laugh, every sigh. By understanding the puppeteer's craft and the audience's response, the director mastered the art of engagement.

You are the  director at any time you choose to be. Instead of a simple spectator or puppeteer, you're guiding, influencing, and orchestrating the dance of neurons and senses in others.

How?

Your thoughts, your ideas, and your ability to construct communications that engage via Surprise are the literal fuel to make engagement happen. It's like...

> Light Switches: Think of each neuron in the brain as like a light switch in your house. When something happens, someone flips the switch "on," and the light (or neuron) lights up. The more switches you flip, the brighter the room.

> High-Fives: Imagine you and your friends are in a line, waiting to give high-fives. When one friend gives a high-five, the next person in line gets excited and gives a high-five too. That's how neurons pass along their excitement.

> Popcorn Popping: Ever watched popcorn pop in a microwave? At first, one kernel pops, and then, suddenly, lots of them start popping all over. Each popping kernel is like a neuron responding when something fun or interesting happens.

When you understand that every brain crafts its narrative based on things you sense, stuff you remember, and ways you react because you've learned them, you grasp the core of communication. By introducing unexpected elements - a unique visual, a profound statement, or even a poignant pause - you can stimulate the anterior cingulate and insular cortex, brain regions responsible for processing new and unexpected information[9]. I like to call them the Surprise Twins. They're always on the lookout for new and unexpected things, ready to jump into action.

Why does this matter? Because Surprises create a momentary dissonance, a break in the ongoing narrative of the mind, giving you, the director, an opportunity to insert the material you need them to fully understand and absorb. While the brain reevaluates and adjusts its story in response to the unexpected element, it becomes more receptive and attentive. You've effectively engaged the audience, capturing their attention, making them hang onto your every word, awaiting the next twist, that concept you want them to focus on!

But this isn't just about startling or shocking. True art lies in the subtlety of the Surprise, in understanding the nuances of your audience's perception, and in crafting unexpected and deeply resonant moments that align with the concept you are communicating. It's about crafting experiences that aren't just heard or seen but deeply felt. Leveraging the science of surprise becomes a powerful tool across diverse fields, creating moments of heightened engagement and receptiveness.

When you deliver a preplanned and brief interruption in the regular thought processes of your audience this draws our attention, because our brain is trying to adjust to the unexpected element. This moment, when the brain is most receptive, is the perfect time to engage an audience, as they're keenly attentive and eager to know what comes next.

### Introduction to Application

**Parenting** - When introducing new habits or behaviors to children, Surprising them with an unexpected reward or turning the process into a fun game can make them more receptive to change. This can also make daily routines like cleaning or studying more engaging, ensuring they're attentive and eager to participate.

**Manager** - If you're introducing a significant change or policy, framing it with an unexpected positive spin or presenting it in a unique, creative manner can ensure team members are more receptive. It can make the news more digestible and employees more adaptable to the change.

**Business Coach -** If a coach wants their client to break out of a rut or consider a new perspective, introducing an unexpected exercise or unconventional method can capture the client's attention. It reinvigorates their thought process, making them more open to new strategies or ideas.

**Selling** - In sales, capturing a potential customer's attention is half the battle. If a salesperson introduces a product or service with an unexpected benefit or presents it uniquely, the client is more likely to be engaged. They'd be keen to learn more about what's being offered, awaiting further details or promotions.

**Education** - Facilitators, teachers, and educators often face the challenge of keeping students engaged. Introducing unexpected elements in lessons, like a surprising perspective or an unplanned field trip, can spike interest and attentiveness, ensuring students are listening and excited about what comes next in the lesson.

By embracing the science of Surprise, you can become a masterful director, choreographing the rhythm of hearts and minds. You can engage, inspire, and influence. In all its unpredictability, the world becomes a theater of endless possibilities, and you direct how it goes from here.

Every great story, every impactful message, is grounded in the unexpected science of Surprise. Harness it, and watch the magic unfold.

## SURPRISE AS A BRAIN PROCESS

What is fascinating about how Surprise is processed in your brain is that IT IS A PROCESS  in your brain: a series of actions or steps taken to achieve a particular end that YOU WILL LEARN!

These actions or steps are now a defined process, a set of steps that must be followed to achieve a goal or expectations. With this you will be able to understand and apply that process to your life.

Imagine a competitive soccer match, with players representing different parts of the brain. Each player has a role, moving fluidly across the field, and coordinating with teammates, all while keeping their eyes on the ball - our expectations.

First to react is our midfielder and the first of our 'Surprise Twins,' the anterior cingulate cortex. Like any good midfielder, it's alert, watching the game's flow, ensuring that passes connect and the rhythm is maintained. When an unexpected play occurs, perhaps an opponent's surprising maneuver, the midfielder first notices, signaling to the team that they need to adjust their strategy.

The goalkeeper, the other 'Surprise Twin,' our insula, assesses the emotional significance of that Surprise. Was that unexpected play a near miss that brought relief, or a spectacular goal from the opposing team that led to disappointment? Like a goalie deciding whether to dive to the left or the right, the insula evaluates the emotional weight of each unexpected event.

Racing on the wings, we have dopamine, always ready to surge forward with a burst of energy. If a surprise move results in a goal for our team, dopamine's pace quickens, amplifying the team's joy and excitement, much like a player would after scoring a goal.

Our big-time defender, the trusty amygdala, is always vigilant, always looking for Surprises that might threaten the team's lead. A sudden counter-attack from the opposition? The amygdala responds, organizing the defense and ensuring the team is safe from threats.

You hear a lot about the amygdala or the amygdalae (since there are two) because they are fascinating brain components. These almond-shaped structures (the word "amygdala" is derived from the Greek word "amygdale," which means "almond") are among the most vigilant members of the brain's ensemble, always attentive, never sleeping. Their primary mission? To keep you safe, day in and day out.

They're like dedicated security personnel, ceaselessly patrolling the perimeters of a vast estate. Eyes and ears never stray, constantly scanning for potential intruders or dangers. Whether it's a looming deadline, an unexpected encounter, or the sudden growl of a lurking predator, their radar picks it up. They are the guardians of our emotional and physical well-being.

When these sentinels spot a threat, they don't just sound the alarm; they rally the entire estate into action. Here's where the autonomic nervous system (ANS) comes into play. Think of the ANS as the rapid response team, always on standby. Directed by the amygdalae, the ANS springs into action, preparing the body for one of four possible responses: fight, flight, freeze, or fawn. It's a primordial mechanism ensuring our survival.

However, there are times when our vigilant guardians may overreact. Imagine a rustling in the bushes. In their determination to keep us safe, it could be just the wind, but the amygdalae might interpret it as a potential threat. This overreaction is what I referred to earlier as an 'amygdala hijack.' Instead of a gentle breeze, the amygdalae might perceive a prowler and trigger an intense fight or flight reaction. Suddenly, your heart races, your palms sweat, and you're ready to bolt or confront.

But why such a dramatic reaction? Evolution has hardwired our brains to prioritize safety. In the wild, it was often better to overreact to a rustling leaf than to underestimate the approach of a predator. Thus, our modern brains still carry this ancient programming. Your brain's most basic functions are to keep you alive and help you thrive.

In understanding the pivotal role of the amygdalae and their interactions with the ANS, we gain insight into our reactions, fears, and instinctual drives.

The strategic genius in our cerebral soccer game is the Prefrontal Cortex (PFC).

In our ongoing soccer metaphor, the Prefrontal Cortex can be considered the team's coach. Positioned off the field, the coach has an overarching view of the match. While the players, or different brain parts, are engrossed in the immediate plays, the PFC is always a few steps ahead, planning, predicting, and strategizing.

Much like a seasoned coach has seen countless matches and can predict the game's flow, our PFC holds our expectations. It considers past experiences, evaluates present circumstances, and predicts future outcomes. It sets the game plan based on these expectations.

Now, when there's an unexpected twist in the match – say, a Surprise goal from the opponent – the coach doesn't just throw in the towel. Instead, he quickly adapts the strategy. Similarly, when our expectations, those held in the PFC, are challenged by a Surprise, our brain adjusts these expectations to accommodate the new information.

During an amygdala hijack, the coach (PFC) might momentarily lose its cool, overshadowed by the impulsive reactions of the players. But, with training and experience, the coach learns to manage these situations better, guiding the team back on track. In real life, we call this self-regulating our emotions and being in charge of how we think and make decisions - maintaining focus even when faced with Surprises or challenges.

To master the game – or your next presentation– one doesn't just need agile players but also a wise, adaptive coach who can integrate the unexpected into the grand strategy, helping the team navigate challenges and emerge victorious.

## Expectations Always Come First

Every soccer match starts with a plan. Before the players even set foot on the field, the coach (our Prefrontal Cortex) has already formed a strategy. This strategy is rooted in expectations. The coach analyzes the opposing team, evaluates their own team's strengths and weaknesses, and recalls past matches. Similarly, in the theater of our mind, our expectations are shaped by past experiences, societal norms, and beliefs we've cultivated over time.

Now, picture a regular soccer fan, Tom. Over time, Tom has watched numerous matches and has developed certain expectations about how the game unfolds. He expects a certain flow, some tried-and-tested tactics, and, of course, some curveballs. Tom's set of expectations mirrors our life expectations. They are our rulebook, our map of how we believe events will or should unfold.

However, like every soccer fan, everyone has a unique set of expectations. Another person might expect aggressive plays because they have watched high-intensity matches, while yet another person, having seen more strategic games, expects careful and deliberate moves. Our personal histories, cultures, and experiences lead to these individual ideas of what to expect.

## Expectation Meets Reality

Now, back to our match. The whistle blows, and the game kicks off. As the minutes tick by, some of Tom's expectations are met – a few standard passes and some defensive plays. But then, out of the blue, a player attempts an audacious bicycle kick, something Tom hadn't expected. Surprise!

This deviation from Tom's prediction is where the spark of Surprise ignites. It's that unexpected bicycle kick during a predictable play. When our map – *our expectation of how things should go* – doesn't align with reality, the amygdala springs into action, signaling the brain that something's different and something better happen NOW!

Let's imagine this scene. A soccer player on the pitch, confronted with a situation that triggers the amygdala, putting them on the edge of an amygdala hijack. Here's how a player might express these responses verbally and physically, how Surprise affects us:

### Fight
*Verbally*: "You think you can intimidate me? Try me!"
*Physically*: Aggressive posture, confronting the person or situation head-on, possibly even leading to a physical altercation or getting in someone's face.

### Flight
*Verbally*: "I can't handle this right now."
*Physically*: Swiftly moving away from the scene, possibly even asking to be subbed out, or avoiding the confrontation by keeping distance on the pitch.

**Freeze**
*Verbally*: Silence or stuttered attempts at communication, unable to formulate a response.
*Physically*: A stunned deer-in-headlights appearance, standing immobile and unsure of the next move on the field.

**Fawn**
*Verbally*: "Hey, I'm sorry, okay? Let's just play the game."
*Physically*: Attempting to appease or placate the aggressor or situation, possibly with pacifying gestures, trying to smooth things over.

It's essential to remember that the amygdala hijack's automatic nature means the player might not even be consciously aware of their initial reaction until after it occurs. They are primal responses designed for survival, deeply embedded in our brains from our ancestral past.

## Adapting and Evolving

Post-surprise, our coach (the PFC) gets busy. Is this new strategy a one-off or something to be integrated into future plays? Should the team's approach change? Similarly, our brain reevaluates and updates our expectation map post-surprise.

For instance, if Ted repeatedly watches matches where players pull off unexpected moves, he might start expecting such spontaneity in future games. His map of a 'typical soccer match' evolves.

## Your Front Row Seat to Mastery

Let's picture the look and energy of a soccer stadium. The roar of the crowd, the anticipation in the air, and the game's rhythm unfolding on the field. Every player, strategy, and move is orchestrated with a purpose grounded in expectations.

In this grand stadium of life, you're not just a spectator but both a player and a coach. The instruments you possess, the intricate parts of your brain, are like the players on that field. They have been training, preparing, and functioning tirelessly to help you navigate your world. Like a star player knows when to dribble, pass, or score, your brain knows when to alert, engage, and Surprise.

## Your Secret Weapon – Surprise

Use Surprise as an unexpected bicycle kick AND a deliberate, calculated move. To communicate more persuasively, to engage your audience – be it a boardroom full of executives, a classroom of students, or a dinner table with family – requires understanding this potent instrument of Surprise. You become the game-changer when you recognize where, when, and how to interject Surprise.

Why is this so powerful? Because knowing the mechanics of Surprise – understanding the brain's response and how it reshapes expectations – enables you to connect, resonate, and engage more profoundly.

Your goals, your aspirations, and your expectations can be met more effectively when you grasp the art of engagement using the science of Surprise as your linchpin. By the end of this exploration, you won't merely be observing the game; you'll be setting the pace, steering the narrative, and leaving your mark on the field.

*"To accomplish great things, we must not only act but also dream; not only plan but also believe."*
*-Anatole France, French poet and writer*

## Science of Surprise Scouting Report

### Expectations
  - The origins of our expectation maps.
  - Recognize how these expectations shape our understanding and reactions to the world around us.

### Brain Instruments
  - Identify the critical components of our brain and how they function in the context of a soccer game metaphor.
  - Grasp the roles of the Prefrontal Cortex and the Amygdala in shaping our anticipations and responses.

### The Process
- Explore how the brain processes unexpected information and events.
- Understand the role of the anterior cingulate and insular cortex, our 'Surprise Twins,' in processing the unexpected.
- The amygdala's role in moments of Surprise.

### Engagement Via Surprise
- How Surprise serves as a tool to capture attention and enhance engagement.
- The art of weaving surprise into communication for deeper connections and better outcomes.

### Practical Application
- Learn how understanding the science of Surprise can revolutionize various professional fields, from parenting to educating.
- Equip oneself with strategies to harness the power of Surprise in everyday interactions and presentations.

### Reality
- Reflect on how our expectations, coupled with the science of Surprise, shape our perceived realities.
- Recognize the balance between our anticipations and the unfolding narrative of our lives and how we can be better directors of our stories.

Before you turn the page, reflect on what you've just read. What was Surprising?

## SURPRISE CAUSES BLINDNESS

Strolling through a busy Farmer's Market on the weekend, the exciting stalls offer an explosion of colors, textures, and sounds. Out of nowhere, a brilliant green and blue dragonfly with wings that seem to refract a world of colors makes its unexpected hissing appearance as it floats effortlessly in front of you, just out of reach. For that split second, it feels like time has halted, drawing your gaze and complete attention to its delicate dance.

Yet, the nature of attention is fickle; it's like a spotlight that can only shine on one thing at a time.

Lost in the mesmerizing path of the dragonfly, it's easy to overlook other unfolding events—the child trying to get your attention, the fragrant aroma of freshly baked bread, or the soft notes of a distant flute from a brusker dressed in balloons. Scientists call this the "attentional blink," a brief period where we might miss the next noteworthy event right after an unexpected one captures our focus.

Our attention operates on two distinct levels. The first is when we willingly decide where to focus (known as top-down attention). The second, more spontaneous kind, is when something out of the blue, like our dragonfly, commands our watch (termed bottom-up attention).

Understanding this could redefine strategies. Consider the perfect moment to introduce a Surprise in a speech or sales presentation.

Researchers have pinpointed that an unforeseen yet irrelevant event (like our fleeting dragonfly) can cause a brief lapse in noticing what immediately follows. They've termed this intriguing phenomenon "Inattentional blindness."[11] Intriguingly, by the second or third brush with our iridescent visitor, the brain recalibrates, less perturbed by its shimmering Surprise, highlighting the brain's ability to quickly adapt and deemphasize repetitive Surprises with no consequential meaning.

If this sounds familiar, it's because you see this all the time:

- The shepherd boy who falsely cried wolf once too often.
- An online personality oversharing every minute detail of their day.
- The local is shrugging off the impending storm, assuring it's another passing cloud.

For a Surprise to captivate consistently, it must constantly evolve. Otherwise, its sheen wears off, and it's greeted with a mental shrug of, "Is this still worth my attention?"

But let's not rush. Let's unpack this.

Diligent scientists and researchers dug deeper, designing a battery of tests to better understand the nuances of Inattentional blindness.

One study aimed to see if this phenomena sprouted solely because the Surprising element was an anomaly amid the unexciting. So, they adjusted the setup, making the surprise element just as familiar as everything else. The result? When the Surprise was no longer rare, the Inattentional blindness affect dissolved.

The takeaway? A Surprise must stand out in a sea of monotony.

A subsequent experiment explored if familiarity bred indifference. Instead of a single recurring Surprise, participants were bombarded with a plethora. Yet, while recovery from the Inattentional blindness effect was rapid, it wasn't as sharp as instances without any Surprising elements.

Every novel Surprise still snagged a slice of their attention.

Then, in an experiment tinted with a twist, researchers had participants zero in on a unique "face" from an array. Some faces were to be overlooked, primarily focusing on one distinct face. But here's the catch: even with instructions to dismiss irrelevant faces, they often missed the crucial one when it followed a Surprising face. It was as if their vision blurred for a moment.

What can we glean from this? Telling someone to overlook a captivating Surprise is akin to asking a hungry salesperson to ignore a hot lead. For instance, if I suggest you not flinch at a Jack-in-the-box's sudden appearance, you'd probably be even more entranced.

Digging deeper still, it wasn't that participants weren't trying hard enough. Once diverted by an unexpected sight, the attention led to them overlooking the primary objective.

Essentially, Surprise doesn't just grab our attention—Surprise hijacks our attention.

Focusing harder isn't the answer. It's not a sheer distraction that makes us miss critical details but our inherent pull toward the unexpected.

All these explorations underscore a pivotal theme: our attention, while easily captured by novelty, is also resilient, acclimating quickly to Surprises, discerning what's paramount from the inconsequential. It's a beautiful dance, with our brain evaluating what deserves its spotlight.

But this much is undeniable—if well-timed and genuine, a masterfully presented Surprise leaves a permanent mark.

# PHYSIOLOGICAL EFFECTS OF SURPRISE

You are nestled comfortably at home, flopped on your plush couch with a book, deeply immersed in an enchanting tale of courage and myth. The gentle cadence of raindrops provides a soothing backdrop, creating an ambiance of serene escapism.

Then, without warning, an explosive BOOM ruptures the tranquility. Lightning's fiery crack has touched close to your safe place. Now, pause and dissect the physiological whirlwind this electrifying event has sparked within you.

The casual ambiance and your leisurely posture are a distant memory in that electrifying moment. It's as if an internal switch is flipped, transforming you from a relaxed couch potato to an alert guardian, primed to face any imminent challenge the tempest might unleash.

Your heart, now racing, thunders in your chest, priming your limbs with surges of oxygenated blood. Your breaths, more rapid, infuse your body with life-sustaining oxygen. A heightened clarity dawns as your pupils expand to capture more ambient light, making the room's cozy dimness incredibly vivid.

Seated atop your kidneys, the adrenal glands — typically silent and inconspicuous — surge into action, releasing a flood of adrenaline into your circulatory system. Newfound vigor courses through you as you tap into a hidden power reserve.

Every fiber of your being is attuned, senses sharpened to a keen edge, orchestrated by the symphony of your autonomic nervous system producing this intricate dance of Surprise within.

This cascade of reactions, spanning mere fractions of a second — as fleeting as the lightning that instigated it — underscores the marvel of our physiological response to Surprise.

### At The Beach With Your ANS

The sun's warmth kisses your skin as you stand on the overhang, overlooking a shimmering blue sea. The exhilaration of the impending cliff dive makes your toes wiggle in anticipation. A rich breath fills your lungs as you prepare to embrace the deep unknown.

As you spring forward, something profound commandeers your physiology. This maestro is none other than the Autonomic Nervous System (ANS), the quiet caretaker of myriad subconscious physical processes: the rhythmic beat of your heart, the gentle ebb and flow of your breath, and the fluttering sensation in your gut.

Yet, the ANS roars into life at this pivotal airborne moment, shifting from a gentle murmur to a roaring crescendo. Its Sympathetic division, the precursor of the "fight or flight" reaction, springs into an energetic ballet.

Your heart pulsates, setting a frenetic rhythm that resonates within your ribcage. Your respiration deepens, drawing in generous draughts of oxygen, readying your body for the plunge. And your gaze? It intensifies, with pupils expanded, drinking in every photon, crystallizing this thrilling experience.

Though the imminent splash awaits below, this sympathetic activation primes you as if preparing to grapple with unseen adversaries. It's the quintessence of your body's inherent wisdom, ensuring survival and optimal reaction, irrespective of the context.

This electrifying alertness and physiological overdrive are not just unique to cliff diving; even the sudden appearance of our benign jack-in-the-box can evoke a similar burst [12]. So, the next time a Surprise sends your heart aflutter, spare a thought for the tireless Sympathetic ANS, your internal, ever-vigilant guardian.

### Eating With Epinephrine

You're immersed in your culinary sanctuary, enveloped in your cherished apron and fingers playfully dabbed with flour. You gently mold the dough for a handmade pasta creation you learned while attending a cooking school from an Italian chef on her farm in Lerici, Italy.

The tantalizing scent of your simmering tomato sauce wafts through the air, a particularly proud moment since these tomatoes were the fruits of your garden's labor. You've eagerly anticipated this culinary moment where your mother's cherished sauce recipe would once again come to life. With every fold and press of the dough, you're swaying to the melodic tunes of Bossa Nova, each note amplifying your joy, and a glass of wine nearby completes the ritual.

In an abrupt discordant shift, the smoke alarm belts out its shrill warning – oh no, the sauce!

The tranquil, meditative culinary dance you were in dissolves instantaneously. Your pulse races, and every sense snaps to heightened vigilance; you might even catch yourself pausing your breath.

Behind this sudden metamorphosis? An adrenaline cascade.

This hormone, epinephrine, springs into action when faced with unforeseen or potentially dangerous situations. Think of it as your body's innate siren, prepping every sinew and neuron for swift and decisive action.

With adrenaline coursing through your veins, your heart drums faster, channeling a surge of oxygen-rich blood to prime your muscles. Your eyes become more receptive, dilated pupils capturing every glint of light, refining your vision to manage the impending challenge. Meanwhile, the intricate dance of digestion gracefully steps aside as your system reallocates its energies to more pressing priorities.

When your culinary exploits veer towards unexpected drama, and you feel that electrifying shock, know that it's adrenaline stepping in, prepping you to navigate the unpredicted adeptly.

## Clubbin' With Cortisol

You're immersed in the hypnotic sounds of an avant-garde blues/funk fusion band at a bustling club. Strobe lights dance in tandem with the beat, while the bass pulses, permeating the atmosphere, the room is accentuated by a saxophone's mournful wail.

The band suddenly introduces a twist as your body syncs with the rhythm, feet tapping and head nodding. They break into an unexpected semi-silence, and the bass drops, transforming the auditory landscape like they've become an entirely different entity playing a piece of utterly foreign sounds.

As the room's energy halts, your heart rate quickens, signaling your body's instinctual response to the sudden change. What's behind this heightened state of alertness? It's cortisol, often dubbed the stress hormone.

Released from the adrenal glands in response to the unexpected switch in rhythm, cortisol prepares your body to react. It's preparing the body for the unforeseen. Cortisol helps increase glucose availability to ensure your brain and muscles have energy. While it gears you up to respond to the change, it's just one part of a complex physiological dance that readies you for whatever the night might bring.

Cortisol is part of a complex hormonal and neural response to stressful or surprising stimuli.

While it's true that cortisol can increase the availability of glucose and enhance certain brain functions, continuously high levels of cortisol (as in chronic stress) can have detrimental effects on health, including impaired cognitive performance, suppressed thyroid function, and decreased bone density, among other things.

### Cortisol in the Conference Room

We've all felt the stirrings of cortisol during moments of sudden attention at work or in class. Imagine you're comfortably seated in an arc of chairs, the air conditioner's refreshing hum contrasting the summer's swelter beyond the window panes. A room full of colleagues surrounds you: some familiar faces, others mere acquaintances acknowledged with hallway or online conference call nods. Running the room is the facilitator, an individual challenged with breathing life into day-to-day topics. Today, she's diving into the nuances of the latest business software.

As the clock's hands march steadily toward the end of the day, terms like 'spreadsheets,' 'pivot tables,' and 'data analysis' meld into an indistinct jargon haze. This 'Sage on the stage' maintains hours of monologic babble. You're doing your best to keep up, yet occasionally, your thoughts meander to the charms of the impending weekend's drive out to the coast and that brewpub on the beach next to an oyster farm.

The droning of the facilitator's voice spikes in intensity as you hear your name piercing the air. A jerk surges through you, charging the boring environment with unmistakable tension. You suddenly become the focal point of every gaze, acutely aware of the spotlight. The facilitator restates her question, this time, you're all ears.

*"In the 17th century, when Sir Isaac Newton discovered the laws of motion, he also had a lesser-known fondness for apples,"* she starts, her eyes twinkling with mischief that doesn't quite align with the serious topic of the day. *"Now, given that you have no access to a time machine nor any historical record of Newton's culinary preferences, can you tell us, with confidence, how many apples Newton ate on the exact day he discovered gravity?"*

Within moments, adrenaline courses through you, pupils widen, heartbeat quickens, and a heightened sense of focus takes over, even though you know it's all in jest [12]. Your body, ever on alert, has surged into action, ready to respond.

Cortisol, in both these scenarios, plays a fascinating role. Whether elicited by an unexpected musical about-face or a whimsical question, it's a hormone that responds to the surprises life throws, powering our body's internal machinery. As you navigate the world, your physiological responses—sometimes unnoticed—guide your every reaction, turning the ordinary into the extraordinary, all through the release of these invisible molecular marvels [13].

### Shifts in the Neuro-Landscape

Dive deeper into the brain's intricate network, and there you'll find the hippocampus, an essential limbic system component, lying adjacent to our previously discussed bouncer, the amygdala. The hippocampus is often hailed as the maestro of memories, seamlessly connecting past experiences with our current context.

Let's focus our spotlight on this impressive memory maestro. Picture yourself in Club Brain, early to a show, watching a predictable yet entertaining comedy warm-up act as Campari & Soda starts to play with your balance. The narrative is familiar, chuckles guaranteed, and the hippocampus confidently sifts through past experiences, assuring you that you know how this story typically goes.

Without introduction, the lights go dark, and a booming sound system shrieks and a horror flick shines on a dropdown screen that appears from nowhere, replacing your anticipated show. The once sporadic giggles make way for eerie echoes. The hippocampus rapidly bridges this unexpected experience with familiar emotions from past frights or Surprises as tension escalates. While the amygdala ensures the emotional intensity is felt, the hippocampus provides context, reminding you of previous times you felt this mix of adrenaline and dread.

The synergy between the hippocampus and the amygdala forms a dynamic duo in Club Brain. As one interprets the emotional weight of the Surprise, the other provides the context, ensuring that our responses are reflexive and rooted in our memory archives. This is why that sudden shift from comedy to horror isn't just startling; it's an immersive experience drawing upon the well of past emotions and learnings [12].

### Enhanced Vigilance

A sudden Surprise shakes our system into heightened vigilance, priming our body to brace itself for unforeseen occurrences. This heightened awareness lets us zero in on the unexpected, ensuring we react aptly.

Example: The walk from your car to the front door. Each footstep is predictable, and every sound is familiar. It's like the ho-hum diddly dum grocery store trip you've done a million times, where the aisles feel like well-trodden paths you can navigate without much thought..

Now, as you're scurrying down your habitual vegetable aisle, an anomaly emerges. An animated, life-sized eggplant boogies away, greeting every passerby with an infectious enthusiasm that only a life-sized eggplant can. Certainly not your usual grocery spectacle!

The dancing mascot isn't just a source of amusement; it flips a switch in your brain. In this moment of astonishment, your cerebrum amps its attentiveness, letting the mascot steal the spotlight while other distractions blur. It's as though your brain has donned a pair of high-powered binoculars, zooming in on this unexpected performer.

This elevated vigilance isn't just a quirk of human behavior. It's an evolutionary tool designed to keep us safe, ensuring we're ever-ready to tackle anything unusual – be it a needling nightshade or more significant, unforeseen events.

### Ah, Ah, Dopamine Delight!

Surprises, especially the pleasant kind, lead to a dopamine release, the neurotransmitter that sets off happiness and enthusiasm in the brain. This delightful chemical shower can turn any moment into a celebration.

**Personal** - You've just finished a challenging workout and all you can think about is a hot shower and some downtime. You walk into your bathroom and flip on the lights... "SURPRISE!" Your significant other has turned the bathroom into a spa oasis, complete with scented candles, relaxing music, and a steaming bubble bath. A delightful shock that melts your fatigue away!

Now, let's journey into your brain. As the shock sets in, it's game time and dopamine, the star player in our previous soccer metaphor, takes a victory lap. This surge of the 'happy neurotransmitter' showers you with feelings of delight and exhilaration. Think of it as a mental fireworks display, a dazzling end to a regular day. It's not just the unexpected party; it's your brain's way of gifting you a happiness bonus.

**Professional** - The office, those spreadsheets, the ticking clock - it's all fading into a monotone blur. Suddenly, your boss hands you an envelope with a grin, saying, "You've earned this." Inside, a promotion letter gleams, turning an ordinary workday into a thrilling triumph.

Here again, dopamine steps onto the field, this time in a business suit, ready to celebrate. With the news of your unexpected promotion, your brain throws its confetti, and dopamine dances to the sounds of its own golden buzzer. It's more than just professional recognition; it's a brain-fueled fiesta, livening up the everyday grind.

The release of dopamine in reaction to a pleasing Surprise, be it a birthday party or a well-deserved promotion, underlines the exciting play of unexpected rewards in our personal and professional lives [12]. These immediate physiological effects of Surprise are not just reflexive but serve as the body's tactical play, priming us to notice, remember, and aptly respond to unforeseen events

# MEMORY & THE ELEMENT OF SURPRISE

To be clear, memory is flawed. You forget what you memorize, which is why our focus is understanding. The Ebbinghaus Forgetting Curve tells us learned information slips out of our memories over time.

Have you ever shared an old story, only to discover that your friends or family recall it differently? That's because our memories don't capture events as exact replicas. They get shaped by our feelings during that moment, our focus, and even how we revisit these memories later on. So, in a sense, our brains tend to recreate events rather than just replaying them.

I'd like to emphasize that the aim of this book, and the use of Surprise for engagement, is to help you communicate in a way that fosters understanding, rather than just rote memorization.

Understanding is more deep-rooted. It's about genuinely grasping the substance of a topic or situation. For instance, remembering the formula to find the area of a circle is one thing. But real comprehension is when you can use that formula to estimate the amount of paint for a round room. You don't forget what you understand.

Think about the old-school education system, designed in an era of factories and assembly lines. The primary goal? Fill students with facts and then test them on how well they could repeat them, assuming this was the accurate measure of learning. Do you remember those nights cramming for exams, only to forget it all shortly after?

Now, imagine our present age, overflowing with information at our fingertips. While there's a place for memorization, it doesn't command the same respect. Today, we value critical thinking, creativity, and adaptability—qualities that won't sprout from rote learning.

### Understanding: Top Business Skill.

Modern teaching methods, like Brain-centric, have evolved to fit our new understanding of learning. Instead of just giving out facts and testing how well they're remembered, these methods ensure learners actively engage with the material. This not only helps in grasping the information but also in analyzing and applying it. Such a method shifts the focus from memorizing to genuine understanding.

So, you've got this big company training its employees the same way for over a decade. Think of it like a traditional classroom setting: students in rows, listening to a lecturer at the front - a classic way many of us learned in school. Now, they tried something new. They redesigned their established learning using Brain-centric Design frameworks. Instead of just spoon-feeding gobs of information, they focused on creating a personal connection for the learner to every core concept needed to efficiently work in that position, using in-person and online methods.

They tested it out with 250 employees - half in the old way and half with this new approach. They tracked how well everyone was learning and even asked them about their job satisfaction. The results? The new method was a game-changer. People not only understood the material, but they were happier and more connected to their job. Plus, the company even saw better returns on their investment.

Bottom line: When companies change their training to match how the brain learns, everyone wins. The employees feel more connected, and the company benefits too.

Consider our discussion about the power of Surprise. In old-school learning, you might have received a bunch of facts about the brain's reaction to Surprises. But, when the content is presented engagingly, you're pushed to grasp the underlying concepts, not just regurgitate facts.

It's essential for you to see that our learning must adapt to our dynamic world. Truly understanding concepts and developing cognitive skills aren't just the latest trends. They are vital for navigating our intricate, fast-paced environment. This approach enables us to shift from merely knowing things to deeply comprehending them. Surprise plays the pivotal role of placing whatever comes next as something more important than everything else.

When something unexpected happens, our brain works extra hard to understand why, involving parts like the hippocampus, which is crucial for memory. This intense brain activity ensures the Surprising event is remembered more strongly than usual. Additionally, the emotions elicited by Surprise can further enhance memory retention. As studies suggest, emotionally-charged moments tend to be recalled more vividly and last longer in our memory.

Surprise, as we've emphasized, profoundly enriches understanding. When confronted with the unexpected, you naturally weave that new detail into your pre-existing knowledge, enhancing your grasp of the world. Surprises are mental jostles, pushing us to re-evaluate and reassess our perception. More than just startling, a surprise piques our curiosity. It demands our focus, urging us to understand its context and significance.

Cognitive dissonance is at the core of this intrigue, a concept introduced by Leon Festinger in the late 1950s. It captures the unease we feel when we encounter data that clashes with our beliefs. Surprises act as triggers for this, urging our minds to find a resolution to the inconsistency.

This dissonance, this conflict, drives us to deep cognitive engagement...deep thinking. We rally our memories, tap into associated ideas, and might even hunt for additional data to comprehend the Surprise, fortifying our neural pathways and amplifying our recall capabilities. We're essentially refining our mental representation of the world. Each unexpected moment becomes part of our vast, personal, intricate mosaic. Integrating these elements compels us to scrutinize our preconceptions, test our convictions, and attain a deeper understanding.

Surprise acts as a formidable ally in our educational journey. It halts our mental inertia, seizes our attention, and stimulates our thinking prowess. It encourages us to harmonize novel insights with our foundational knowledge, solidifying our neural bonds and enriching our comprehension. Through Surprise, we're constantly fueled and guided in our perpetual quest for knowledge.

# TELEPHONE & WHAT'S NOT FORGOT

Imagine the well-known game of Telephone, reimagined within the vibrant backdrop of a contemporary business conference or an engaging corporate workshop. Telephone is where words flow as swiftly as the scrolling headlines on a financial news channel.

You've assembled your team in an executive boardroom setting, eager to partake in this cerebral challenge. This is a critical mission to relay a top-secret communique from one division of the enterprise to another, where each individual becomes an indispensable link in this communication relay.

Our corporate game's prime directive?

The message must be singular, embodying the principle that no two innovative strategies ever unfurl identically within an organization. As the game kickstarts, the initiator discreetly shares a cryptic statement, such as,

*"Marketing praises the Finance team's algorithms. Finance boasts unparalleled data interpretation. HR is perplexed by talent scouting. The CEO is a chess prodigy."*

Now, spotlight on the next participant. Their task? To grasp the core of the whispered intelligence and transmit it forward. But wait, there's a twist! Remember that time during a pivotal video conference when a temporary loss of signal made the CEO sound like she was asking for a chessboard layout rather than the annual growth projections?

As the hushed words shift from one participant to another, they evolve – mirroring the dynamic flux of a business strategy in a volatile market.

Upon completion of the communication cycle, anticipation runs high as the last participant unravels their take on the initial statement. The room resonates with a mix of anticipation and amusement, reminiscent of a game-changing product's unveiling.

And the result? Often, the concluding rendition is a whimsical blend of humor and unexpected interpretations. Let's roll out the red carpet for the final reveal...

*'Marketing is enamored by Finance's algorithmic dance, while the CEO and HR are locked in a strategic game of chess!'*

Whisper Relay with a corporate twist serves as a lively metaphor for the unpredictable yet delightful nature of interdepartmental communications. While it underscores the perils of miscommunication, it also highlights the fun and merriment inherent in human interactions.

A cutting-edge study [14] explored deeply into the mechanics of the Whisper Relay game. Traditional research often centered around the fidelity of the relayed message's content. Yet, here's a twist! The spotlight isn't just on the message's substance but its emotional resonance!

Reflect on this: the sheer joy when Surprising your partner with an unplanned getaway or reuniting with a family member after prolonged separation. In a comprehensive study involving numerous repetitions of relayed stories, an enlightening trend emerged–while the specifics of a tale may evolve or vanish over iterations, the essence of Surprise embedded in the story remains strikingly stable!

Researchers contend that it's the emotional roller coaster that truly lies at the heart of captivating tales. It's less about chronicling events and more about preserving that spark of astonishment, ensuring it's faithfully passed to the subsequent recipient.

Here's the kicker: With an impressive 2,389 participants in the mix, the research illuminated that tales aren't just factual records. They're emotional journeys, blending details with feelings, creating stories that enrich our collective consciousness.

Effective communication is more than a transfer of information; it's about embracing the delightful unpredictability of narratives and ensuring the element of Surprise remains undiminished.

# SURPRISE & EFFECTIVE LEARNING

For effective education and self-improvement, the combination of Surprise and Effective Learning is essential. Effective learning empowers you to adapt, grow, and succeed in a world that doesn't stand still. It enhances personal and professional development, boosts problem-solving and critical thinking skills, and enriches life experiences. By embracing effective learning, you're better equipped to navigate challenges and seize opportunities.

Just as a skilled chef meticulously pairs ingredients to enhance.a dish's flavor, facilitators, educators, and trainers must thoughtfully intertwine Surprise with their presentation methods to truly captivate and educate their audience. This isn't a serendipitous occurrence; it requires planning, foresight, and a basic understanding of your audience. Before unveiling new information, considering the element of Surprise ensures not just the dissemination of knowledge but its lasting imprint on the learner's mind.

This heightened attention allows for better information encoding, making the Surprised content more memorable.

**Interrupting the Predictable** - The human brain is efficient, often predicting patterns to conserve energy. When a Surprise interrupts these patterns, it disrupts our cognitive predictions, forcing us to pay closer attention, ensuring the learning material isn't glossed over or forgotten.

**Surprise and Curiosity** - The unexpected nature of Surprise naturally piques our curiosity. We want to know why something doesn't align with our existing knowledge or expectations.

**Filling Knowledge Gaps** - Recognizing something unexpected also indicates a gap in understanding. The natural inclination is to fill that gap, which promotes exploration and self-directed learning.

**Driving Questions** - Driving questions, stemming from moments of Surprise, serve as pivotal points in the learning journey. When encountering an unexpected twist or revelation, it's natural to wonder, "Why did that happen?" or "How does that work?". These aren't just inquiries; they manifest innate human curiosity. They propel learners into a state of investigation, pushing them to seek answers and deepen their understanding.

At the core of these driving questions is the principle of intrinsic motivation. Unlike extrinsic motivation, which relies on external rewards or threats, intrinsic motivation comes from within. The internal drive pushes someone to do something out of genuine interest or personal satisfaction. ***When intrinsically motivated learners engage with the content not because they have to but because they want to.***

So, how do driving questions fuel intrinsic motivation? Simply put, they create a personal connection between the learner and the information. Instead of passively receiving knowledge, learners are actively seeking it out. The question becomes a challenge, a puzzle to solve. This quest for answers becomes personally meaningful and satisfying. Each discovery or piece of understanding achieved in the process is not just another fact to memorize but a rewarding step in the learner's journey.

Additionally, in an educational setting, driving questions foster a culture of exploration and critical thinking. Instead of rote memorization, students are encouraged to ask questions, seek out answers, and build upon their existing knowledge. The learning space becomes dynamic and learner-centric, where each individual's curiosity guides their learning trajectory.

**Emotional Enhancement**- The powerful catalyst of Surprise for emotional enhancement and effective learning is well-documented by Leonard Mlodinow in his enlightening book "Emotional," which focuses on the indispensable role emotions play in our decision-making processes. Contrary to the long-held belief that emotions and rational thinking are at odds, Mlodinow asserts that emotions are vital for our well-being and are as crucial as logical thought. This understanding strengthens the idea that the emotional stimulation spurred by Surprise can deeply embed learning experiences.

When we experience Surprise, it often triggers a rush of emotions, ranging from curiosity to excitement or even apprehension. These emotional responses compel us to seek answers, explore the unknown, and understand the unexpected. Such a drive, stemming from an emotional reaction, ensures that the learning process is cerebral and visceral. As Mlodinow suggests, our emotions evolved over millennia and are nature's tools, helping us navigate complex scenarios and make decisions even without complete information.

Connecting this to the concept of 'driving questions' we discussed prior, when Surprise elicits questions like "Why did that happen?" or "How does that work?" It's not just the brain seeking logical answers. There's an emotional undertone urging us to find a resolution, to achieve a sense of understanding and satisfaction. This intertwining of emotion with the quest for knowledge makes the learning experience richer and more memorable.

Mlodinow's exploration into how emotions help us connect better with others sheds light on collaborative learning environments. When learners experience Surprise collectively, they share a common emotional experience. This shared emotionality can foster collaboration, mutual understanding, and a deeper collective exploration of the subject at hand.

Embracing the emotional enhancement that springs from Surprise doesn't just make learning effective; it makes it holistic, bridging the gap between reason and emotion and ensuring that learning experiences are stored in memory and felt deep within.

**Using Surprise for Growth** - Utilizing Surprise in learning experiences can encourage learners to go beyond passive information intake. It can promote active engagement, problem-solving, and critical thinking, ensuring the information is retained better. It also fosters personal and intellectual growth as individuals are more likely to connect new information with prior knowledge, analyze data critically, and approach subjects with an open and explorative mindset.

Moreover, integrating Surprise for the learners' autonomy,

mastery, and purpose supercharges the learning experience. Autonomy grants learners the freedom to chart their path, making the journey of discovery even more personal and resonant. Mastery ensures that this journey isn't just about accumulating knowledge but refining and perfecting one's skills. And when coupled with Purpose, learners find a deeper motivation, as they understand the broader significance and impact of their learning. The confluence of Surprise with this triad first brought to light by Daniel Pink offers a holistic approach, making every learning moment not just memorable but also meaningful and impactful.

Surprise acts as a catalyst, amplifying our learning experiences, triggering curiosity and promoting exploration, transforming the learning process into an ongoing journey of discovery and personal development. As we get more familiar with this relationship, we begin to see the vast potential of integrating Surprise into educational and communication strategies, ensuring every opportunity is personally worthwhile and rewarding.

# TIMING SURPRISE

Introducing Surprise hinges profoundly on its timing. Surprises naturally jerk us out of our expectations, drawing our gaze towards the unforeseen. Surprises can amplify engagement, captivate attention, and imbed messages in our memories when aptly wielded. However, if mishandled, they might baffle or even estrange the audience.

Our brain's intrinsic response to the unexpected is at the heart of the potency of Surprise. When confronted with something unanticipated, our brain emits a burst of dopamine, the chemical messenger linked with delight and reward. Furthermore, this unexpected turn of events lights up the amygdala, our emotional processing center, making such incidents hard to forget.

The criticality of timing in Surprises manifests in diverse ways.

## Flow of Information

During a presentation or discourse, striking elements or events can be strategically placed to punctuate essential junctures, marking moments you desire to be etched in the audience's mind. This could be at the outset to seize attention, the culmination for a resounding finale, or at pivotal shifts in the storyline.

Consider the timeless fable of "The Tortoise and the Hare." An overzealous hare, oozing confidence, contrasts with a steadfast tortoise whose pace wouldn't turn heads. The hare's complacency sees it snoozing while the tortoise trudges on. Yet, the real twist isn't the hare's realization of the tortoise's proximity to victory but the eventual triumph of the tortoise. This unexpected climax, a product of the tortoise's unwavering commitment and the hare's poorly judged break, reinforces the undeniable importance of the timing of Surprise.

Drawing from this, whether initiating a dialogue, wrapping up a proposition, or during a pivotal moment, masterfully timed Surprises can seize attention, emphasize an argument, or even swing the balance to one's advantage.

## Surprise & Audience Anticipation

How an audience responds to a Surprise often hinges on their prevailing mental state and what they're anticipating. When an audience's attention starts to wane, a cleverly placed Surprise can reel them back in, refocusing them on your content. On the flip side, if they're already engrossed, a Surprise can elevate their experience, making your content even more unforgettable.

Imagine you're settled in for a rom-com like "When Harry Met Sally." You're immersed, riding the waves of humor and sentiment, already predicting the love story's trajectory. Yet, you're hooked, mainly because of the relatable characters and the unfolding narrative.

Ah, let's talk about that diner scene, shall we? Picture this: the scene starts like any other in the movie. But then, out of nowhere, Sally, brought to life by the ever-talented Meg Ryan, decides to go for the dramatic, putting on a performance that's nothing short of theatrical. The diners around her? Their jaws practically hit the floor. And we, the unsuspecting audience, were just as gobsmacked. It wasn't your run-of-the-mill romantic comedy moment. Oh no, this scene chucked the rulebook out the window. And because of its audaciousness and sheer unexpectedness, it's become the sort of movie moment we find ourselves reminiscing about, even years later. Who would've thought a casual diner rendezvous could leave such an indelible mark?

"I'll have what she's having."

What sets this scene apart isn't just its shock value and impeccable timing. It's dropped into the plot when viewers are thoroughly invested, turning an already engaged audience into an utterly captivated one.

Drawing from this, embrace the' Sally' strategy whenever you're in the spotlight - be it a presentation, a lecture, or a sales pitch. With an audience already leaning in, a well-positioned Surprise can transition your content from simply being memorable to being etched in their memory.

## Timing In The Broader Context

In sales or negotiation, strategically timing a Surprise can dramatically change the interaction dynamics. Unfurling an unexpected piece of information at the right moment can tilt the balance in your favor, confound your counterpart, and lend you a distinct advantage.

Consider the story of David and Goliath. Most know the tale of the young shepherd boy going up against a towering, armored giant. With his imposing stature and vast experience, Goliath was the overwhelming favorite. Everyone expected a swift victory for the giant. Meanwhile, David, armed only with a sling and a few stones, seemed to stand no chance.

Yet, in a move no one saw coming, David swiftly and skillfully used his sling to target Goliath's most vulnerable spot: his forehead. The timing of David's action, combined with the sheer audacity of his approach, caught Goliath entirely off guard. Against all odds, David's timely maneuver resulted in the giant's downfall.

This age-old tale underscores the potency of a strategic Surprise. Like David, who transformed a seemingly hopeless situation with a single, well-timed action, professionals can use the element of Surprise in negotiations or sales to redirect the conversation, re-engage a listener, and drive home a specific point that needs to be understood. In the grand communication theater, the right Surprise combined with impeccable timing can transform the game.

**WARNING**: It's essential to proceed with judgment. All Surprises aren't created equal. Ill-conceived or poorly timed Surprises can incite adverse reactions, leading to stress, distrust, or hatred, and could compromise relationships or dilute the potency of your message. The timing and nature of Surprise should be keenly assessed before deployment.

## Ready For A Surprise?

Isn't it fascinating how our brain is essentially a future-predicting machine? As you breeze through this text, your noggin' is sneakily trying to outguess what comes next, relying on your vast personal library of past experiences—like a detective anticipating the culprit's next move based on old case files.

Let's put this Sherlock-level anticipation to the test with a Surprise mental experiment. Ready?

Complete this sentence: ***"She poured herself a large cup of ____."***

"Tea"? "Coffee"? Those are the usual culprits. But imagine if I blindsided you with "gravy." A bit left field, right? You didn't see it coming, and your brain's alarm bells are ringing just like that.

What we've tapped into here is called the "orienting response." Picture your brain doing a double-take, exclaiming, "Hold up! That wasn't in the script!"

And it's not just about sneaking in a quirky word; it's all about when it waltzes in. Tossing "gravy" at the start doesn't have the same zing. The key is the element of genuine Surprise, which jolts the brain into high gear.

This brainy magic trick does more than amuse – it latches onto our attention, sharpens our focus, and boosts our memory. The best part? This all goes down faster than you can say, "Squirrel!"

Timing, as they say in comedy and brain science, is everything. When serving up Surprises, considering the ebb and flow of your narrative, tuning into your audience's vibes, and gauging the broader scene can make all the difference. Who can forget a well-timed cup of gravy?

This quirky gravy example brings to mind an anecdote from my days as a radio salesperson, where the element of Surprise played an unexpected role in my early success at the sales game. In the energetic '80s, I devised a strategy to craft personalized commercials for prospective clients rather than 'smile & dial' hoping every tenth call resulted in a meeting to possibly convince them my radio station could bring them business. My process? Dive deep into research about the prospect's business, chat with their clientele, and maybe even indulge in secret shopping. Armed with insights, I'd head back to the studio and create what I believed was a show-stopping commercial that would bring them new customers from my radio audience.

Dale Carnegie, best known for his iconic self-help book, "How to Win Friends and Influence People," first published in 1936, believed that hearing one's own name is the sweetest sound in any language. Taking that to heart, I tried to think from a prospect's perspective. Did this prospect really want to listen to me wade through endless facts about listening habits, CUME numbers, antenna power, and reach? No! He was after customers. And so, I embarked on a mission to weave each prospect's name into compelling narratives set against a backdrop of dynamic music, captivating sound effects, and outstanding audio production. My ready-to-play radio commercial (spec spot) wasn't about positioning my station against another with statistics; I was about crafting an auditory experience so alluring it acted as the siren's song I knew the business needed—an irresistible call to potential customers.

I excitedly played one such spec spot for a prospect one day using my trusty boom box. As the snappy story on that cassette about "Lonestar Chili Saloon on Emerson Pike, right next to Tony Pitt's Hyundai!" filled the room with visions of this joint hoppin' with new customers, the growing enthusiasm of a few employees who started the gather to hear the spectacle elevated. But then, the needle scratched. The prospect, thrust from his revelry, almost shouted, "Hold on! We're beside Emerald Chevrolet, not Tony Pitt's Hyundai!"

The sheer Surprise on his face! I'd mistakenly fumbled the location in the commercial. But it was this accident that turned out to be a blessing. The prospect was now fully invested, and needed the error rectified.  My response? "Not a problem! We'll change it this afternoon, and you'll be featured on tomorrow's morning show." His anxiety over potential customers mislocating his business due to the wrong address shifted the narrative. Rather than being pitched, he was now in problem-solving mode.

I left with a new advertiser in my pocket and a valuable lesson learned. The magic of an 'unintentional' error added a twist to my pitch. Every spec spot I crafted had a 'deliberate' sprinkle of misinformation from then on. Just enough to stir the pot and spark engagement.

# WHAT WAS SURPRISING?

Brain-centric frameworks are changing the game in impactful communication. By first emotionally resonating with the audience and then delivering the message in sync with how the brain naturally processes information, comprehension is ensured.

Anchoring its ethos are the Cognitive 3Rs - Reflect, Revised Thinking, and Report Out — each with the same three questions embedded within that have reverberated through every arena whose communications have consequences. The questions within never change impacting classrooms and boardrooms alike, turning them into places where people can learn fearlessly.

Each question dodges our brain's bouncer, the amygdala, and caters to our natural curiosity managed within the gift of planned reflection.

The first reflective question, "What was Surprising?" holds a transformative power that's reshaping the landscape of understanding and learning performance. I want to fully explain its magnitude because, believe me, the effectiveness and applicability of this simple question is unparalleled.

Consider "What was Surprising?" as the ultimate "plot twist" for our minds. Just as a sudden turn in a riveting tale keeps you glued to every word, this question engages your brain in a similar fashion. It beckons the mind to explore the uncharted and welcome the unforeseen. And here's the magic: our brains are wired to hold onto Surprises. When confronted with the unexpected, the brain latches onto it, engraving it into our memory.

But why spotlight this question among the Cognitive 3Rs? Its brilliance lies in its universality and personal resonance. Imagine a colleague sharing a challenging situation or recounting an event sequence. By simply asking, "What was Surprising?", you invite a deeply personal reflection. The answer will always be unique to the individual, ensuring that they feel truly listened to and acknowledged.

The impact of this seemingly simple question on communication is profound. It's altered the way we approach managing situations and has brought about a revolution in educational methodologies.

By prioritizing personal insights and individual discoveries, it's not just about the transfer of information anymore. Now, it's about forming meaningful, personal connections with that information. And when your audience finds personal relevance in what they're considering information is absorbed and assimilated.

To say that "What was Surprising?" has changed the educational game would be an understatement. Its lasting influence on learning performance ensures that it will continue to shape and refine the way we engage with knowledge for generations to come.

## Scaffolded Reflection Articulated

During this reflection time, we always pose three consistent questions in a set sequence, offering a typical duration of two minutes for responses. This quiet two-minute span allows learners to organize their thoughts, jot them down (clearing their immediate memory), and translate their in-the-moment thinking onto paper. This process sets a clear starting point or benchmark for their understanding of the presented material.

## QUESTION ONE

### What Was Surprising?

This first question given immediately after experiencing multiple perspectives on the challenge of the moment, might seem simple on the surface, but oh boy, it's like a master key to unlocking how our brain loves to operate. Let's dive into why this seemingly innocuous question is basically a cheat code for the mind.

**Curiosity and Attention** - Our brains are a bit like toddlers – endlessly curious and always on the hunt for the next shiny thing. If something's surprising, our brains are on it. By asking this question, you're simply giving your brain the green light to do what it does best: zoom in on the intriguing stuff.

**Memory Encoding** - Remember that time you saw something so unexpected you couldn't forget it? That's your brain giving VIP treatment to surprising info. With "What was surprising?", we're basically rolling out the red carpet for memories to stroll right into the long-term storage.

**Neural Plasticity and Learning** - Our brain is no static machine; it's more like Play-Doh. Show it something surprising, and it starts reshaping, forming new connections. This question nudges your brain into its "let's adapt and evolve" mode.

**Emotional Engagement** - There's a reason viral videos often have 'shocking' or 'surprising' in their titles. We're hardwired to feel something when confronted with the unexpected. By identifying what caught you off guard, you're ensuring your emotions are in the driving seat, making the whole learning experience stickier.

**Problem-Solving and Creativity** - Ever had a surprise twist in a movie that made you rethink the entire plot? That's what this question does for learning. It challenges you to think outside the box, to piece things together creatively.

**Attentional Filter** - We're bombarded with information daily. Our brain, playing the role of a top-notch bouncer, decides what gets the VIP entry to our conscious mind. Surprises? They get the fast pass. By focusing on the surprising elements, you're making sure the key takeaways aren't lost in the crowd.

"**What was Surprising?**" isn't just a question; it's THE Question.

In the world of sales, which we are all a part of, the moments immediately following a pitch are crucial. Traditional sales tactics might prompt a representative to ask, "Do we have a deal?", effectively cornering the prospect into a binary decision: a 'Yes' or 'No'. This can create pressure and may lead to hasty decisions, or worse, resistance from the prospect who feels rushed into a commitment.

Now, imagine replacing that with the question, "What was Surprising?". This seemingly subtle shift in approach can make a world of difference in the trajectory of the conversation. Why?

**Personal Reflection** - Asking "What was Surprising?" nudges the prospect to reflect on the pitch from a personal standpoint. Instead of being pressed into an immediate decision, they are given a moment to process the information, relate it to their needs, and articulate their thoughts.

**Feedback Opportunity** - This question provides an invaluable opportunity for feedback. The prospect might bring up a point they found particularly compelling, or perhaps something they hadn't considered before. This can give the salesperson insights into what resonated most with the prospect and what areas might require more attention.

**Avoids Pressure** - Instead of pushing the prospect into a corner, this approach fosters an open dialogue. The salesperson demonstrates genuine interest in the prospect's thoughts, making the conversation more of a collaborative discussion rather than a transactional negotiation.

**Deepens Connection** - When a prospect shares their feelings about the pitch, it offers the salesperson a chance to further tailor their approach, address concerns, and deepen the relationship. It moves the dynamic from merely a vendor-buyer relationship to a more consultative and trusted partnership.

**Strategic Follow-Up** - Based on the prospect's response, the salesperson can strategically steer the conversation. For instance, if a prospect found a particular feature surprising, the salesperson can expand on its benefits, perhaps securing the deal by emphasizing that specific point.

In Sales, "What was Surprising?" serves as a powerful tool to shift the conversation from a binary decision-making process to a more nuanced, insightful exchange.

## QUESTION TWO

### What Did I Already Know and Now See Differently?

This isn't about rehashing old facts. It's about rediscovery, like rewatching a movie and spotting details you missed the first time. Our brains love to re-evaluate and re-connect the dots, and this question gives them just the workout they need and aligning with the brain's processing of information:

**Schema Activation and Modification** - The brain organizes knowledge into schemas, mental frameworks that help us understand and interpret the world. When encountering new information, the brain tries to fit it into existing schemas. By asking, "What did I already know but now see differently?" We activate relevant schemas and encourage individuals to revisit and modify their existing mental models based on the new information. This process enhances understanding and promotes more accurate perceptions of the world.

**Metacognition and Reflection** - Metacognition refers to thinking about one's thinking process. The question prompts individuals to engage in metacognitive reflection by assessing their previous knowledge and comparing it to the new perspective. This metacognitive activity fosters critical thinking and self-awareness, leading to deeper insights and improved cognitive flexibility.

**Cognitive Dissonance Resolution** -The question often leads to the experience of cognitive dissonance, which is the discomfort arising from conflicting beliefs or viewpoints. When individuals realize their previous understanding differs from the new information, they are motivated to resolve this dissonance. This process can drive further exploration, research, and deeper integration of the new perspective.

**Neural Connectivity and Memory Consolidation** - Recalling existing knowledge and linking it to newly acquired information strengthens neural connectivity in the brain. The act of revisiting and restructuring previous knowledge enhances memory consolidation, making the updated knowledge more accessible and retrievable in the future.

**Lateral Thinking and Creativity** - The question promotes lateral thinking, encouraging individuals to approach the topic from different angles and consider alternative viewpoints. Within this reflection period, this second question stimulates creative thinking and fosters a more open-minded approach to learning by challenging preconceived notions.

**Application of Learning** - When individuals see something they already know in a new light, they are more likely to apply this updated knowledge in various contexts. Brain-centric frameworks leverage this aspect to ensure that the learning experience is not isolated but can be transferred and applied in real-world situations, leading to a more practical and meaningful understanding of the subject matter.

**Cognitive Growth and Adaptation** - The brain's ability to adapt and grow in response to new information is vital for cognitive development. Encouraging individuals to see existing knowledge differently facilitates cognitive growth and promotes intellectual flexibility, helping individuals become more adept at learning and adjusting their beliefs based on evidence.

"What did I already know but now see differently?" is ingeniously designed to align with various cognitive processes. It capitalizes on schema activation and modification, fosters metacognition and reflection, resolves cognitive dissonance, enhances neural connectivity and memory consolidation, stimulates lateral thinking and creativity, promotes learning application, and drives cognitive growth and adaptation.

# QUESTION THREE

### Question 3: What Do I Still Need Help With?

This isn't about admitting defeat, but rather embracing growth. It's an invitation to reflect, team up, and tap into collective wisdom. No one's pretending to have all the answers. Instead, there's a camaraderie, a collective "we're in this together" vibe but it's cool if you lay back a bit. Aligning with how the brain processes information is well documented.

**Metacognitive Awareness** - The question "What do I still need help with?" prompts individuals to engage in metacognitive awareness by recognizing their knowledge gaps and limitations. Metacognition involves understanding one's cognitive processes, and this question encourages individuals to reflect on what they don't yet understand fully.

**Active Learning and Inquiry** - Individuals become more proactive in their learning process by identifying areas where they need assistance. This question stimulates curiosity and inquiry, as individuals are motivated to seek out resources, ask questions, and actively engage in the learning process to fill in their knowledge gaps.

**Memory Consolidation through Goal Setting** - When individuals recognize their need for help, they form clear learning goals. This process of goal setting enhances memory consolidation and retrieval, as the brain organizes information around the identified objectives, making it easier to remember and apply later.

**Neural Plasticity and Skill Acquisition** - Acknowledging areas that require further assistance primes the brain for learning and skill acquisition. Neural plasticity, the brain's ability to reorganize and form new neural connections, is optimized when there is a conscious effort to improve in specific areas. The question encourages individuals to embrace learning and enhance their cognitive abilities.

**Emotional Intelligence and Humility** - Recognizing the need for help is an act of emotional intelligence and humility. Emotions play a significant role in the learning process, and being open to seeking help fosters a positive learning environment. By acknowledging that they don't have all the answers, individuals can create a more receptive mindset for learning.

**Social Learning and Collaboration** - The question encourages individuals to seek help from others, promoting social learning and collaboration. Working with peers or experts who can provide guidance and support enhances the learning experience and can lead to deeper understanding and retention of knowledge.

**Feedback and Iterative Learning** - Identifying areas that need assistance allows individuals to receive feedback on their understanding. Constructive feedback facilitates iterative learning, where individuals can refine their understanding through multiple iterations, leading to more robust and accurate knowledge.

**Personalized Learning Experience** - Everyone has unique strengths and weaknesses in their knowledge. By recognizing what they need help with, individuals can tailor their learning experience to focus on areas that will significantly impact their personal and professional growth.

"What do I still need help with?" strategically aligns with various cognitive processes. It fosters metacognitive awareness, promotes active learning and inquiry, enhances memory consolidation through goal setting, optimizes neural plasticity and skill acquisition, encourages emotional intelligence and humility, facilitates social learning and collaboration, enables iterative learning through feedback, and creates a personalized learning experience.

By incorporating these cognitive elements, you empower individuals to become active, self-directed learners, fostering continuous improvement and growth in their understanding and knowledge.

By posing the three non-amygdala hijack-producing questions - "What was surprising?", "What did I already know but now see differently?" and "What do I still need help with?" - we unlock the doors to an immersive and psychologically safe learning environment.

With any communication for consequence, engagement is the key that unlocks the treasure trove of understanding. When individuals are genuinely engaged, their cognitive faculties fire on all cylinders, and learning becomes a joyous adventure..

By leveraging the power of this framework, you unlock the gateway to an exciting realm of discovery, where your audience willingly embraces the wonders of what you are communicating, one Surprise at a time.

# SURPRISE: THE ART

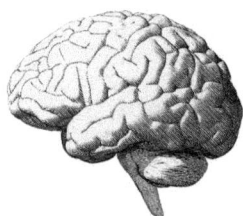

# SURPRISE IS NO SURPRISE

The Science of Surprise examines the systematic understanding and study of how our brains and bodies react to unexpected events and encompasses the physiological, neurological, and psychological responses that occur when something deviates from our expectations. On the other hand, the Art of Surprise is about the intentional creation and delivery of unexpected moments to engage, evoke specific emotions or achieve certain outcomes. It's the skill of crafting and timing Surprises for maximum impact, tailored to a given audience or situation. To clearly define the differences:

**Science of Surprise** - The biological and psychological study of our reactions to the unexpected.
**Art of Surprise** - The skillful crafting and delivery of unexpected moments for emotional or strategic impact.

In the heart of World War II, Europe was choking under the oppressive grip of Hitler's Third Reich. The dark cloud of war seemed impenetrable, so the Allies had little chance to pierce the fortress of Europe. But something was astir beneath the visible panorama of dread and desperation. A scheme was in the making, a plan so audacious it might just turn the tides of the war.

It was the cloak-and-dagger world of Operation Fortitude. The narrative sold to Hitler was one of a direct assault on Pas-de-Calais. The decoy? The loud and brash General Patton, leading a phantom army complete with inflatable tanks and an elaborate stage of misleading radio chatter. But this was mere sleight of hand, a magician's distraction, while the real trick unfolded elsewhere.

When the dawn of June 6, 1944, broke, the world held its breath. Normandy beaches came alive not just with the sounds of war but with a revelation, as a masterclass in the strategic use of Surprise shifted the axis of World War II.

Fast forward to technology, an arena ripe for Surprise and innovation. OpenAI introduced the world to a new creation, an Artificial Intelligence (AI) so powerful that it was almost eerie.

Its name? ChatGPT.

When it was first introduced, many viewed it as an upgrade to the existing language models, a modest improvement at best. However, the Surprise was waiting in the wings.

As people interacted with ChatGPT, they discovered its uncanny ability to generate coherent responses and simulate a conversation with a human. It was not just an AI; it was an AI that could write, 'speak,' and emulate the complexity of human thought.

As you can see from these examples, the Art of Surprise requires manipulation and deft control of anticipation and expectations, but its principles are not confined to the annals of history or grand stages. These recollections are tools you can use, lessons you can learn from, and implement in your world.

I'll show you.

In a negotiation scenario at work, you might use a similar tactic as the 'red herring' used in World War II to divert attention from your main objective until you're ready for the reveal. This is not about deceit but rather strategic engagement to maximize the outcome.

But what about emotional intelligence? How does that play into Surprise?

Take the example of a parent planning a Surprise birthday party for their child. The key here is understanding, predicting, and managing emotions. You can use this principle in your relationships, workplace, or social circles.

By empathizing with the other party and managing your own reactions, you can tailor a Surprise that resonates, delights, and fosters a connection.

On to an instructional designer constructing an online course with a Surprise twist at the start, let's say, an unexpected video or an interactive game. This is where understanding cultural context and standards comes into play. The Surprise works because it's designed for the audience.

It is always about the audience, the learner, and their brain.

Always.

How do you apply this?

If you're tasked with leading a project at work or organizing a community event, factor in who your audience is. Understand their cultural and contextual background. Tailor your strategies, presentations, or interactions to incorporate elements that Surprise and engage *them*.

### Plan For The Outcome

Preceding every communication you need to clearly articulate the following or you'll be wasting everybody's time. You need to not only know what your audience is walking away with, but how you will measure the success of your presentation. To wit:

- What will my audience walk away with? What will they understand and be able to assimilate?
- How will I measure the success of this communication?
- What two things must my audience understand to make that happen?

When you know these attributes about what you are about to communicate, you can see how planning the appropriate Surprise, when, and for what reason, becomes self-evident.

The power of planning the Surprise extends beyond the pages of history books or the dramatic turns of pop culture; it finds relevance in our daily lives, interactions, and objectives.

# TYPES OF SURPRISE

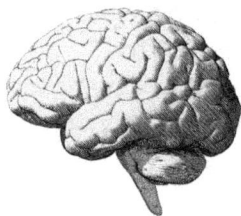

## SURPRISES: GENERAL & SPECIFIC

Surprise has an array of flavors and intensities that give your dish, your communications, depth and distinction. To truly enthrall and persuade, you must learn to blend types of Surprise, each with its unique aroma and zest, with culinary mastery.

Fortunately, all Surprises fall nicely into two categories - General & Specific. Distinguishing its distinct types is at the heart of mastering the Art of Surprise.

### General Surprise

In the following pages, we introduce you to five distinct General Surprises, each casting its own captivating and distinct resonance. As you devour this book, we will unveil each one's unique essence and artfully guide you on seamlessly weaving them into your daily narrative. Prepare for a transformative journey where every chapter presents a richer engagement & communication ideal.

**Positive Surprise** brings joy and delight; they're the uplifting moments we cherish.

**Negative Surprise**, on the other hand, invokes challenges or setbacks, demanding resilience.

**Neutral Surprise** stands in the middle ground, neither particularly elating nor disheartening, yet still capturing attention.

**Foreshadowed Surprise** - these are hinted at, allowing the audience to anticipate, creating a sense of suspense.

**Unexpected Surprise** come without warning, catching us completely off guard and often leaving the most profound impact.

These five types are the fundamental canvas upon which every Surprising moment is crafted. Each holds immense value in communication and is essential for fostering genuine engagement.

# Specific Surprises

Specific Surprises abound, much like the array of spices in a chef's kitchen or the diverse hues on an artist's palette. Integrating them into your communication adds precision, catalyzing distinct forms of engagement tailored to your message's requirements.

To whet your appetite, consider this random sampling of four Specific Surprises as unique additions that can enrich and elevate your communications.

**Delightful Surprise** is like an unexpected hint of flavor in a dish. These are the moments that bring joy and make the audience feel valued. They're the tiny garnishes that transform a good story into a great one.

**Informative Surprise** challenges existing beliefs, akin to discovering a fresh way to use a familiar ingredient. It opens up avenues of knowledge and solidifies the key messages you wish to convey.

**Intriguing Surprise** keeps the audience guessing, much like that secret ingredient you can't quite pinpoint but makes the dish unforgettable. It encourages deeper engagement and exploration.

**Shocking Surprise** is the game-changer, the bold twist in the tale. Use this with discernment. It's like a jalapeno - powerful when used correctly but overwhelming if mishandled.

Specific Surprises, of which there are dozens, are the intricate brushstrokes that bring the canvas of Surprise to life. Each one, nuanced and distinct, adds depth and texture to our communications. They capture attention, evoke emotion, and ensure our messages resonate deeply. Every Specific Surprise engages specifically, allowing us to connect with our audience on a more intimate and memorable level.

Mastering these facets of engagement is about understanding your audience, knowing when to introduce a twist or a turn, and expertly seasoning your narrative.

As you internalize the potential of these elements, this guide will become indispensable.

Just like the core ingredient of any dish, your communications need the right seasoning. And there's no seasoning quite like Surprise to make a message memorable. Let's break down how our sampling of four Specific Surprises specifically affect engagement:

**Delightful Surprise** *makes audiences savor each moment*
**Informative Surprise** *enriches your narrative*
**Intriguing Surprise** *keeps them wanting more*
**Shocking Surprise** *propels them into action*

Your curiosity is piqued because these Surprises resonate. You're thinking, "This speaks to my situation!"

Because this book is about understanding & applying Surprises in your life, now let's take the same four example Specific Surprises and see them at work.

**Delightful Surprise** - Imagine attending your regular team meeting, expecting the same old agenda. But today, your manager begins by announcing an impromptu half-day off. This Delightful Surprise makes you savor the moment and fosters a positive work environment where employees feel valued and are motivated to contribute further.

**Informative Surprise** - During a presentation on the company's quarterly performance, instead of the usual charts and figures, your colleague introduces a lesser-known market trend or a new tool that could revolutionize your work. This Informative Surprise enriches the narrative, making everyone in the room re-evaluate strategies and look forward to implementing new ideas.

**Intriguing Surprise** - You're at a workshop, and just when you think you know what's next, the facilitator introduces a mystery guest speaker or an unexpected hands-on activity. This Intriguing Surprise keeps everyone on their toes, sparking conversations and ensuring everyone is tuned in, eager to see what unfolds next.

**Shocking Surprise** - During a brainstorming session on increasing productivity, a team member shares a staggering statistic about wasted time or an anecdote about a massive project failure at another company due to a minor oversight. This Shocking Surprise is a wake-up call, propelling the team into immediate action to avoid such pitfalls in your organization.

Do these scenarios sound familiar or, better yet, enticing? It's because these Surprises resonate with our everyday experiences in the workplace. They remind us that banal routines can be transformed with a touch of creativity and intention, and significant impacts can be achieved.

This book illuminates, demonstrates, and articulates these techniques, equipping you with a toolkit of Surprise to enhance communication, foster engagement, and drive results. Real-world examples will clarify their potential, guiding you to master the art of Surprisation in any professional situation.

It's time to fine-tune your craft.

# GENERAL SURPRISE

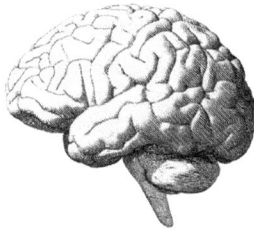

## GENERAL SURPRISES ARE FOUNDATIONAL

**Positive**, **Negative**, **Neutral**, **Foreshadowed**, or **Unexpected**
*The strategic application is your key differentiator.*

Evidence of the impact of the General Surprise is robust. A Harvard Business School study revealed that integrating Surprise into presentations boosted audience retention by 37% by maintaining focus and challenging assumptions. Likewise, McKinsey's research underscores how high engagement levels, often fueled by Surprise, can lead to a 21% advantage in profitability.

But Surprise is not confined to shock value and enterprise acknowledgement. Surprise is engineered to cultivate an atmosphere that encourages innovation and deep connection. The five General Surprises and their core principles we'll explore next.

Beyond General Surprise, we'll launch a thrilling series of guided rabbit holes into the Specific Surprise, uncharted territory of transformative tools that hold the potential to reshape professional and personal interactions providing a competitive edge.

As you read each one, imagine seamlessly weaving and tactically planning these into your daily professional and personal life, moving beyond dull presentations and meetings, and crafting experiences that engage and leave a lasting impression. That's our goal here.

There is a mind-expanding journey ahead. Prepare to uncover new instruments of engagement on every page, apply them across the various levels of engagement, and revitalize your strategies. The real exploration is about to begin, and this book is your map for this fascinating world.

## POSITIVE SURPRISE: UNLOCK JOY!

Positive Surprise is an engagement dynamo: a motivator, connector, and amplifier, supercharging learning and performance. And its power is both tangible and scientifically grounded.

Surprising, right?

Our brains crave unpredictability. A study titled "The Neural Basis of Surprise in Humans" from Nature, 2001, provides enlightening insights. Participants engaged in a rigged game of chance. While they thought their choices led to outcomes, the results were predetermined. Findings? When Surprised by outcomes, the brain—specifically the nucleus accumbens, the reward center—lit up, proving that Surprise isn't just delightful; it challenges us, compels us to adjust, and spurs creativity.

Now, consider the specific power of a Positive Surprise. You pull up to the window of a drive-up coffee shop, ready to pay for your order. The cashier beams, "The person in the car ahead of you already covered your coffee. They just wanted to brighten someone's day."

A swell of gratitude and warmth envelops you. "Wow, that's so thoughtful!" you respond, genuinely touched by this random act of kindness.

This spontaneous gesture stimulates the brain's pleasure centers, prompting the release of dopamine, the pleasure neurotransmitter. The experience becomes a cherished memory, a bright spot in an otherwise routine day. The sheer unexpectedness not only elevates your mood but also reaffirms the goodness that exists around us, with no strings attached.

The dopamine release would help you remember this event, and you might even be more likely to be generous to others.

The real-world applications are extensive. A simple box of pastries can disrupt monotony in offices, forging connections and augmenting employee morale. In classrooms, an instructor can switch a typical quiz with one laden with humor and intriguing facts, making learning a joyous affair. Positive Surprise isn't about grandiosity but about crafting moments that spark joy, curiosity, and connectivity.

Reflecting on Maya Angelou's words, "People will forget what you said... but people will never forget how you made them feel." Positive Surprise etches unforgettable feelings, enhancing engagements.

The practical implications are far-reaching. Zappos' plans a tactic of happiness by randomly upgrading shipping for customers. The delightful early arrival brings immediate joy and a lasting positive brand association. Strategies such as historical reenactments, staggering facts, or spontaneous games can amplify engagement and memory retention in educational spaces.

Tailoring to your audience, understanding their predispositions, and pacing your Surprise can transform your engagements. Like an artist visualizing the masterpiece before the first brushstroke, effective engagement demands understanding the audience and meticulous planning. Surprise then becomes purposeful, strategically interwoven to optimize engagement and learning.

### Apply It: Delivering a Positive Surprise

The secret to crafting an impactful Positive Surprise lies in meticulous planning. Here's your blueprint:

**Know Your Audience** -The foundation of a powerful surprise begins with understanding your audience. Familiarize yourself with their interests, current knowledge, and what they anticipate. This accommodation will help you curate Surprises that genuinely resonate. You are a mystery author, planting clues throughout, only for readers to be delightfully shocked by the ending.

**Strategic Placement** - Don't go overboard and pile up all the Surprises at the beginning. Instead, sprinkle them thoughtfully across your content. Understanding this ensures consistent engagement, much like breadcrumbs leading your audience deeper into the narrative or lesson.

**Align With Objectives** - Every surprise should serve a purpose. Are you explaining a tricky concept? Perhaps an unanticipated demonstration or analogy can shed new light. If you're trying to persuade, a Surprising testimonial or a compelling piece of data might be your ace in the hole.

**Simplicity is Key** - Not every Surprise needs a drumroll. A quaint fact, a light-hearted story, or a provoking question can be just as effective. The secret sauce? Planning these nuances in advance and integrating them where they can best amplify engagement.

**Practice Makes Perfect If You Practice Perfect** - Regularly incorporating these planned Surprises' becomes an instinctual part of your communication strategy. The resulting reactions - grins, sudden realizations, and bursts of interest? Indicators of success.

The aim here  isn't surface level or injecting fun into learning or communication. It's about forging connections, enhancing memory retention, and amplifying impact.

I'll give you an idea by taking a typical business meeting (a stakeholder update meeting) and planning a Positive Surprise in it prior to the meeting taking place and using the steps I just outlined.

By introducing Positive Surprises in the following manner, managers can fill an environment of anticipation, enthusiasm, and trust among stakeholders. The element of Surprise, when aligned with project objectives, will transform a routine update into a memorable moment of validation and motivation.

## Apply It: A Manager's Guide

**Understand the Stakeholders** - Before the meeting, take a moment to reflect on who's attending. What do they expect from this project update? What are their main interests or concerns related to the project? The Big Idea?

**Build Anticipation** - Begin your presentation with a statement that hints at the Positive Surprise. "By the end of this presentation, you'll discover a surprising fact that we're excited to share."

**Pepper the Updates** - Rather than rushing into the Positive Surprise, give regular updates first. This maintains a rhythm and builds further anticipation. Perhaps you can hint at a number that's improved or a milestone reached sooner than expected, but don't reveal it just yet.

**Surprise with Relevance** - Introduce your Positive Surprise when discussing a critical project objective. Let's say you've achieved a significant project milestone weeks ahead of schedule or under budget. Frame it as, "While we initially projected X, we're thrilled to report Y!" and present the data or the testimonial supporting this.

**Keep It Straightforward** - The Positive Surprise doesn't need to be extravagant. It could be as simple as sharing a testimonial from a satisfied end-user or an unexpected benefit that's emerged from the project.

**Reflect on the Impact** - After revealing the Surprise, take a moment to discuss its implications. How does this early milestone completion accelerate other parts of the project? How does a happy end-user testimony validate the direction the project is taking? Fill in those blanks.

**Cultivate Consistency** - Aim to incorporate such moments in future project updates. Not only will stakeholders start looking forward to these meetings, but it'll also create a culture of expectation for positive news, pushing teams to consistently deliver.

Over time, you'll find that this strategic use of Positive Surprises becomes second nature. The smiles, the 'aha' moments, and the spark of curiosity you see in your audience are the rewards that make it worth the effort. **You are witnessing engagement.** That is a surprise worth planning for.

## NEGATIVE SURPRISE: EMBRACE THE NEGATIVE

When we hear the word Surprise our minds often drift to pleasant memories – a Surprise birthday bash, a breathtaking scenic vista, or the exhilaration of an amusement park ride. However, Surprise also comes in darker shades: the unexpected challenges and discomforts that jolt us from complacency. These are our Negative Surprises.

You might wonder, "Why incorporate Negative Surprise in my presentations or teachings?" The answer lies deep within our brain's evolution. Historically, our minds were crafted to emphasize threats that could jeopardize our survival. This ancient alert system means that we naturally pay more attention to and vividly remember the negative.

This quality is what gives Negative Surprises their unique strength. A sudden plot twist, a frank critique, or an unforeseen market plunge grips our attention, compelling us to think, reassess, and remember: **You're learning what not to do and how to react.**

As you might imagine, wielding Negative Surprises demands finesse. You should never dishearten or inflict harm. Instead, Negative Surprise should spark engagement and deeper insight. A facilitator might use a difficult problem to disrupt complacency, nudging the group towards innovative thinking. A manager could share disappointing news, not to demoralize but to highlight growth areas and rally the team for better strategies. It's akin to a piquant spice – intense, memorable, but used judiciously.

In harnessing Negative Surprises, the balance between challenge and support is paramount. Presenting this Surprise should kindle resilience and curiosity, not dread. When executed adeptly, Negative Surprises become invaluable tools, pushing us to think on our feet, adapt swiftly, and fortify our resilience — essential attributes in a rapidly evolving world.

Let's first example a few global Negative Surprises for your vocabulary and then show you what transpired from each. After that, we'll give you the 'How To' on setting up Negative Surprises on your own.

## Harnessing the Potential of Negative Surprises

**Apollo 13 - Disaster Turned Triumph** - In 1970, the Apollo 13 mission faced a near-catastrophic Negative Surprise when an oxygen tank exploded, threatening the lives of the astronauts onboard and sending mission control into high alert. However, this adverse event also ignited unprecedented collaboration, creativity, and resilience. NASA's ground team swiftly formulated a life-saving plan, turning this mission from a potential disaster into a testimony to human ingenuity. The lesson? Preparedness, resilience, and collaborative problem-solving can turn emergencies into defining moments of success.

**Kodak's Missed Opportunity** - Kodak, a giant in the film photography realm, faced an unexpected challenge when its engineer, Steve Sasson, birthed the digital camera in the 1970s. Viewing this groundbreaking innovation as a Negative Surprise, Kodak sidelined it to protect its established film market. In doing so, they missed a pivotal shift in the industry. The lesson here is clear: Embracing and adapting to Negative Surprises, rather than resisting them, can shape industry revolutions and maintain market leadership.

**The Socratic Method - A Pedagogical Power Tool** - The Socratic method, a teaching approach rooted in challenging the learner through probing questions, exemplifies the educational potential of Negative Surprises.

> **Harvard Law's Approach** - Envision a law student, confident in her grasp of a case study. As class begins, she's posed a question from an angle she hadn't anticipated. This method, employing Negative Surprise, pushes her to rethink, refining her analytical abilities and deepening her grasp of legal intricacies.

> **Elementary School Perspective** - Consider elementary students introduced to Columbus's expedition from a standard viewpoint. A twist comes when they're prompted to

view the event from the Native Americans' perspective. This shift broadens their historical perspective and nurtures empathy.

**In the Corporate World** - Extending the Socratic method to corporate training, IT professionals might be presented with an unanticipated challenge—developing software for those less tech-inclined, forcing them to step outside their expertise bubble, resulting in more inclusive and intuitive products.

Each instance emphasizes the transformative power of a Negative Surprise. They underscore that, when approached constructively, such Surprises can enhance engagement, cultivate deeper understanding, and drive growth.

The crux is leveraging these moments as catalysts for progress rather than setbacks, a process that requires mindfulness, adaptability, and resilience. Here are actionable steps to help you navigate and capitalize on these unexpected challenges.

## Apply It: Navigate and Capitalize the Negative Surprise

**Embrace the Emotion** - Recognize and validate the immediate emotions (shock, disappointment, or confusion) a Negative Surprise brings. Give yourself or your team a moment to process before reacting.

**Reframe Perspective** - Instead of viewing the Surprise as a setback, see it as an opportunity. "What can I learn from this?" or "How can this lead to improvement or growth?"

**Seek Root Causes** - Dig deep to understand the root cause of the surprise. What overlooked elements contributed to this situation? Understanding causes can turn the event into a learning opportunity.
**Collaborate & Brainstorm** - Gather a team or seek advice. Group problem-solving can lead to innovative solutions and new perspectives, making the most out of the surprise.

**Take Strategic Action** - Devise a plan to address the immediate challenges. Then, consider longer-term actions that can prevent similar surprises or better equip you to handle them.

**Document & Reflect** - Keep a record of surprises and your responses to them. Regularly review this log to identify patterns and areas for improvement, ensuring future readiness.

**Foster Resilience** -Cultivate a growth mindset, both individually and within your team. Accept that challenges are inevitable but can be harnessed for growth. Celebrate the wins that come out of managing Negative Surprises, no matter how small.

**Continuous Learning** - Engage in ongoing education and training. Not only will you be equipped with skills to handle surprises, but you can also prevent them through foresight.

**Communicate Openly** - Foster an environment where communication flows freely to quickly identify and address issues, converting potential setbacks into constructive dialogues.

**Stay Adaptable** - The world is constantly changing. Remaining flexible and open to change means you're better poised to pivot and evolve in the face of surprise.

Again, it's not the Negative Surprise but how you respond to it that defines the outcome. With preparation, a growth mindset, and a proactive approach, you can transform unexpected challenges into moments of growth and innovation.

Recognizing that a Negative Surprise is inevitable makes mastering your response even more crucial. It's not a matter of "if" but "when." And when it does arrive, your readiness and agility in navigating it will prove your salt. By equipping yourself with knowledge and strategies, you not only mitigate its impact but seize it as an opportunity to demonstrate resilience, adaptability, and forward-thinking. The true test of self-leadership lies in turning unforeseen setbacks into springboards for progress.

## Applied: Unexpected Project Setback

Andrea manages a global branding agency in Canada and has been leading a creative team to develop a brand campaign for a major client. They've spent weeks gathering data and designing creatives. A day before they're set to present, Andrea finds out the client has dramatically changed their product features, rendering their work irrelevant - a significant Negative Surprise.

### Leveraging the Negative Surprise for Progress

**Embrace the Emotion** - Andrea calls an emergency team meeting. She acknowledges the shock and frustration everyone is feeling and provides a safe space for the team to vent and process their immediate emotions.

**Reframe Perspective** - Instead of panicking, Andrea says, "This is a challenge, but it's also an opportunity for us to showcase our adaptability and depth of skill. How can we turn this around to impress the client even more?"

**Seek Root Causes** -She contacts the client's liaison to understand the reasons behind the sudden change. Andrea learns that market feedback prompted the product changes.

**Collaborate & Brainstorm** - The team pools their ideas. They discuss how they can salvage aspects of their current campaign and adapt it to the new product features.

**Take Strategic Action** - The team decides to retain the campaign's core message but modifies the visuals and feature descriptions. They work in shifts to ensure they're ready for the presentation.

**Document & Reflect** - After the presentation, Andrea makes a note of the events. She reflects on how they might maintain more regular check-ins with clients in the future to avoid such last-minute shifts.

**Foster Resilience** - Andrea praises her team for their quick adaptability and hard work, creating a positive narrative around the challenge and fostering resilience among her team members.

**Continuous Learning** - She schedules a team debriefing session to discuss lessons learned and explores training sessions on agile project management to better handle such curveballs in the future.

**Communicate Openly** - Andrea meets with the client to establish better communication protocols, ensuring that her team remains informed about significant changes.

**Stay Adaptable** - Moving forward, Andrea incorporates a more flexible structure in her project timelines, allowing for potential last-minute modifications.

The result? Not only does the team successfully present an adapted marketing campaign, but Andrea also strengthens her team's resilience, adaptability, and rapport with the client. This unexpected challenge evolves into a powerful demonstration of their capabilities.

## NEUTRAL SURPRISE IS PURE ENGAGING MAGIC

Neutral Surprises don't send shockwaves through your life; instead, they sprinkle it with moments of pause and intrigue. They break the monotony without causing a stir, like finding an unfamiliar coin from another country among your change or witnessing a shooting star on an otherwise regular night.

They're not filled with the adrenaline rush of a Positive Surprise or the wallop of a Negative one, but they still capture a fleeting moment of your attention and wonder.

Neutral Surprises pop up more often than we realize.

Stumbling upon a book in a store you didn't know you were looking for, hearing an unfamiliar yet catchy tune from a passing car, or even bumping into an old friend in an unexpected place. These incidents neither elate nor dismay; they just... are. They add texture and layers to our experiences without dramatically altering our emotional landscapes. If Neutral Surprises were an algorithm, the following is open source:

### <u>Neutral Surprise = Nothing Positive or Negative</u>
### Just Are

Understanding and using Neutral Surprises can be incredibly effective. Imagine you're in a meeting, and it's dragging on with the same monotonous agenda points. Suddenly, the facilitator flashes an intriguing, unrelated image on the screen or shares an unrelated anecdote. It doesn't directly contribute to the topic at hand but revitalizes the energy in the room, refreshing everyone's focus.

Similarly, you could introduce a seemingly unrelated fact or story in the middle of any communication for engagement. It might not directly relate to the core material, but it breaks the routine and sparks curiosity, making the overall experience more memorable.

For instance, I recently read about newly discovered ruins in Egypt where they found honey in jars thousands of years old that's still edible. This gives me a fresh Neutral Surprise to weave into a narrative when the chance arises.

## Apply It: Neutral Surprise

**Facilitator**: Pauses and says, *"Did you know honey never spoils? Archeologists have found honey pots in ancient Egyptian tombs that are over 3,000 years old and still perfectly good to eat."*

**Participant A**: *"Really? That's fascinating!"*

**Participant B**: *"I had no idea! What does that have to do with cognitive-communication, though?"*

**Facilitator**: Smiling, responds, *"Well, not much directly. But think of it this way: just as honey can stand the test of time, so too can the impact of our words. What we say, how we say it, and when we say it, can resonate with others for a very long time. So, choosing our words carefully is crucial and ensuring that our communication is understood and persuasive."*

Neutral Surprises serve as reminders that life isn't just about the highs and lows but also about the moments of wonder in between. They bring about a spontaneous curiosity, making the ordinary seem just a little more extraordinary; life's delightful footnotes add richness and depth to our stories without shifting the main narrative.

Neutral Surprises have a unique way of maintaining engagement; they're like the unexpected pause in a conversation that refreshes the communication without changing its course. They may not pack the emotional punch of Positive or Negative Surprises, but they're effective in keeping things lively. As mentioned, you find them everywhere if you realize they are there for you to notice and put in your private mental pantry.

Picture a seasoned salesperson during a product demonstration to a potential client. The conversation is focused on specifications, pricing, and features.

In the middle of the pitch, the salesperson shares an unrelated yet captivating story about their adventure while traveling to a remote village, encountering a unique local tradition. This story has no direct link to the product or the sales pitch, but it injects a brief moment of wonder and intrigue.

And the connection to the sale? There isn't one.

It's simply a refreshing pause, a neutral surprise, breaking the routine of the pitch. It doesn't lead to a selling point or objection handling; it's just there to reinvigorate the conversation and keep the potential client's attention engaged.

It's an artful pause that maintains the emotional connection between the salesperson and the prospect, and in the world of sales, oftentimes, that's precisely what's needed.

How I longed for the literature professor who starts strumming a guitar and crooning Bob Dylan during a lecture about post-modernism.

*"You don't need a weatherman
to know which way the wind blows..."*

At first glance, the impromptu seems out of place amidst the analysis of literary works. However, it offers a breather, reminding students of the era's broader themes of change, protest, and adaptability - all encapsulated in Dylan's lyrics. Postmodernism is suddenly connected to Bob Dylan's passion. We are connecting dots, uh, learning lobes of the brain.

Neutral Surprises interrupt the routine, reinvigorating curiosity without drawing strong emotional responses and that's key. The central discourse is still on literature, but these unexpected moments shine a different light on the subject, and a different perspective, making the presentation more captivating and leaving a lasting mark on the students' memories.

*?huh ,ffuts looc ytterP*

See how easy that was? It's not always about the highs and lows; sometimes, the middle ground can be just as effective.

Consider a scenario that happens more each day then we realize. In this example, where a salesperson named Jennifer calls a potential client, Dr. Schall, from the pharmaceutical sector, illustrating how a Neutral Surprise might unfold for effect.

**Jennifer**: Good morning, Dr. Schaal. I'm Jennifer from BioFuturePharma. Thank you for taking my call.

**Dr. Schaal**: Good morning, Jennifer. I've only got a few minutes, so let's get straight to it.

**Jennifer**: Of course, Doctor. I'll keep it brief. BioFuturePharma has some exciting new developments in neurodegenerative disease treatments that I think could greatly benefit your practice.

**Dr. Schaal**: I'm listening, but bear in mind I've heard plenty of sales pitches. What makes yours different?

**Jennifer**: Well, let's put it this way, Doctor. Can you guess how many chemical compounds the average snail produces?

**Dr. Schaal**: Snails? I have no idea. What does this have to do with neurodegenerative treatments?

**Jennifer**: It might seem unrelated, but bear with me. The average snail produces around 80 unique chemical compounds, many of which have significant pharmaceutical potential.

**Dr. Schaal**: That's... surprising, I must admit.

**Jennifer**: Indeed. Now, let's take our surprising friends, the snails, and relate them to our work at BioFuturePharma. We're exploring several marine species, including snails, for their unique compounds. One of them shows excellent potential as a treatment for neurodegenerative diseases.

**Dr. Schaal**: That's unexpected... Tell me more about this.

### Step By Step: Crafting a Neutral Surprise

**Know Your Audience** - Dive deep into understanding whom you're engaging. What do they anticipate? What mild surprise would intrigue them without evoking extreme emotions?

**Pinpoint Your Goal** - Why are you introducing this surprise? Is it to rekindle interest, segue into another topic, or seamlessly transition between discussion segments?

**Ideate Surprise Elements** - Think creatively. What can serve as a neutral surprise? Perhaps an intriguing statistic, an unexpected visual, or a brief topic detour.

**Gauge the Likely Impact** - Anticipate your audience's response. You're aiming to capture their interest without sending them on an emotional roller coaster.

**Craft Your Communication** - Ensure the surprise blends seamlessly with your ongoing content or conversation.

**Deploy and Refine** - Set your strategy in motion. Observe the audience's engagement and modify your techniques based on their feedback.

While Neutral Surprises might be understated, they pack a punch in recapturing attention. They're valuable allies in the intricate dance of sustained engagement. And they can happen anywhere, anytime, or when needed. Set your RAS and you'll see them everywhere.

### In the Heart of a Quilt Shop

The magic of connection often unfolds when you least expect it. On a serene day in a local coffee haunt, I chanced upon a chat with 'Mickie.' Her words were so captivating it felt like getting lost in a melodious tune. A master Quilter, Mickie unraveled tale after tale filled with Neutral surprises.

One particular technique she shared was the "Disappearing 9-Patch Quilt". In the quilting world, the traditional "9 patch quilt" is akin to the comfort of home – nine squares sewn in a 3x3 grid, humble yet timeless.

But then comes the twist – the "Disappearing 9 Patch". With a quilter's sleight of hand, the traditional block morphs into a tapestry of complexity. It's a trick of rearranging, leaving the beholder assuming a maze of sewing intricacies. The simplicity behind the perceived complexity is the heart of the Neutral Surprise - it intrigues but doesn't swing emotions intensely.

For those attuned to the nuances of quilting or those enamored by its beauty, this technique stands as a beacon of curiosity. It gently beckons, asking them for more, perhaps even challenging them to adopt the trick.

## An Encore from Yesteryears

As we stroll further into Neutral Surprises, let's drift into an era where music was the world's muse. The year was 1985, and the event - Live Aid - was a mission helmed by Bob Geldof and Midge Ure, aiming to bring solace to Ethiopia's famine-hit souls.

Enter Queen, and the bar of expectations was skyscraping. Yet, Freddie Mercury did the unexpected in a weave of melodies – an impromptu call-and-response with the audience. It wasn't a dazzling curveball nor a disheartening twist but a Neutral Surprise that rekindled the crowd's spirit.

This seemingly fleeting moment is now etched in rock annals as one of its grandest. Mercury's act that day stands testament to the power of Neutral surprises in keeping audiences riveted. It serves as a reminder that even in the explosive world of rock, there's a place for the gentle allure of Neutral Surprise.

## On the Horizon

Our foray into Neutral Surprises might be drawing to a close, but the odyssey of engagement is far from over. Ahead lies the uncharted waters of Foreshadowed and Unexpected Surprise, where anticipation meets the unforeseen, promising to redefine engagement. The tale of Surprise is only beginning to unfold, and I'm thrilled about the revelations ahead.

## FORESHADOWED SURPRISE, ANTICIPATED REVELATIONS

By the way, that last sentence on the prior page foreshadowed this one. :-)

Since you can, picture yourself immersed in a gripping novel. The storyteller crafts an atmosphere dense with suspense and uncertainty. Clues are gently sprinkled, hinting at a looming revelation. You feel it, a crescendo of anticipation.

*"Amid the tales of twisted fate and intrigue, I subtly guide your curiosity. Like delicate droplets, whispers of what's to come dot the narrative. The aura brims with suspense. It clings to you, beckoning toward that foretold climax. And when it unfurls, even with the hints, it resonates like a sudden clap of thunder, jolting yet oddly expected."*

And even with its foreshadowed nature, it startles you when that moment dawns.

*"As the story culminates, emotions flood, clarity emerges, and revelations resonate. Time converges, and clarity emerges, leaving behind the tantalizing suspense in favor of deep resonance. The tale's inhabitants, who've become familiar figures in your mind's theater, remain indelible, their narratives echoing the exhilarating journey you've traversed together. And even with every clue, every hint, the finale still leaves an imprint, a mark of the enigma that was this tale."*

Such is the allure of Foreshadowed Surprise - a voyage of expected yet unexpected moments, where hints don't diminish the surprise but amplify its impact.

Envision a group of budding sales recruits gathered for their introductory training at a prestigious tech corporation. The atmosphere is charged with hopeful anticipation. Their day, they assume, is chalked out with theoretical modules, slideshows, and interactive exercises: their facilitator, a renowned sales veteran known for his out-of-the-box techniques, steps forward.

"Let me kick things off with an anecdote," he commences, unfolding a narrative of an ambitious sales novice. With every word, he intersperses glimpses of the novice's unconventional tactics and the astonishing outcomes they birthed.

He illustrates a landscape where one behemoth dominates the market. Yet, the tale describes how this fresh salesperson carved a niche for his fledgling venture. The facilitator vividly paints the image of the relentless grind, networking marathons, and unyielding sales pitches. Yet, a shadowy hint persists — a masterstroke strategy played in the backdrop, though he cleverly conceals it.

The recruits hang on to every word. The young salesperson's journey resonates with them, while the mystery strategy's allure holds them captive. The atmosphere thickens with suspense.

As dusk nears, after the recruits are equipped with a barrage of sales tactics, the facilitator finally unveils the mysterious game-changer: the salesperson's knack for transforming customer endorsements into riveting sales narratives.

The reveal, though subtly hinted, catches them off guard. They'd envisioned a tech marvel or a radical sales methodology. Yet, what they got was uncomplicated, centered around customer feedback, and brilliantly impactful.

Employed masterfully by the trainer, Foreshadowed Surprise became the lynchpin that captivated the recruits from start to finish, ensuring the tale's core message was imprinted deeply in their professional psyche. While they sensed a looming revelation, its simplicity, and effectiveness delivered an unforgettable impact.

Sounds counterintuitive, doesn't it?

Think of a film maestro subtly hinting at a plot twist that evades the conscious grasp of the audience, or a magician teasing an upcoming act, only to astonish viewers with an outcome they didn't see coming.

Foreshadowed Surprise are the backbone of literature, cinema, and drama storytelling. They weave tension and engagement, holding viewers in eager suspense.

**Step-by-Step: Crafting the Foreshadowed Surprise**

**Lay the Groundwork** - Kickstart with a riveting story, event, or idea tailored to your audience's interests and expectations.

**Sow the Clues** - Gently weave hints, cues, or tantalizing bits of information into your narrative, pointing subtly toward the impending twist.

**Heighten the Drama** - Deepen the narrative tension as you proceed, deploying pacing, tone, or further breadcrumbs that pull your audience deeper into the story.

**The Big Unveil** - When the moment is ripe, unveil the surprise with gusto at your narrative's zenith, ensuring it gratifies the buildup.

**Reflection & Linkage** - Afford time for your audience to digest the Surprise. Then, circle back to the overarching message or objective, anchoring the twist and its associated lesson in their consciousness.

This template is versatile and suitable for various scenarios, such as developing an instructional course, curating a business pitch, or scripting an advertising stint. The essence is to sustain engagement, immerse the audience, and amplify their absorption.

Suppose our backdrop is a routine sales convention. The familiar goal? Motivating the team towards a novel sales protocol aimed at escalating client loyalty. Yawn. Spice it up with a Lil' Foreshadow.

**Lay the Groundwork** - Initiate the conference with a gripping chronicle of the firm's most illustrious sales maven with an unparalleled client loyalty record. Make this account vivid, emphasizing the salesperson's distinctive flair and triumph.

**Sow the Clues** - Intersperse subtle allusions that this sales ace possessed a covert modus operandi, an unparalleled client interface style in the enterprise. Keep them guessing.

**Heighten the Drama** - Enrich the narrative with more of the sales virtuoso's retention feats, accentuating the enigma of their modus operandi. Incorporate lighthearted anecdotes of peers endeavoring to emulate this elusive approach.

**The Big Unveil** - At the climax of curiosity, disclose that this covert strategy mirrors the very sales methodology the firm intends to adopt. It's not mere legend but a tested blueprint soon to be everyone's mantra.

**Reflection & Linkage** - Pause for the revelation to settle. Next, bridge it to the essence of client loyalty, the merits of the fresh sales plan, and its alignment with the firm's broader goals. Promote dialogue, solicit queries, and clarify each member's contribution to this plan's realization.

This approach guarantees the sales crew's unwavering engagement, intertwining company heritage with the novel sales blueprint and strengthening collective resonance and insight.

To Illustrate... One of cinema's most iconic foreshadowing instances remains the "I am your father" bombshell in Star Wars Episode V: The Empire Strikes Back. Clues sprinkled throughout Episode IV: A New Hope and into The Empire Strikes Back insinuate a profound bond between Darth Vader and Luke Skywalker. C'mon!

There's a scene from Pitch Perfect, the movie, where Beca tells Jesse about Darth Vader that illustrates this brilliantly.

**Beca**: I've never seen Star Wars.

**Jesse**: What?

**Beca**: I know, I know. It's a sin. But I've never been into sci-fi.

**Jesse**: Well, you're missing out. It's the greatest story ever told.

**Beca**: I'm sure it is. But I don't know, the whole "Darth Vader is Luke's father" thing just seems too predictable.

**Jesse**: What? No, it's not predictable at all! It's a total twist!

**Beca**: I mean, come on. It's so obvious. The guy's got a black cape and a voice like Darth Vader. 'Vader' in German means 'father'. His name is literally Darth Father. It's just too easy.

**Jesse**: But that's what makes it so good! The twist is so unexpected that it's actually believable.

**Beca**: I don't know. I just don't see it.

**Jesse**: Well, you should watch it sometime. You might be Surprised.

In literature, Shakespeare's Romeo and Juliet stands out as the OG of Foreshadowed Surprise. The prologue itself declares the "star-crossed lovers" destiny, setting the tone for their tragic culmination.

It's pivotal to grasp that foreshadowing and Surprise seem inherently opposing. While foreshadowing preempts the audience, Surprise is inherently unforeseen. However, in masterful storytelling, they harmoniously coexist: events, even if subtly foreshadowed, can astonish when they materialize, yet in hindsight, the indicators had been ever-present.

What comes next is unexpected.

# EMBRACING THE ELEMENT OF UNEXPECTED SURPRISE

At its core, Unexpected Surprise is that moment that comes out of left field, leaving us stunned, our perceptions shifted, even if briefly. They're the plot twisters, the dramatic crescendos, the sudden climaxes. While they might seem haphazard, when wielded with finesse, Unexpected Surprises can be compelling in sparking interest and maintaining engagement.

There's a corporate session progressing as usual – with reports, strategies, and routine forecasts. But then, out of the blue, the CEO announces a radical change where attendees, without any forewarning, are randomly grouped for an impromptu workshop. Such scenarios serve as system shake-ups, necessitating rapid recalibration to an evolving situation. A few stand-out examples:

**The Sudoku Wave** - In the puzzle realm, the world received an unexpected jolt with Sudoku. Wayne Gould introduced this relatively obscure Japanese number game to The Times in Britain in the early 2000s. The outcome? A global craze. It's astonishing how a humble number grid entranced so many, underscoring that novelties, regardless of their simplicity or intricacy, can evoke widespread wonder.

**Spotify's Wrapped Magic** - Every year's end, Spotify pulls a delightful rabbit out of its hat, presenting users with a bespoke roundup of their year in music. This surprise deepens users' bond with the platform and fuels social media buzz as users flaunt their musical timelines.

**Google's April Foolery** - April 1st and Google have a fun love affair. The tech giant revels in Unexpected Surprises, rolling out whimsical product announcements and playful games. These jests bolster Google's user engagement, making the brand more relatable and endearing.

The power of Unexpected Surprises is undeniable. When artfully deployed, they can turn the ordinary into extraordinary, making experiences unforgettable.

## The Art of the Unexpected Surprise

Unexpected Surprise challenges us to step out of our comfort zones, pushing past the monotony of everyday routines. They stir us to adapt swiftly, reevaluate preconceptions, and embrace fresh viewpoints. When orchestrated thoughtfully, these moments disrupt the status quo and invigorate our minds, offering a refreshed lens through which we view the world. More critically, they prime us for absorbing new insights.

Mastering the element of Unexpected Surprise is nuanced. It hinges on deeply comprehending your audience's psyche, anticipations, and limits. It isn't about sheer shock value. Instead, it's about introducing an element of wonder that broadens their understanding, capturing their imagination and sustaining their attention. Whether it's a revelation in a storyline, a dramatic strategy pivot, an impromptu challenge, or a Surprise guest, the essence of Unexpected Surprise lies in the thrill of the unanticipated, coupled with its ability to captivate and engage.

### Step-By-Step: Crafting Unexpected Surprises

**Audience Insight** - Grasp your audience's psyche. Understand their expectations and gauge the thresholds of their comfort zones. What thrills one demographic might not resonate with another.

**Objective Clarity** - Pinpoint what you aim to manifest with your Unexpected Surprise. Is it about etching a memorable episode, triggering a paradigm shift, or infusing enthusiasm?

**Design the Novelty** - Contemplate avenues to infuse a twist into your story or presentation. The crux is to interweave something surprising yet pertinent and impactful.

**Anticipate Reactions** - Strategize the aftermath of the surprise. Perhaps facilitate a discourse, open a Q&A avenue, or introduce a reflective activity.

**Assess and Refine** - Post-deployment, gauge the surprise's resonance. Did it enhance the engagement quotient? Elicit feedback and utilize it to refine future strategies.

### Apply It: A Speaker's Approach

Alan, a renowned public speaker, was tasked with addressing a conglomerate of young entrepreneurs at a business symposium. Here's how he applied an Unexpected Surprise...

**Audience Insight** - Alan recognized that his audience comprised millennials and Gen-Z entrepreneurs who had grown up in the digital era and were likely jaded by the typical, cliched entrepreneurial success stories. They craved fresh, authentic narratives and insights and would immediately tune out anything they deemed irrelevant or redundant.

**Objective Clarity** - Alan's 'Big Idea,' what he wanted his audience to walk away with, was to impress upon them the importance of resilience in entrepreneurship. However, instead of merely recounting familiar tales of business moguls, he aimed to introduce a powerful, Unexpected Surprise to drive the point home and ensure it lingered in their memories.

**Design the Novelty** - Instead of starting with a usual PowerPoint slide or a predictable anecdote, Alan began with a live performance of a sand artist illustrating a story. As the artist drew, Alan narrated the tale of a little-known entrepreneur from a small village, emphasizing the obstacles they overcame that weren't just business-related but also deeply personal and cultural. The visual representation through sand art and an unusual narrative served as an unexpected treat for the eyes and ears. Alan ensured every learning lobe of the brain was connected to this story.

**Anticipate Reactions** - Alan paused after the performance and story, allowing the audience to process and absorb the tale. He then transitioned into an interactive Q&A, asking them, "What was surprising?" "What did you already know but now see differently?" and "What do you still need help with?". The blend of a powerful narrative and inviting participation ensured the audience was not just passive listeners but active contributors.

**Assess and Refine** - Post-session, Alan sent out digital feedback forms to gauge the impact of his presentation, focusing on the Unexpected Surprise element. The response was overwhelmingly positive, with many attendees expressing a profoundly personal appreciation for the novel approach. They felt seen, heard, and, most importantly, deeply engaged.

By carefully weaving in an Unexpected Surprise and following through with cognitive frameworks, Alan managed to capture the attention of a hard-to-impress demographic and left a lasting impact beyond the confines of the conference hall.

While Unexpected Surprise can undoubtedly captivate, they must remain cohesive with the overarching theme or message. Their role isn't to detract but to augment. The most effective Unexpected Surprises enthrall and seamlessly align with the central narrative, reinforcing rather than detracting from it.

When employed discerningly and purposefully, Unexpected Surprise metamorphoses into formidable engagement catalysts, etching indelible imprints, fostering rich dialogues, and propelling deeper immersion and thoughtfulness.

# SPECIFIC SURPRISE

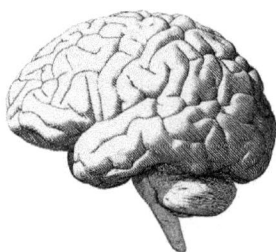

## THE WONDER OF SPECIFIC SURPRISE

As you now know, a General Surprise is an unexpected event or revelation that can be experienced by anyone, regardless of their background or context. It's broad and universal in its appeal, like suddenly seeing a rainbow after a rainy day.

In contrast, a Specific Surprise is tailored to a particular individual or group based on their unique experiences, expectations, or knowledge. It's a more personalized form of the unexpected, like receiving a Surprise gift that's been on your wishlist for a long time.

Surprise is as essential to our lives as the very air we breathe. Its presence is felt in the chills down our spine, the gasps of amazement, the laughter of joy bursting from your granddaughter, and even the tears of discovery. But the magnitude of Surprise we encounter in our lifetime is vast and incredibly varied.

I've crafted umpteen unique shades of Surprise for you. Like a drawer full of spices to spiff up a dish, each Specific Surprise with its own distinct flavor and aroma, ready to elevate your communication.

Imagine your communications as a dish.

These Specific Surprises are the spices that add nuance, elevate the essence, and provide a twist where you least expect it. From Aesthetic Surprises that tickle the senses to Cognitive ones that challenge our perceptions and Emotional Surprises that add warmth, each contributes to refining our communications.

Just like cumin, chili powder, and oregano are commonly used in Mexican cuisine, Cognitive, Linguistic, and Conceptual Surprises will provoke an individual cognitive shift.

Know what you need your audience to walk away with and plan your Surprises for the effect you desire. It is that easy. If you know what you want, it's easy to spice it.

The key is knowing which one, when and how much to sprinkle on, just like cooking, and creating a memorable dish that resonates with everyone at the table.

# AESTHETIC SURPRISE
*Magic Hidden In Plain Sight*

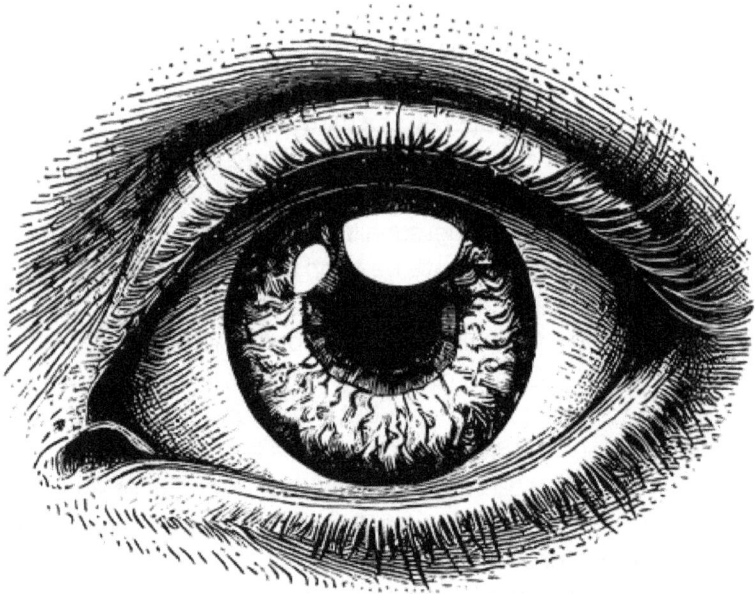

Aesthetic Surprise beautifully encapsulates the crossroads where art, human emotion, and design converge. It's that heart-skipping moment, that delightful burst of wonder, when an ordinary sight, sound, or experience transforms, presenting itself in an unexpectedly mesmerizing manner. Whether through a visual treat, a harmonic resonance, an evocative phrase, or even an event's unanticipated choreography, the effect is the same – sheer sensory enchantment.

Picture Aesthetic Surprise as the intriguing surrealism of Dali's drooping clocks amidst the predictability of everyday life or Banksy's thought-provoking graffiti punctuating a city's concrete canvas. It's the stirring emotion of Beethoven's Symphony No. 5 piercing a room's stillness.

It is not exclusively reserved for grand artistic expressions; its beauty can be found and harnessed in the most ordinary moments, turning them extraordinary. We can enrich our daily experiences by tapping into its allure, fostering creativity, innovation, and deepened understanding.

Now, let's translate this into a professional setting.

Imagine yourself as a team leader tasked with revamping those monotonous weekly updates. Introducing Aesthetic Surprise could transform the atmosphere and invigorate the team's mindset. Maybe one week, the confines of the boardroom are exchanged for the serene surroundings of a local garden. The following week, PowerPoint slides take a back seat, replaced by vivid tales celebrating the team's victories and learning moments. With each unforeseen twist, the workaday transforms, making every meeting an eagerly awaited event rather than a tedious obligation.

Shifting your lens to your personal life, picture your roles at home. Weekly chores like Saturday tidying sessions could quickly devolve into grumbles. But what if Aesthetic Surprise is sprinkled into the routine? Suddenly, that vacuum isn't just a household appliance—it's a device capturing ghosts one week and extracting extraterrestrial beings the next. My kids loved this! The routine morphs into exciting escapades by weaving narratives, ensuring tasks are completed amidst giggles and imaginative play rather than reluctant sighs.

Older kids? It's late, well past the agreed curfew time, and your teenage child is yet to return. The house is veiled in silence, interrupted only by the insistent tick-tock of the clock, and a simmering worry rises within you. Conventional wisdom might dictate a stringent punishment or the temporary seizure of their treasured smartphone.

But tonight, you opt for a less traveled route to teach a lasting lesson minus the hostility.

As the door finally creaks open and your teenager steps in, they brace themselves for the anticipated storm of disapproval. But instead, a gentle scene unfolds before them. The kitchen is bathed in a soft, inviting glow, and there you sit, calm and composed, Spotify softly playing a chill playlist, a plate of their favorite late-night snack centered on the table.

The stern lecture they had mentally prepared for is absent. Instead, you gesture for them to join you. With a look of bewilderment, they sit opposite you, their tense shoulders beginning to relax.

"Tough night, Champ?" you start with curiosity rather than

criticism in your voice. Gradually, you begin recounting tales from your rebellious teenage days— missteps, wild adventures, and lessons learned.

"I remember a night much like this," you reminisce, a hint of nostalgia coloring your words. "Back when I was your age, I, too, felt that rules didn't apply to me. That evening, I quickly learned that every choice has repercussions, affecting me and those who loved and waited for me."

This sudden shift—from an anticipated reprimand to a heartfelt sharing of experiences—etches the intended lesson far more profound than any lecture could. Your child is nudged to reflect on their actions, not from a vantage point of defiance, but from one of mutual respect and understanding. Through the art of 'Aesthetic Surprise,' they gain a deeper appreciation for responsibilities and connections.

Let's head down a woodland path.

You're walking through a forest, each step bringing a sense of the known, predictable rhythm. The path is familiar, and the sights and sounds are ones you've encountered countless times before. Just as you've settled into the comforting embrace of routine, Aesthetic Surprise gently tugs at your senses, urging you to view the world with fresh, childlike wonder. It asks you to pivot, shift your gaze and recognize the magic beneath the surface of the everyday.

Aesthetic Surprise isn't only about a breathtaking vista suddenly emerging around a bend; it's a transformative lens that reveals hidden intricacies and overlooked splendors in our day-to-day lives. It unveils the wonders tucked away in the folds of the ordinary, turning the mundane into something truly magical.

By welcoming Aesthetic Surprise into our lives, we move from a static canvas to an ever-evolving mural of experiences. The ordinary moments are now punctuated with unexpected bursts of delight and newfound appreciation because you frame them that way. We often frame Aesthetic Surprise as 'being present.'

The beauty of Aesthetic Surprise isn't just in the initial bang of the unexpected but in the cascading waves of inspiration and exploration it ignites. It encourages us to stretch beyond our comfort zones, revel in the new, and dance to the unique tune of our individuality.

At its core, Aesthetic Surprise is more than just a moment of astonishment. It too is a catalyst, urging us to challenge the boring, ignite creativity, and infuse our daily lives with spontaneous bursts of joy. Life can be cinematic only if we take charge of its direction and narrative. You can take charge.

Now, immerse yourself in a cinematic short story that embodies the essence of 'Aesthetic Surprise.'

### Linda's Unveiling: Art That Brought a Town Closer

Linda lived her days in tiny South Prairie, cushioned between undulating hills and a shimmering creek. She was the ever-smiling librarian to her neighbors, ready with a book recommendation. But beyond those reading glasses was a world few knew, brimming with vibrant hues and secret pigs. By day, she shared tales; by night, she painted them, always adding her hidden signature: a pig, sometimes multiple, subtly tucked away in the scene.

Each evening, Linda would retreat to her basement studio. Walls adorned with canvas after canvas revealed her prowess. Yet, these treasures stayed confined, away from the world's gaze.

With "Art in the Park" approaching, the town buzzed in anticipation. While others prepped, Linda felt no desire to showcase her art, enjoying the solitary embrace of her paintings.

Having chanced upon Linda's secret, Greg, a renowned photographer who believed the town and world should witness such brilliance, displayed one of Linda's pieces without her knowledge.

The day arrived, and as townsfolk admired various artworks, Linda's depiction of South Prairie drew them in. Her portrayal was familiar, yet enchanted, with every stroke narrating a story. Amidst the admiration, keen eyes began spotting the whimsical pigs subtly hidden within, adding another layer of delight.

The revelation was transformative. A wave of awe swept the crowd when Linda was recognized as the artist. From then on, Linda wasn't just the local librarian. She was their town's illuminating force, weaving deeper connections among its people with her hidden pigs and vibrant tales.

## COGNITIVE SURPRISE
*Bursting Bubbles of Assumed Knowledge & Beliefs*

Cognitive Surprise is the concept cousin of Aesthetic Surprise, but while the latter thrills the senses, Cognitive Surprise engages the brain in a quick-step dance of epiphany. It's THE lightbulb moment, a burst of understanding when the pieces of a complex puzzle suddenly fit together, when a novel idea blooms, or when an elusive concept finally makes sense.

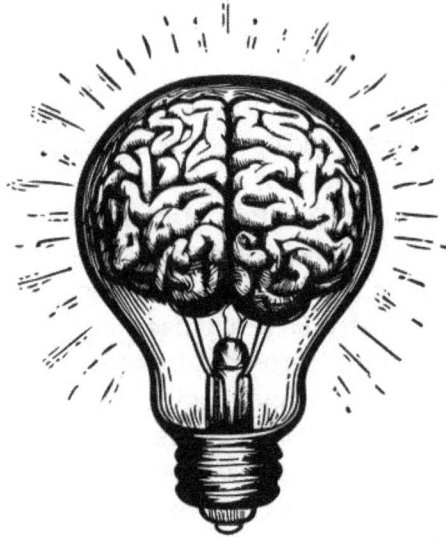

Cognitive Surprise is the unexpected joy of learning, the satisfying shock of sudden understanding.

As you step into the role of an educator or team leader, you wield a mighty tool of influence: Cognitive Surprise. As grounded in educational psychology, the concept leverages our brain's natural responses to unpredictability and novelty to boost learning and engagement.

Groundbreaking research in education, such as those conducted by Dr. Kieran O'Mahony and his 'Brain-based Classroom,' Dr. B. Price Kerfoot on 'Spaced Education' and the brain-centric works of Dr. Renate N. Caine, have underscored the potency of Cognitive Surprise in reinforcing learning.  These educational insights have stressed the significance of unpredictability and novelty in instruction, proving that they boost recall and understanding and stimulate curiosity and a thirst for knowledge.

Brain-centric is an instructional model that harnesses the natural learning mechanisms of the brain. It views the learner as a brain owner and not merely a student, creating learning experiences that align with how the brain processes and retains information.

One key aspect of Brain-centric  is its emphasis on presenting new information as discoveries, effectively incorporating elements of Cognitive Surprise throughout its revolutionary simple framework for presenting any concept to another with deep understanding. As learners navigate the curated flow, they encounter Surprise strategically placed to deepen understanding and enhance retention throughout by presenting for uncovery. And because of the model's alignment with how the brain processes information, it's co-created in the learning space.

This approach is steadily gaining recognition on a global scale, transforming classrooms, corporate training environments, sales presentations, and business management alike. With its understanding of the brain's workings and its effective use of Cognitive Surprise embedded in the framework, Brain-centric is setting a new direction in the field of education.

As an educator or team leader, you can catalyze transformative learning experiences. Your role is pivotal in imparting knowledge and igniting curiosity, fostering a lifelong love for learning, and shaping future leaders.

At work, instead of presenting solutions, try presenting problems. Encourage your team to wrestle with the issues at hand. Let them struggle, experiment, and be faulty. And when they piece the puzzle together, the solution will be a moment of Cognitive Surprise - far more rewarding than any ready-made solution.

You often hear the reply, "I didn't think of that." following a Cognitive Surprise.

As a parent, Cognitive Surprise transforms your child's learning experience. For instance, instead of explaining how a caterpillar transforms into a butterfly, have them observe a live caterpillar, its pupation, and eventual metamorphosis. The first-hand experience and the discovery process can lead to a decisive moment of Cognitive Surprise and a deeper understanding of nature's miracles.

Cognitive Surprise is far from just the dramatic reveal or the climactic twist; instead, the intricate dance leading up to that pivotal moment makes it truly meaningful. It's a calculated process that requires meticulous orchestration of the learning environment, carefully curating each detail, each clue that builds up to the moment of revelation.

Think of it as composing a symphony of learning, where each note and beat plays a role in creating a rich, layered understanding. Like a potter at the wheel, the educator meticulously shapes and molds the cognitive experience, setting a deliberate pace and rhythm that keeps the learners engaged, intrigued, and ever on their toes. And they like it.

This unfolding process closely mirrors how an engaging narrative is built. Each chapter, each character interaction, and each plot twist builds on one another, creating a complex web of interconnected ideas and themes. It's about creating a rich context, developing the landscape within which the learners navigate, and uncovering for them an intellectual journey toward a nuanced understanding of the subject.

The Cognitive Surprise is the crescendo, the high point where all the carefully laid out pieces fall into place, causing a shift in understanding. 'I knew that, but now I know this!' But the power of the Surprise is as much in the journey leading up to it as it is in the Surprise itself. The journey, the anticipation, the suspense — these elements make the moment of revelation deeply personal and impactful, facilitating understanding and promoting retention and application of the learned concept.

Cognitive Surprise is the carefully constructed path that uncovers information for the learner to discover. If Cognitive Surprise were a recipe, you have to use the right ingredients in the proper amount and in the right order, which I will outline next.

## Step-By-Step: How to Craft a Cognitive Surprise

**Context Setting** - Begin with a common managerial challenge: a chaotic, unproductive meeting scenario where everyone talks over each other, and the discussion goes off on tangents. Make it relatable, reminding them of situations they've likely experienced in their professional roles.

**Layering Information** - Introduce the 'facilitation' concept without defining it outright. Pose a thought-provoking question, such as, "What if there were a way to ensure each voice is heard, every agenda item is covered, and the meeting concludes with actionable outcomes?" This will hook their interest.

**Building Anticipation** - Share anecdotes of meetings that transformed from chaos to coherence. Keep the key factor – the facilitator – a mystery for now. Their curiosity about this transforming factor will grow.

**The Reveal** - Unveil that the hero of these anecdotes was a facilitator. Define what facilitators do and how they ensure an inclusive, focused, and productive meeting, essentially becoming the lighthouse in the stormy seas of chaotic gatherings.

**Cementing Understanding** - Culminate this learning journey with a hands-on exercise where they get to experience the role of a facilitator in a mock meeting. This immersive activity will consolidate their understanding and enable them to grasp the nuances of facilitation.

There's a specific power to this Surprise. It informs, it engages and motivates. It triggers a spark of insight that can lead to ongoing curiosity and continuous learning. In the classroom, the office, or the living room, aim for those Cognitive Surprise moments.

## Apply It

Fletcher addresses the staff...

"Let's reflect, for a moment, on the meetings we attend. Are they as productive as you want? Or do they dissolve into a chaotic conversation with numerous tangents and unmet objectives?"

After a pregnant pause, he continues. "Let's acknowledge it; we've all been there. Now, let's imagine a scenario where every voice is heard, every topic is addressed, and clear action points emerge by the end. Go ahead, imagine it. I'll be quiet for thirty seconds."

Half a minute later, Fletcher states, "Sounds like a dream?"

"Now, consider a situation where a high-stakes project meeting transforms from a whirlpool of diverse ideas to a finely-tuned orchestra producing a clear, unified plan. We've all been there too! Think back on a time when you met with a group and everything started discombobulated and finished like a masterpiece."

Fletcher again was silent, allowing the room to get into the moment of a magical meeting they took part in.

"Are you intrigued about transformations like the one you're thinking about, right now, happen?"

He raises his voice in excitement. "Brace yourself for the big reveal: the change agent is a skilled 'facilitator'! A facilitator navigates the flow of conversation, meets them where they are, utilizes multiple perspectives, manages time effectively, and gives time to reflect, collaborate, and discuss the shift in their understanding of what they used to know but now see differently."

The room is smiling and in agreement, but Fletcher now makes it real.

"Let's experience the value of the facilitator! We'll all now engage in a mock strategy session where each of you will don a facilitator's hat. Feel the challenges, experience the power, and understand the difference that effective facilitation can bring to your leadership toolkit."

## CREATIVE SURPRISE
*Crafting Novelty to Illuminate and Engage*

Creative Surprise is that unexpected twist in a communication, a stroke of genius in a presentation, or a splash of color on a blank canvas that evokes a gasp, a chuckle, or a moment of reflection. It's a form of Surprise that doesn't just startle or catch someone off-guard; it inspires, excites, and ignites the imagination. It's the reason we remember a story long after we've heard it, why we're drawn to a piece of art, or why a lecture becomes an experience rather than just another monologue.

At its heart, Creative Surprise is the art of delivering information or an experience in a way that's not just new, but novel and ingenious. Think of it as the difference between telling someone a fact and telling them a story. The fact might be forgotten, but a well-told story with an unpredicted twist? That stays. That resonates. And more than that, it engages.

Imagine you're a history teacher, trying to impart to your students the gravity of the Apollo 11 moon landing in 1969.

**Typical Approach** - "On July 20, 1969, Apollo 11, piloted by astronauts Neil Armstrong, Buzz Aldrin, and Michael Collins, landed on the moon. Neil Armstrong became the first human to set foot on the lunar surface."

While this fact is undeniably significant, it's presented in a straightforward and expected manner. For someone who has heard of the moon landing multiple times, this might feel repetitive and easy to tune out.

**Creative Surprise Approach** - "Imagine it's 1969. You're sitting in your living room with your family, the room dimly lit by a single bulb, all eyes fixed on a small black and white television. The static-filled screen shows a space-suited figure descending a ladder. The room is silent, the world is silent. And then, through the grainy visuals and crackled audio, you hear: *'That's one small step for man, one giant leap for mankind.'* At that moment, you're not just watching history; you're living it. Neil Armstrong, a man from Ohio, is walking on the moon, and you're walking right there with him."

The Surprise approach isn't just providing a fact. It paints a picture, placing the audience right into the scene. It brings in elements that are familiar - a living room, a family gathering, the hum of an old television. But then, it introduces the novel aspect, the Surprise - the experience of witnessing a monumental event. By turning the fact into a narrative and adding sensory elements and emotions, it becomes engaging and memorable.

This difference exemplifies Creative Surprise. Instead of stating a fact, you craft an experience. In doing so, you've made it resonant and engaging.

If you're looking to harness the power of Creative Surprise, whether it's for a pitch, a classroom, or even a casual chat, the trick is to weave in elements that are both familiar and novel. Start with what your audience knows, but introduce it in a way they wouldn't expect. This could be as simple as using an unconventional metaphor for a common idea or showcasing a well-known concept through a new lens.

It's a bit like when you're strolling through a familiar park, a route you've taken countless times, and suddenly, you spot a new art installation. You've walked past that very spot so often, and now, here's this captivating piece, unexpected and fresh, right in the midst of the familiar. That's what we're talking about with Creative Surprise.

For instance, think of the simple concept of 'time'. It's familiar, something we all grasp. Now, if I were to describe it as "the rhythm to which every heartbeat synchronizes," it takes that common idea and presents it in an unexpected light. The familiarity is there, but so is the novelty.

Think of that park the next time you're preparing a presentation or looking to explain something. Start with the familiar path but introduce an unanticipated piece of art. Your audience will not only appreciate the scenery but will be drawn to that new, intriguing 'thing' – the essence of what you're trying to convey...like the earlier mentioned astronaut.

Online and Digital, as vast as that it is, offers a unique playground for the power of Creative Surprise. In this universe where another diversion is perpetually a mouse-click away, the introduction of the unforeseen becomes paramount. Imagine the momentary shift of an unexpected animation in an e-learning course or the delightful intrigue of a novel sound byte in a podcast. Such moments yank your audience back to the forefront, captivated.

But here's a pivotal point: the art of Creative Surprise should amplify your message, not overshadow it. It's not about creativity for its mere thrill but about using it to bolster your core message. A misplaced Surprise, one that muddles rather than illuminates, could very well backfire.

The nuance in wielding Creative Surprise effectively comes from how well it reinforces your core message. For example, you're giving an online seminar about the importance of mental health. Your slides are well-designed, the statistics compelling, and the narrative personal. About halfway through, you shock your audience with a sudden loud buzz and a flashing screen that reads, "Wake Up!"

At first glance, it's an astonishing Creative Surprise. It slaps the audience out of their passivity, makes them alert. But here's where the caution comes in: Did that loud buzz serve the message, or did it cause undue stress that could detract from a topic that's inherently about reducing stress and send them into an amygdala hijack? Did it amplify the message of the importance of mental health, or did it dilute it by introducing an element of anxiety?

The power of Creative Surprise isn't just in its capacity to awaken; it's in its ability to enlighten, to complement your message so that your point isn't just made, but felt. In this case, a better Surprise could have been to pause for a guided one-minute breathing exercise in the middle of your talk on mental health. It would be unexpected but harmoniously aligned with the subject at hand, reinforcing the importance and accessibility of self-care and mental wellness.

The lesson here isn't just to Surprise for the sake of surprising; it's to do so in a way that fortifies your core message, making it more impactful and long-lasting in the minds and hearts of your audience.

### Step-By-Step: Build An Effective Creative Surprise

**Step 1** - Identify your Big Idea, the key takeaway or message you wish to convey to your audience. This will be the foundation on which you'll build your Surprise.

**Step 2** - Brainstorm a *Potential Surprises List*, various ways you could introduce a Surprise. Visual aids, auditory cues, interactive elements, personal anecdotes. Don't filter yourself too much at this stage and make ideas visible.

**Step 3** - Evaluate each Surprise. For every Surprise you've conjured, ask:
- *Does this align with my core message?*
- *Will it enhance the audience's understanding or appreciation of my message?*
- *Is there a risk it might detract or confuse?*

**Step 4** - Test It Out. If possible, share your chosen Surprise with a small group or trusted colleague for feedback. This will give you a sense of how well it's received and whether it bolsters your primary message as intended.

**Step 5**: Fine-Tune. Based on feedback and personal reflection, refine your Surprise. Adjust its intensity, timing, or delivery method to ensure it's perfectly calibrated to serve your core message.

**Step 6** - Integrate & Deliver. Embed your Surprise seamlessly into your presentation, lesson, or communication piece. Ensure its placement feels natural and its execution is smooth.

**Step 7** - Reflect After Delivery. After you've presented your material, take a moment to assess:
- *How did the audience react to the surprise?*
- *Did it make the intended impact?*
- *What can be improved for next time?*

The objective of a Creative Surprise is not just to be stunning, but to meaningfully accentuate your message, making it resonate deeply with your audience. Through this iterative process, you'll not only master the art of this Specific Surprise but also the craft of impactful and effective communication. It's a bit of work, but with a ton of return.

# CONCEPTUAL SURPRISE
*Redefining Ideas and Upending Existing Frameworks*

In the massive flexibility of Surprise, Conceptual Surprise stands distinct. Rather than being a bump or epiphany, it fundamentally transforms our understanding of the world. It's akin to realizing the sun doesn't revolve around the earth. It's understanding gravity as more than just a force, but a warping of space-time.

This form of Surprise, much like the grand reveal of a magician, shakes our core beliefs, recalibrating our perceptions. While it often underpins major scientific theories and societal shifts, Conceptual Surprise is also deeply woven into our daily experiences. Consider walking a familiar route and discovering an unnoticed path – that sudden awareness is the essence of this Surprise, nudging us to unlearn and relearn.

In life's grand narrative, Conceptual Surprise acts as a riveting plot twist, spurring contemplation and expansion of our worldview. Slowly but profoundly, it influences our choices, attitudes, and behaviors.

In a workplace setting, cultivating an atmosphere ripe for Conceptual Surprise is akin to rolling out the red carpet for innovation. Imagine being a software project manager. Rather than sticking strictly to traditional methods, you champion curiosity, exploration, and occasionally, gentle defiance of convention. This could lead to innovative coding techniques or fresh troubleshooting strategies.

See yourself as a leader managing an environment of intellectual exploration, where groundbreaking ideas are born and celebrated. Here, you're not just a manager but a cultivator, tending to the fertile ground of innovation. We're churning out new ideas and challenging the old. It's the demolition of assumptions and the construction of new insights.

Within this nurturing environment, Conceptual Surprises bloom, signaling breakthroughs that can redefine industries. The unanticipated solutions and pioneering methodologies all stem from this audacious culture.

By shaping such a space, you instill intellectual courage within your team, preparing them to embrace ambiguity and venture into new territories. They become not respondents to change, but its architects.

As a parent, embedding Conceptual Surprise can expand your child's thinking horizons. Just shake up a family game night with a complex riddle. These simple activities nudge anybody to challenge assumptions and see the world differently.

**Riddle**:
The more you take, the more you leave behind. What am I?
**Answer**:
Footsteps.

For children, Conceptual Surprise serves as a guidepost towards critical thinking. It equips them with the tenacity to challenge, the hunger to explore, and the imagination to conceive the inconceivable. And it is so simple to initiate and needed.

In professional life, Conceptual Surprise propels you and your team into uncharted territories, fostering innovation and creativity. It's where established notions crumble and fresh insights emerge.

As a leader, you are urged to break from the familiar, rethink conventions, and blueprint novel concepts. You learn the value of knowledge's fluidity, the importance of adaptability, and the strength in embracing change.

Consider the Monarch butterfly. Each year, this seemingly

delicate creature embarks on a remarkable 3,000-mile migration, navigating various terrains and weather challenges. It doesn't resist change; it flows with it. Adapting to its environment, the Monarch teaches us resilience, the importance of flexibility, and the sheer power of transformation. Just as this butterfly embarks on its transformative journey, a leader must be ready to evolve, embrace change, and chart new paths.

Conceptual Surprise is more than an experience; it's a lifestyle. It ensures life remains a perpetual puzzle, an ever-evolving journey, and a ceaseless learning adventure.

Fashioning a Conceptual Surprise is an art and requires curiosity, patience, and a willingness to venture outside your comfort zone. Embrace the process, and remember that the journey often holds as much value as the destination. And it's a helluva journey to pull off a Conceptual Surprise, but it can be done by combining creativity, intellect, and insight to catalyze profound shifts in understanding.

**Step-By-Step: 13 Steps to Craft the Conceptual Surprise**

1. **Deep Research & Learning** - Begin by immersing yourself in a topic. Understand existing beliefs, norms, and knowledge structures. Identify the conventional wisdom that is ripe for challenge.

2. **Question Assumptions** - Play the devil's advocate. Challenge existing paradigms and beliefs. Ask questions that others might overlook or take for granted. "Why?" is a powerful tool.

3. **Cross-disciplinary Exploration** - Look for inspiration in unrelated or loosely related fields. Oftentimes, revolutionary ideas emerge from the intersection of seemingly unrelated disciplines.

4. **Seek Diverse Perspectives** - Engage with individuals from different backgrounds, professions, and cultures. Their unique viewpoints can offer fresh insights and challenge your existing notions.

**5.  Create Safe Spaces for Ideation** - Foster environments where unconventional ideas are welcome. Encourage open dialogue, brainstorming, and a judgment-free zone for exploration.

**6.  Encourage Play and Experimentation** - Sometimes, playful exploration without the pressure of immediate results can lead to the most profound discoveries.

**7.  Iterative Testing** - Before presenting a new concept, test it in various contexts. Refine and adjust based on feedback. This iterative process ensures the Conceptual Surprise is robust and impactful.

**8.  Use Storytelling** - Narratives can be potent tools to introduce and explain complex concepts. Craft a compelling story that illustrates the Conceptual Surprise in a relatable and engaging manner.

**9.  Present Contrasts** - Highlight the difference between the old paradigm and the new one. Contrasting the "before" and "after" can amplify the impact of the Surprise.

**10. Seek Feedback and Adjust** - Once you introduce the Conceptual Surprise, gather feedback. Understand how people are receiving and interpreting it. Refinements might be necessary to make the concept more straightforward or more impactful.

**11. Stay Open to Continuous Learning** - Even after introducing a Conceptual Surprise, remain receptive to new information. A hallmark of intellectual growth is the recognition that understanding evolves over time.

**12. Celebrate the Unconventional** - Embrace and celebrate ideas that defy norms. The more you appreciate the unconventional, the more you become attuned to potential Conceptual Surprises.

**13. Document and Share** - Ensure that the process and the outcome are documented, shared, and made accessible. This establishes credibility and allows others to build upon the idea.

Building upon the **13 Steps to Craft the Conceptual Surprise**, let's make visible two succinct examples—Sales and Business.

### Sales - The Reverse Pitch

Traditionally, a sales pitch involves a salesperson presenting a product or service to a potential client, attempting to highlight its features and benefits. The Conceptual Surprise? Flip the script. Instead of pitching the product, sales reps ask potential clients to "pitch" their problems, challenges, and desires.

**Client**: "Wait, so you want me to pitch to you? That's a new one!"

**Sales Rep**: "Absolutely! Consider me your audience today. Let's hear what keeps you up at night, and maybe, just maybe, I've got the bedtime story to help."

This Surprising shift prioritizes understanding the client's needs and crafting solutions tailored to them. It reframes the sales process as a collaborative dialogue rather than a one-sided presentation.

### Business Pivot - From Gaming to Health

Imagine a company initially dedicated to creating addictive mobile games. The company took a Surprising pivot after recognizing the increasing screen time and sedentary lifestyle issues. They leveraged their gaming expertise to develop engaging fitness apps, making workouts feel like thrilling in-game challenges.

**Developer 1**: "With all our game expertise, we could get folks moving more than just their thumbs."

**Developer 2**: "Are you suggesting we swap 'Couch Conquest' for 'Cardio Challenge'?"

**Developer 1**: "Exactly! Let's make breaking a sweat as thrilling as breaking a high score."

Instead of just entertaining their audience, they promoted health and wellness. This dramatic shift from gaming to promoting an active lifestyle showcases a Conceptual Surprise, demonstrating the company's agility and commitment to addressing pressing societal challenges.

Ultimately, the real Surprise lies not just in conceptual shifts but in the tangible, measurable outcomes these shifts produce.

STEP-BY-STEPS
TEMPLATES
TRAINING

## CULTURAL SURPRISE
*Experiencing a Different World Through Others' Eyes*

Cultural Surprise is a moment of learning and growth. When we encounter something from another culture, it challenges our assumptions and opens our eyes to new possibilities. It can be a powerful and transformative experience.

Like a scene from a movie, Cultural Surprise can be intense and visceral. It can leave us feeling amazed, challenged, or even touched. It can also be a source of conflict and confusion. But it is ultimately an opportunity for growth and understanding.

Just as a biographer can help us to understand a person's life, cultural Surprise can help us to understand the world around us. It can teach us different ways of thinking, feeling, and behaving. It can help us to appreciate the diversity of human experience.

When we experience Cultural Surprise, we must confront our biases and assumptions. We may realize that we have been taking our own culture for granted or that we have been making assumptions about other cultures that are not accurate. It is a challenging experience but can also be an opportunity for growth and learning.

For example, imagine you are an American traveling to Japan for the first time. You may be Surprised to see that people eat with chopsticks, take their shoes off before entering a house, and bow to each other as a greeting. These customs may seem strange to you at first, but they are perfectly normal in Japanese culture.

*Cultural Surprise is a gift.* It is a chance to expand our horizons and become more open-minded. It is an opportunity to connect with people from different cultures and build understanding bridges.

Cultural Surprise can play a crucial role in fostering inclusivity and enhancing communication in your professional life. Imagine working in a multicultural team where people come from different backgrounds and have different ways of doing things. You might be surprised when a colleague from Japan initially avoids eye contact during conversation, a cultural norm showing respect contrary to Western norms. Understanding these nuances can deepen your relationships, create a more harmonious working environment, and lead to better collaboration.

As a leader, you can use these moments to foster a more profound sense of cultural sensitivity in your team. You might arrange a "Cultural Day" where each team member presents something unique from their culture. The day would be filled with surprises, from cuisine, music, and dance, to lesser-known traditions and customs, helping the team bond over shared experiences.

As a parent, exposing your children to other cultures and their surprises can be a fun and effective way of teaching them empathy and broad-mindedness. It could be as simple as making a traditional dish from a different country and explaining its origins. Or perhaps reading bedtime stories from different cultures, letting their imaginations run wild across the plains of Africa, through the bustling streets of India, or over the Great Wall of China.

The magic of Cultural Surprise often lies in its capacity to challenge societal norms, provoke thoughtful critiques, and spur transformation. It's like reading the seminal works of sociologist Erving Goffman, whose dramaturgical analysis presented society as a stage where people enact roles that counter or support societal norms.

"In our everyday life, we are all actors on the stage of society," Goffman famously wrote. This perspective prompts us to view Cultural Surprise as a societal interplay, an opportunity to challenge, alter, and shape norms.

Research also backs the transformative potential of Cultural Surprise. According to a study published in the Journal of Cross-Cultural Psychology (Bennett, 1993), experiences outside our cultural framework can catalyze shifts in our perspective and behaviors. Such shifts, the study suggests, are the kernels of cultural adaptation and understanding.

Let's imagine a conversation that illustrates this idea:

"Hey, Alex, remember when you visited Japan last year?" Maria asks during a team meeting.

"Yes, absolutely. It was an eye-opening experience," Alex responds, his face lighting up at the memory.

"You were surprised when you learned about the 'omotenashi' tradition, right?" Maria queries further, referring to the Japanese concept of wholehearted hospitality.

"Yes, indeed! The level of service and attention to detail was mind-blowing," Alex acknowledges, "It made me rethink our approach to customer service."

Here, Alex's encounter with 'omotenashi' serves as a Cultural Surprise that reshapes his understanding of customer service, illustrating how such Surprises can alter our perspectives and instigate changes in our behavior. In such instances, we are not mere spectators of diversity but active participants in evolving cultural norms and societal landscapes.

Cultural Surprise lets us question our norms, widen our understanding, and deepen our connections with others. In our increasingly globalized world, it is an asset for any professional and a priceless lesson for the younger generation. So, open the door to Cultural Surprise, and let the world Surprise you.

## EPISTEMIC SURPRISE
*Unearthing Hidden Depths of Knowledge and Ignorance*

Epistemic Surprise, a term coined by cognitive psychologists, refers to an unexpected event or experience that challenges our existing knowledge or belief systems. It's the "aha" moment that comes when our assumptions are upended, and we are forced to reconsider our understanding of a subject. It's as if the curtain of our cognitive theater is suddenly drawn back, revealing a stage we didn't even know existed.

**Fun Fact** - Epistemic literally means *'the pin that shakes the earth.'*

In exploring the depth of Epistemic Surprise, you cannot help but consider the words of Albert Einstein, who once said, "The most beautiful thing we can experience is the mysterious. It is the source of all true art and science." This sentiment reflects the crux of Epistemic Surprise – the ability to relish in the mysterious and the unknown.

The seminal work of Thomas Kuhn, "The Structure of Scientific Revolutions," offers insight into the potency of Epistemic Surprise. Kuhn argues that scientific advancement isn't a steady, cumulative process but rather a series of peaceful interludes punctuated by intellectually violent revolutions, which he refers to as "*paradigm shifts*." In essence, these shifts are the ultimate Epistemic Surprise, changing the course of science and, by extension, our understanding of the world.

In your professional life, encouraging a culture that welcomes Epistemic Surprise can be game-changing. Here's a practical scenario: You're leading a brainstorming session, and instead of seeking conventional ideas, you encourage outlandish, even outrageous, ones. This "anything goes" approach allows team members to step outside their intellectual comfort zones. And when an idea that initially seems too 'out there' starts to make sense, that's Epistemic Surprise in action – shaking up the status quo and leading to innovation.

Dan Cable, in his book "Alive at Work," talks about the 'seeking system' that drives us to explore, learn and adapt. By harnessing Epistemic Surprise, you are essentially activating this 'seeking system,' fostering a work environment that is vibrant, dynamic, and continually evolving.

As a parent, fostering Epistemic Surprise is about instilling a sense of curiosity and a love for learning in your child. It's about creating an environment where questions are celebrated, and "I don't know" is seen as an exciting opportunity rather than a deficiency.

For instance, during a weekend outing, you could turn a simple walk in the park into a voyage of discovery. Engage your child in observing and questioning the natural world - why are leaves green? Why do birds sing? And then, instead of supplying the answers, guide them on a journey to find the answers themselves.

The psychologist and philosopher William James once remarked, "The art of being wise is the art of knowing what to overlook." I say, with Epistemic Surprise, the wisdom might be in not overlooking. Instead, by inviting the unexpected and reveling in the unknown, we allow ourselves, and those we mentor, to experience the thrill of learning and the joy of discovery.

When somebody says they're an 'Out of the Box' thinker, Epistemic Surprise is how  they entertain themselves while experiencing the world. They (we) live outside any box.

Think back to the COVID-19 reality we all lived through. As surreal as it was, many amazing things sprung from those locked-up, mask-wearing days of Tiger King and grave concerns on every media.

Epistemic Surprise serves as a powerful catalyst for innovation, creativity, and learning. By embracing and fostering these Surprises in our professional and personal lives, we allow ourselves and those around us to engage more deeply with the world, continually evolve our understanding, and, ultimately, lead more enriched lives.

Need more?

Imagine this scene: you're at home, puzzling over a piece of IKEA furniture that you're trying to assemble. The instructions seem cryptic, the pile of odd-shaped panels, screws, and dowels intimidating. Frustration begins to mount as you struggle to understand how everything fits together. Suddenly, an unexpected guest pops in — your seven-year-old niece. She glances at the chaos, picks up a couple of pieces, and casually comments, "Oh, this piece goes here, right?" As she slots the piece into the exact spot you were struggling with, you are struck with a sense of "Epistemic Surprise." You're astounded by her insight, but this surprise also prompts a paradigm shift in your thinking.

No longer are you relying purely on the instruction manual or your previous experiences with furniture assembly. Instead, you are now more open to unusual, creative solutions. You start looking at the pieces from different angles, trying out unconventional connections. Suddenly, the process of assembly becomes less tedious and more of an exploration of possibilities.

That is the power of Epistemic Surprise. It disrupts your existing beliefs and assumptions, forcing you to seek new knowledge and understanding. It encourages you to break out of the routine, the usual ways of thinking, thereby sparking creativity and innovation. In the grand scheme of things, these Epistemic Surprises can fuel advancements in various fields —

from technology and science to art and philosophy. It's like a sudden lightning bolt, illuminating a path that was previously hidden in the dark.

Get your geek on...

## Surprised 'Top Ten' Epistemic Surprises

**Discovery of Quantum Mechanics** - This fundamentally changed our understanding of physics, introducing the concept of wave-particle duality and uncertainty at the atomic and subatomic level.

**Einstein's Theory of Relativity** - This was a major Surprise that redefined our understanding of space, time, and gravity.

**The Structure of DNA** - Watson and Crick's discovery of the double helix structure of DNA was a major Surprise, leading to revolutions in biology and medicine.

**Heliocentrism** - The Copernican revolution, which proposed that the Earth revolved around the Sun and not vice versa, was a major epistemic surprise in astronomy.

**Plate Tectonics** - The discovery that Earth's crust is composed of large plates that move was a Surprise that changed our understanding of geology and Earth's history.

**The Expanding Universe** - Edwin Hubble's discovery that the universe is expanding, and not static or contracting, was a significant surprise in cosmology.

**Evolution by Natural Selection** - Darwin's theory of evolution was a major surprise that transformed our understanding of the diversity and interrelatedness of life on Earth.

**Germ Theory of Disease** - The idea that many diseases are caused by microorganisms was a major surprise in medicine.

**The Discovery of Radioactivity** - The unexpected discovery that certain elements spontaneously emit radiation transformed our understanding of atomic physics.

**Fermat's Last Theorem Proof** - After over 350 years, the proof of this theorem by Andrew Wiles was a surprise that significantly advanced our understanding of mathematics.

This list is far from exhaustive, and the ranking of "Top Ten" would likely vary from person to person, depending on their perspective and field of interest. It's here to give your occipital lobe another perspective on a new term, Epistemic, and relate that to surprise to form a new thought we'll call Epi, Epi Stemic, Epistemic surprise: The pin that shakes the earth; The thought that stirs the brain; The Paradigm Shift.

Scientific research constantly unveils astonishing revelations, each enhancing our grasp of the universe in thrilling, unforeseen ways. It's crucial for us to remain receptive to these unexpected findings, reflect on them personally and, when relevant, collectively, evolving as a result.

## EXISTENTIAL SURPRISE
*Life's Unexpected Twists Challenge What We Are*

Existential Surprise, a profound and often jarring form of Surprise, involves the sudden, unexpected encounters that challenge our fundamental beliefs about existence and our place in the world. These Surprises can reshape our perspective on life, making us ponder our purpose, values, and relationships with others.

Existential philosophers like Jean-Paul Sartre and Albert Camus spent their lives grappling with the meaning of existence, the absurdity of life, and the concept of freedom. These philosophical explorations can serve as a framework for understanding Existential Surprise. Sartre's famous saying, "Existence precedes essence," encapsulates the idea that we first exist, encounter ourselves, and then define our meaning or purpose.

In a professional context, Existential Surprise is rare but can profoundly impact when they occur. It might come in a career crisis, a startling revelation about your professional path, or a newfound understanding of your true passion or calling.

Existential Surprise, while uncommon, can occur when we least expect them. They strike at the core of our being, altering our perceptions about ourselves, our roles, and the world around us. They push us to question the status quo and reevaluate our life's trajectory, often leading us down paths we might never have anticipated.

Consider the real-world example of Jeff Bezos, the founder of Amazon. Bezos was comfortably situated in a successful Wall Street job in the early 1990s when he first heard about the exponential growth of the Internet. This revelation prompted what can be described as an Existential Surprise, making him reevaluate his career path. After much deliberation, he unexpectedly decided to quit his high-paying job, move across the country, and start an online bookstore out of his garage. This move seemed irrational and reckless to many at that time. However, Bezos's existential realization that he would regret not participating in the Internet revolution led him to take that risk. Today, Amazon stands as one of the most influential companies in the world, and Bezos's surprising career shift underscores the transformative potential of Existential Surprise.

In another instance, consider the case of Ray Kroc, the man credited with turning McDonald's into a global franchise. Before McDonald's, Kroc was a struggling milkshake machine salesman in his 50s, far from the path to success. However, a surprising encounter with the McDonald brothers and their efficient fast-food operation led to an Existential Surprise for Kroc. Intrigued by their model, he proposed franchising their brand nationally, a suggestion that would eventually revolutionize the fast-food industry and transform Kroc's life. This surprising turn of events in Kroc's professional life dramatically illustrates the potential impact of Existential Surprise on our career trajectories.

Consider the story of Vera Wang, a name synonymous with high-end bridal wear. Before diving into the fashion industry, Wang was a figure skater and journalist. However, her struggle to find a suitable wedding dress for her wedding sparked an Existential Surprise, leading her to venture into bridal fashion design at 40. Today, she is one of the most prominent names in the industry, showcasing how an Existential Surprise can catalyze a complete shift in professional paths.

Bezos, Kroc, and Wang experienced surprising moments in all these examples that dramatically shifted their professional lives direction. They faced existential questions, reconsidered their careers, and made decisions defining their legacy. These moments highlight the potential magnitude of Existential

Surprise and their power to redefine our life paths.

You may be working in a high-paying corporate job, but one day, during a volunteering activity, you're surprised by the deep satisfaction you derive from helping others. This encounter can challenge your previous belief about the importance of money and status, pushing you to rethink your career and perhaps even shift towards a more service-oriented profession.

My radio career began as a morning disc jockey in 1987 after many years in the US Army in public affairs, broadcast, and reporting. Although I was successful and having a great time as a civilian hosting the morning show at Rebel 100 FM in Nashville, I noticed that the salespeople and management would start walking in at around 9:00 AM every morning when I was getting off the air after an 8-hour day of show prep, music selection, and commercial break preparation. They had better hours, clothes, cars, and houses and went out for two-hour lunches. Even though I was aware of all this, I overlooked it until I accidentally fell into sales.

I had an idea for a promotion for the radio station and asked the sales manager to package it up so it could happen. She told me she could make it happen if we had a sponsor to pay for it and said that if I could find one, we'd have a promotion. She handed me a piece of paper with what I needed to get a sponsor to pay and a list of businesses she thought might make good sponsors and told me, "Get one of them."

Let some business capitalize off my idea and bring this fun promotion to life on the air seemed easy enough.

After I got off the air, I started calling them, beginning with a local beer distributor. "I have an idea for you that will sell a lot of your beer, and everybody would think it's cool." I met with them, got the sponsorship, gave it to my sales manager, and within a week, we had a ski boat on the Cumberland River promoting Pabst Blue Ribbon, playing alternative rock, and having a great time.

About a month later, my career-changing Epistemic Surprise scrambled me like a raw egg.

I pick up my paycheck at HR, and there are TWO checks with my name on it. One was my salary, and the other I had no idea what it was, but it was about three times my salary and had my name on it. Human Resources confirmed I received my monthly radio DJ salary, and that other check was something called a 'sales commission.' And according to HR, that was the first of three because my promotion sponsor, Pabst, committed to sponsoring the ski boat for the summer.

After another conversation confirming this with the sales manager, I entered the sales world full-time every day after I got off the air. Sales equals money, and I wanted it.

Such moments are beautifully captured in Clayton M. Christensen's book, "How Will You Measure Your Life?" where he encourages individuals to look beyond traditional markers of success and consider what brings them genuine fulfillment and joy.

Let me point out that, at the time, genuine fulfillment and joy WAS money. Gordon Gekko, the wealthy, unscrupulous corporate raider, was topping the box office with Wall Street, and Donald Trump's first book, Trump: The Art of the Deal, had just been released. In the late 1980s, money was seen as the key to happiness, and this attitude was reflected in popular culture.

- A focus on material possessions and financial success characterized the rise of the yuppie culture.
- The popularity of business-themed movies and TV shows, such as Wall Street, The Apprentice, and Dallas.
- The increasing emphasis on wealth and status in advertising, my profession then.

- The rise of the self-help industry promised to teach people how to achieve financial success and personal fulfillment.

*"As the twig is bent, so grows the tree."* -Seneca

Existential Surprise is particularly significant when you're a parent. They might occur when your child takes an unexpected path or when you discover new depths of love, patience, or sacrifice you didn't know you were capable of. For instance, imagine your child, who has been focused on academic pursuits, suddenly shows a profound passion for music or art. This change can challenge your beliefs about success and happiness, forcing you to reconsider the values you want to impart.

Existential Surprise is reminiscent of Rilke's advice in "Letters to a Young Poet": "Live the questions now." They invite us to be comfortable with uncertainty, question our assumptions, and be open to redefining our understanding of the world and our place in it.

Existential Surprise serves as a reminder of the dynamism of existence. Introspection, encouraging personal growth, and, most importantly, underscoring the beautiful unpredictability of life are the benefits it delivers. Embracing these Surprises can enhance our capacity for understanding, empathy, and adaptation in our personal and professional lives.

# INTERPERSONAL SURPRISE
*The Unplanned Plot Twists in Human Relationships*

Interpersonal Surprise summarizes those unexpected moments and revelations within our interactions and relationships with others. This Surprise is centered around human behavior, interactions, and the unexpected revelations or outcomes in these encounters. It's about the realization that the people we know well can still Surprise us - with their thoughts, actions, depths, growth, and sometimes, secrets.

Interpersonal relationships, as underscored by scholars like Irwin Altman and Dalmas Taylor in their Social Penetration Theory, are dynamic and fluid. As relationships deepen, more layers of the 'self' are revealed, often leading to a Surprise. Such instances of Interpersonal Surprise can redefine relationships, altering our understanding of the other person and, often, of ourselves.

Let's navigate this concept within a professional context first. Think about a scenario where a colleague, whom you've always considered quiet and introverted, suddenly takes the lead in a meeting and displays a level of charisma and eloquence you hadn't seen before. Or, think of an employee who consistently meets expectations but suddenly comes up with an innovative idea that changes the trajectory of a project. These are examples of Interpersonal Surprise in a workplace setting.

Interpersonal Surprise can foster a sense of appreciation and recognition, contributing to a positive workplace environment. It allows individuals to demonstrate their unique talents and abilities, often Surprising their colleagues and making the professional environment dynamic and engaging.

**Meeting Attendee 1** "Did you see how Vikram led the meeting today? He was so confident and eloquent!"

**Meeting Attendee 2** "I know! I've always seen him as quiet and introverted. I had no idea he had such excellent public speaking skills. He was truly surprising and impressive. He's a hoot!"

Such surprises can transform workplace dynamics, often leading to a deeper appreciation of diversity and encouraging a culture of inclusivity. Being open to these surprises creates an environment where people feel valued for who they are, promoting a deeper sense of commitment and engagement.

**Manager** "Susan, your idea was a game-changer in today's project meeting. It was unexpected but seriously, very innovative."

**Susan** "I'm glad you liked it. I thought it was high time to step up and contribute something out of the box. I appreciate that it was well-received."

### Orchids & Dandelions

In the context of Interpersonal Surprise, it's crucial to consider the groundbreaking research by W. Thomas Boyce and Bruce J. Ellis on biological sensitivity to context, which underpins Boyce's Orchid and Dandelion theory. This theory proposes that some individuals (Orchids) are highly sensitive to their environment, responding dramatically to positive and negative experiences. Conversely, others (Dandelions) are less reactive, maintaining relative stability regardless of environmental changes.

As a parent, you may observe that one child (an 'Orchid') may respond to family dynamics, school environments, or societal shifts with heightened emotional reactions or perceptible behavioral changes. In contrast, another child (a 'Dandelion') might easily navigate these same circumstances, showing little change in mood or behavior. These individual differences may seem bewildering, even concerning. However, they represent natural variances in biological sensitivity to context, how you feel and react to the space you are in, essentially embodying Interpersonal Surprises within your family system.

Recognizing these unexpected variations and tailoring your parenting approach to suit your 'Orchid' or 'Dandelion' child can be invaluable. It enables you to support their unique needs effectively, aid in building their resilience, and contribute positively to their development. Understanding Interpersonal Surprises is not merely about acknowledging differences but celebrating each child's unique individuality and responsiveness to the world around them.

As we move into the professional arena, we must understand that these same 'Orchid' and 'Dandelion' children grow into adults who bring their unique biological sensitivities into the workplace. While childhood is a crucial period for development, the attributes associated with being an 'Orchid' or a 'Dandelion' do not simply evaporate upon reaching adulthood.

An 'Orchid' employee may react to professional environments, team dynamics, or changes in leadership with heightened emotional responses or noticeable shifts in productivity. Conversely, a 'Dandelion' employee may navigate these same professional landscapes effortlessly, their performance and disposition relatively unaffected by such shifts.

This understanding has profound implications for managers and team leaders. Instead of expecting uniform responses to changes and challenges, leaders can cultivate 'greenhouse' environments that accommodate and nurture their employees' sensitivities. These include creating conditions allowing 'Orchids' to thrive — be predictable, consistent and kind. Provide positive reinforcement, foster supportive relationships, and ensure a sense of safety and stability. Simultaneously, it requires harnessing the resilience of 'Dandelions' —encouraging their adaptability, promoting their strength, and leveraging their ability to thrive in various circumstances.

Recognizing and responding to these Interpersonal Surprises can facilitate collective intentionality — a shared sense of purpose and alignment within the team, allowing leaders to leverage their teams' diverse strengths and sensitivities, building an inclusive culture that supports 'Orchids' and 'Dandelions.'

In this way, leaders can effectively cultivate high-performing teams characterized by mutual understanding, respect, and shared commitment to achieving common goals.

Interpersonal Surprise is a testament to the richness and complexity of human relationships. It's a reminder of the potential for growth, evolution, and depth in each of us. Embracing such Surprise in our professional and personal lives enriches our interactions, deepens our understanding of others, and allows us to celebrate the expanse of human experience.

## LINGUISTIC SURPRISE
*The Magic When Words Take Unexpected Turns*

Linguistic Surprise refers to unexpected moments or realizations in our use and comprehension of language. It could be an unconventional use of a word, a pun, a play on words, a newly learned word or phrase in a foreign language, or even a revelation about the roots and connections between words in the same or different languages.

In a professional setting, Linguistic Surprise may occur when you're exposed to industry jargon or terminology that's new to you, presenting an unforeseen challenge to your understanding and communication. Similarly, if your work involves international communication, learning an unfamiliar phrase or cultural nuance in another language might be a delightful surprise, enhancing your intercultural communication skills.

Studying Linguistic Surprise brings us to the fascinating intersections of language, cognition, culture, and human evolution. It helps us appreciate the beauty and complexity of language – the most potent tool for human communication and connection.

While Dr. Seuss is indeed renowned for his playful and inventive use of language, creating numerous delightful surprises in his rhymes and narratives; the title of "the most famous linguistic Surprisator" might arguably belong to none other than the Bard himself, William Shakespeare.

Shakespeare was a master of linguistic Surprise, using his unparalleled command of language to surprise, delight, and challenge his audiences continually. He invented hundreds of new words and phrases, many of which we still use today, like "break the ice," "green-eyed monster," and "wild goose chase." He also pioneered many innovative linguistic techniques, such as using soliloquies to reveal a character's innermost thoughts and emotions. This creative use of language allowed him to explore complex ideas, evoke powerful emotions, and craft intricate plots filled with unexpected twists and turns.

In his plays, he often used the element of Surprise to significant effect. From the shocking murder of King Duncan in "Macbeth" to the sudden, tragic ending of "Romeo and Juliet," Shakespeare's works are filled with unexpected plot twists that continue to surprise and captivate audiences even today.

> All the world's a stage, and all the men and women merely players.

And, of course, who can forget the Surprise endings of his comedies, where misunderstandings are cleared up, lovers are reunited, and everything is resolved in the most unexpected and satisfying ways? These moments of dramatic reversal, where everything is suddenly seen in a new light, represent the essence of Linguistic Surprise.

When we communicate for effect, we can take inspiration from Shakespeare's innovative use of language. Just as he continually surprised his audiences with new words, unexpected plot twists, and surprising character revelations, so too can we use the element of Surprise to engage learners, stimulate curiosity, and foster deep understanding. By presenting information unexpectedly, we can create moments of discovery and insight that make learning a truly transformative experience.

### 'To Be, Or Not To Be' soliloquy from Hamlet

*"To be, or not to be: that is the question:*
*Whether 'tis nobler in the mind to suffer*
*The slings and arrows of outrageous fortune,*
*Or to take arms against a sea of troubles*
*And by opposing end them."*

Hamlet ponders the fundamental question of existence itself, weighing the pains and troubles of life against the unknown of death. But it's not the Surprise subject matter. Shakespeare's phrasing, rhythm, and choice of words are all carefully crafted to create a sense of introspective suspense and existential uncertainty, reflecting Hamlet's internal struggle.

For example, "to be, or not to be" telescopes Hamlet's dilemma. It's concise, direct, and deeply profound, expressing a complex existential question in just six words. It's unexpected in its simplicity and depth, instantly drawing the audience in and setting the tone for the rest of the soliloquy.

Shakespeare's works demonstrate the power of Linguistic Surprise to engage the audience, provoke thought, and elicit strong emotional responses. By incorporating elements of Surprise into our communication and teaching strategies, we can create a more engaging, memorable, and impactful learning experience. In that spirit, let's continue to Surprise, innovate, and explore the limitless possibilities of language and learning.

A Linguistic Surprise is a word or phrase that is unexpected in a given context. It can add emphasis, create interest, or be playful with language. I began this book with a Linguistic Surprise because I needed a term to accurately describe the intentional and deliberate use of Surprise, in its many forms, for a desired result:

**Surprisation**: /sər͵prīzā'SHən/ **noun**
The act or process of strategically implementing unexpected feelings or reactions that enhance engagement, awareness, or inspire a shift in perspective, often resulting in deeper connections or insights.

## Use Linguistic Surprise

Linguistic Surprise captivates audiences, especially during presentations. It sparks curiosity, ensuring your message resonates and keeps listeners engaged.

Be playful with language. Linguistic Surprises can also be used to be playful with language. Adding a touch of humor or personality to your communication makes you real. It can also help to break the ice and make people feel more comfortable with you.

To underscore my argument, I'll overload the above paragraph with Linguistic Surprise below:

Twist your tongue with tantalizing tales! With Linguistic Surprises, words waltz whimsically, bringing bursts of bubbly banter. Infusing humor and a pinch of personality? Now that's the secret sauce to melting icy walls and weaving a warm rapport. Dive into this delightful dance and watch the world wobble with wonder!

As you can see, Linguistic Surprise can be overdone. Use sparingly. Words carry deep personal emotions, often unnoticed. Selecting unconventional terms isn't just a linguistic maneuver; it's beckoning innate curiosity and our hunger for fresh insights. While we might toy with expressions, we truly aim to captivate, challenge perceptions, and elevate conversations. Let language enhance your shared experiences.

## NARRATIVE SURPRISE
*The Unexpected Twists in Life's Unfolding Story*

Narrative Surprise refers to unexpected turns and twists in the stories we create, consume, or participate in. They are the unexpected twists and turns in a story that keeps audiences engaged, invested, and eager to see what happens next. Whether it's a shocking plot twist in a movie, an unexpected character revelation in a novel, or a sudden cliffhanger in a TV show, these surprises keep the narrative fresh and compelling. They capture the receiver's attention, provoke emotional reactions, and stimulate discussion long after the story has ended. Without these unexpected elements, stories can become predictable and lose their appeal.

Narrative Surprises are the heartbeat of compelling storytelling in the entertainment world. The shake of unexpectedness in the narratives, from Hollywood to hallway, shapes our understanding of the world and ourselves.

Narrative Surprises at work can happen when an ongoing project takes a turn no one predicted or a corporate strategy leads to unforeseen results, like the rise of Netflix. Initially, it was just a DVD rental-by-mail service, but it took an unexpected turn with streaming and then another with original content production. These Narrative Surprises changed not just the story of Netflix but the entire narrative of the entertainment industry.

Ken Burns's style often reveals unexpected facets of historical events or figures, redefining our understanding of those subjects, making us question our preconceived notions, and encouraging a more nuanced, comprehensive perspective.

For instance, in his documentary, "The Vietnam War," Burns features multiple viewpoints from soldiers, civilians, and policymakers from both sides of the war. One particularly striking moment occurs when former North Vietnamese soldier Bảo Ninh recollects his experiences. His unexpected narrative portrays not just the stereotypical enemy combatant but a complex, relatable individual, contributing to the emotional toll of the war, stating, "We were all terribly wounded...not so much in our bodies as in our souls."

Another instance includes when Burns highlights the role of

Vietnam War protesters and presents their perspective as more than just anti-war activists. He features a moment when Bill Zimmerman, an anti-war activist, described the activists' mission as "returning the war" to the U.S. public, a phrase encapsulating the activists' intention to make the distant war a pressing, inescapable reality for American civilians. This perspective was a striking departure from the conventional depiction of protesters as disorganized and reactive, revealing a well-thought-out strategy for social change instead.

Narrative Surprises are why I became a Walter Isaacson fan. His biography of Benjamin Franklin is full of moments that suck your eyes onto the page, adding depth and unexpected insights into Franklin's life. One standout narrative surprise in Isaacson's "Benjamin Franklin: An American Life" is his portrayal of Franklin's relationship with his estranged loyalist son, William, during the Revolutionary War. While most of us are familiar with Franklin's revolutionary spirit and diplomatic actions, the deep personal rift between father and son, accentuated by their political divide, is an emotional twist. The realization that such a revered figure had to navigate profound personal challenges amidst a political revolution adds a layer of complexity and humanity to Franklin's story. Isaacson's ability to unveil these lesser-known aspects of Franklin's life makes his narrative enlightening and engaging.

Such Narrative Surprises challenge our understanding and force us to reevaluate our perspectives, a hallmark storytelling approach. Through these surprises, these thinkers don't just relay history or any communication; they make us rethink it.

Reflecting on parenting, Narrative Surprises can be insightful moments where our children's trajectories divert from the paths we might have predicted for them, presenting delightful revelations.

For instance, imagine you are an accomplished musician and naturally expect your child to share your passion for music. However, one day, your child comes home from school excitedly about a new plant they've studied in their biology class. To your surprise, this sparks a profound fascination with botany, leading them to spend their free time researching different plant species, nurturing a home garden, and even dreaming of becoming a botanist. This unexpected shift in interest, a clear Narrative Surprise, provides a new perspective on your child's unique interests and potential.

Growing up, my Dad always called eggs "cackleberries." As in, "Get out there and pick those cackleberries." I grew up on a farm, which was Pop's way of making chores fun. Give them a fun name.

These examples demonstrate how Narrative Surprises, both in our children and ourselves, can become enlightening and transformational moments, offering a deeper understanding of personal growth, potential, and individuality. They serve as reminders of the unpredictable and dynamic nature of life. They make stories more engaging, add depth to our experiences, and enrich our understanding of ourselves and the world. These Narrative Surprises encourage us to remain adaptable and open-minded, like climbing a mountain of a cloud.

Always use Narrative Surprises. Just as a negotiator uses negotiation, be a Surprisator using surprisation.

## NATURAL SURPRISE
*When Mother Nature Reveals Her Hidden Wonders*

Natural Surprises are those moments of awe, astonishment, and enlightenment we experience with the natural world. These could be unexpected findings in scientific research, sudden natural events, or simply an individual's encounter with the beauty and mysteries of nature.

- The sudden blooming of a rare flower in your home garden
- An unexpected meteor shower during a camping trip
- Discovering an unusual bird species while bird-watching
- Witnessing the Northern Lights for the first time
- Experiencing an earthquake, tornado, hurricane
- Encountering a frog under a toadstool.
- Seeing a double rainbow after a storm
- Observing the transition of a caterpillar into a butterfly
- The breakthrough moment a new species is discovered
- The awe-inspiring view of the Milky Way on a clear night

Natural Surprises can significantly impact various sectors, particularly science, technology, and environmental policy. For example, the discovery of the Ozone hole over Antarctica in 1985 was a substantial Natural Surprise that prompted global environmental action. Scientists were shocked to find a steep drop in ozone levels in the stratosphere, which led to the eventual ratification of the Montreal Protocol to phase out the production of ozone-depleting substances.

# Get Outside

Employing the power of Natural Surprise in your business and professional life can significantly boost engagement, motivation, creativity, and overall productivity. Here's how:

**Inspiration for Innovation** - The intricate workings of nature have been the source of inspiration for numerous innovations. For example, the science of biomimicry applies nature-inspired solutions to solve complex human problems. Encourage your team to look to nature for inspiration - the unique properties of a plant, the efficiency of an ant colony, and the flight mechanics of birds - these could all ignite a spark for your next Big Idea.

**Reconnecting with the Bigger Picture** - Natural Surprise often helps us step back and appreciate the larger perspective, reminding us of our place within the grand scheme of things, helping reduce work stress, and fostering a more resilient mindset in the face of challenges. Seriously, get outside.

**Team Building** - Organizing team activities in natural settings - like a hike or a beach cleanup - can provide opportunities for a Natural Surprise that enhances team building, shared experiences, and foster a sense of shared responsibility and teamwork.

**Enhancing Workspaces** - Bringing elements of nature into the workplace - such as plants, natural light, or nature-based art - can create an environment that stimulates Natural Surprise and contributes to improved mental well-being, creativity, and productivity.

**Embedding Sustainability** - Witnessing the wonders of nature can inspire a more profound commitment to sustainable business practices. For instance, a company-wide viewing of a nature documentary could be a starting point for conversations about sustainability and corporate social responsibility, especially if you unpack the experience using the Cognitive 3Rs.

**Mindfulness and Focus** - Nature-based mindfulness practices, like forest bathing or mindful gardening, can lead to moments of Natural Surprise, helping to improve focus, creativity, and overall mental health, which can translate to enhanced work performance.

**Learning and Development** - Use the concept of Natural Surprises in your learning and development programs. For example, discuss case studies of innovations inspired by nature to stimulate out-of-the-box thinking.

There is a very specific reason my home is located on the banks of a river and my office window looks out on the river's moods, the geese and beaver, the salmon runs...every day is a Surprise. My goal is to assist you in cultivating a Greenhouse atmosphere that encourages Surprise, curiosity, and continuous learning, using nature as a muse to fuel creativity, engagement, and a shared sense of purpose.

Speaking of cultivating, incorporating gardening into our daily or weekly routines can yield unexpected Natural Surprises and a host of benefits which I'll outline, particularly regarding brain health, creativity, and productivity.

### Cognitive Gardening: Planting Seeds of Brilliance

**Surprises in Nature's Processes** - Gardening is a dynamic process full of surprises. The sudden sprouting of a seed, the first flower bloom, or even the appearance of a ladybug can bring moments of joy and Surprise. These natural surprises can stimulate curiosity, awe, and a sense of achievement.

**Stress Relief** - Numerous studies have shown that gardening reduces stress, anxiety, and depression. It offers a break from high-intensity work environments and provides an opportunity to engage with nature, contributing to overall well-being and productivity. The Surprise of seeing a plant thrive due to your care can be incredibly satisfying and uplifting.

**Mindfulness and Focus** - Gardening requires attention to detail, patience, and a present mind - all key components of mindfulness. This act of mindfulness with plants can lead to better focus and productivity when returning to work tasks. As a bonus, the sensory experiences associated with gardening—such as the smell of fresh earth or the texture of leaves—can lead to surprising sensory delights. I look forward, each year, to the scents of the tomato plants when the tomatoes are ripe.

**Fosters Creativity** - The garden can be a canvas for creative expression, deciding where to plant certain flowers, designing the layout, or dealing with unexpected gardening challenges. These tasks stimulate creative thinking, which can be translated into your work.

**Physical Activity** - Gardening involves physical activity, which is known to boost mood, reduce stress levels, and improve cognitive function, leading to better work performance and productivity.

**Learning Opportunities** - Gardening can also teach valuable lessons that can be applied in the workplace, such as the importance of regular care (akin to consistent effort), the effects of changing environments (adaptability), and the rewards of patience.

Gardening 'Brain Breaks' offers an immersion in a world full of Natural Surprise that boosts your mental well-being and improves your work performance and productivity. As a parent, you can introduce your child to the Natural Surprises in your backyard, local park, or through nature documentaries. When a child first notices the stars, finds a hidden nest in a tree, or marvels at a rainbow, they experience Natural Surprise.

Natural Surprises are why aquariums – those at home and those we consider a destination event – exist. These experiences instill a sense of wonder and curiosity about the natural world and an early appreciation for its importance and the need to protect it. They are the heartbeats of our planet that can be felt in the rhythm of our own lives, whispering the beauty and complexity of the natural world into our conscious experience.

## PERSONAL SURPRISE
*The Unexpected Turns in Your Life's Journey*

Personal Surprise refers to the unexpected events, revelations, or experiences that significantly impact our personal lives. Sometimes, random things happen, like Surprise meetings or discovering something new about yourself. These are those.

### Personal Business

Personal Surprises can come in the form of sudden career changes, unexpected promotions, or perhaps revelations about one's passion or lack thereof.

Planning and administering Personal Surprise in a professional setting is a delicate art, as it requires a careful balance of professionalism and personalization. The intention should always be to uplift, appreciate, and motivate individuals while fostering a positive work culture which is no small feat in how business has evolved. *Kid Gloves needed as we progress*

**Identifying Personal Interests and Preferences** - The key to a successful Personal Surprise is understanding the individual's interests, preferences, or needs subtly through general conversations, observing work habits, or gathering feedback from colleagues.

**Setting the Right Context** - Personal surprises must be contextually appropriate and always respect the individual's comfort and boundaries. For example, if a team member has just completed a successful project, Surprising them with a token of appreciation related to their interest could be appropriate.

**Selecting the Surprise** - The Surprise itself should be thoughtful and meaningful. It could be as simple as a handwritten thank you note, a book from an author they admire, or time off for a personal endeavor.

At Google, "peer bonuses" allows employees to award small bonuses to colleagues for good work as a surprise recognition of their efforts.

In a smaller company, a manager might surprise a team member with concert tickets after learning of their passion for music as a thank you for their hard work on a recent project.

By carefully curating and administering Personal Surprises, leaders can foster a work environment that recognizes and appreciates the individuality of its team members, which can boost morale, productivity, and employee retention.

## Personal Parents

As a parent, Personal Surprise often materializes in your journey of raising a child. It could be your child demonstrating a surprising skill or trait or you discovering an untapped well of patience, creativity, or love within yourself. Parenting itself is a series of Personal Surprises as you navigate the unpredictable waters of raising another human being.

As a parent, you'll often encounter Personal Surprise in raising your child. These moments can be when your child suddenly reveals an unexpected way of thinking or when you discover within yourself a new perspective or approach to parenting. Each step in bringing up a child is like navigating a maze filled with surprising turns that challenge and reshape your thinking.

In the enlightening read "Brain-Based Parenting: The Neuroscience of Caregiving for Healthy Attachment," the authors offer a fresh perspective on parenting by focusing on our own mental processes and understanding the workings of the young mind. How it reframes our view of personal surprises in child-rearing:

**Rethinking Reactions** -Instead of reacting to a child's behavior on impulse, the book nudges parents to pause, reflect, and understand the 'why' behind their own and their child's responses.

**Unanticipated Insights** - Realizing that every Surprise, whether it's your child's unexpected reaction or your newfound patience, can be a chance to learn and grow cognitively.

**Mental Flexibility** - The book highlights the value of adapting and changing our thinking patterns as parents. When faced with a Surprising situation, it encourages parents to think anew instead of sticking to old methods.

**Evolving Together** - Because you do. Using Personal Surprise as stepping stones, parents and children can develop together, advancing a relationship built on mutual understanding and cognitive growth. Through this lens, parenting becomes more than a series of actions and reactions. It's a dynamic dance of minds, with every Surprise serving as an opportunity to make our brains stronger and smarter.

### Personal Education

The world would be better if our educational system adapted Dr. Kieran O'Mahony's "The Brain-Based Classroom." The Brain-Powered Classroom offers a fresh way for teachers to use what we know about the brain to make school more engaging and meaningful. Understanding our brains are unique places full of joy, drive, and the ability to feel good about ourselves is a much better mindset to have at school versus if you can remember some detail of some war somewhere that has no application in your life, ever.

With O'Mahony's guide full of brain-friendly methods, teachers can create a classroom where students love to learn and can handle challenges. These new ideas will help teachers keep the peace, avoid problems, and focus on assisting students to feel good and understand each other better.

Teachers and parents flock to this resource, revolutionizing education.

"This is crusader work. Dr. O'Mahony is rowing against the current, but this important book will stand the test of time."
—Terry Bergeson, Washington State Superintendent of Public Instruction (former) and Interim Dean (retired) of the School of Education and Kinesiology at Pacific Lutheran University, USA.

## PHYSICAL SURPRISE
*The Astonishing Feats and Limits of the Body*

Physical Surprise is an integral part of our relationship with our bodies. It can refer to the sudden revelation of physical capabilities we didn't know we possessed, Surprising changes our bodies undergo, or unexpected physical reactions to external factors; something as simple as discovering that you can row a boat, touch your toes when you've never been able to before, or something more profound, such as the astounding resilience our bodies can demonstrate when facing accidents, illness or aging.

Dean Karnazes, famously known as the 'Ultramarathon Man,' is one such story. He discovered his incredible endurance capabilities quite unexpectedly. After a birthday party, on a whim, he decided to run; he ended up running all night, covering thirty miles. This astonishing revelation of his physical capacity led him to a career as a renowned endurance athlete, authoring books such as "Ultramarathon Man: Confessions of an All-Night Runner."

Another powerful example lies in the realm of rehabilitation. People who have experienced severe injuries or strokes often have to relearn basic physical skills. In this process, they can experience astonishing progress, illustrating the brain's plasticity and the body's capacity for recovery, shocking the individuals and their medical teams. Neuroscientist Norman Doidge's book "The Brain That Changes Itself" is filled with astounding stories of physical recovery, highlighting how adaptive our bodies can be.

The interplay of Personal and Physical Surprises altered the trajectory of my life and deepened my understanding of human resilience. A serene motorcycle ride with my daughter through winding backroads, with dreams of a lively rodeo ahead, was brutally interrupted when a car disregarded a stop sign and slammed into us. This sudden tragedy catapulted us over 100 feet into a remote ditch, grappling with grave injuries. My daughter faced the immense challenge of broken bones from her hip to her ankle and a severe concussion. At the same time, I confronted a slightly more distorted reality: reattaching an avulsed arm and adjusting to life with an amputated leg below the knee.

Yet, amid this darkness emerged beams of unwavering strength and resilience. A decade on, my daughter, having fully recovered, earned a barrel-racing scholarship at Texas A&M and soared in her professional life. As for me, I found myself asking: why do some sink into despair following such tragedies while others, like my daughter and I, unearth a previously unknown strength and vigor? I believed the answer lay in the untapped power of our thoughts and our untutored ability to harness them. This belief ignited my quest into the realm of cognitive neuroscience, and here I stand today, a testament to the transformative power of both challenges and the mind.

In another shade of the spectrum, Physical Surprise can also be associated with the effects of aging or disease. Someone might be shocked to find they can no longer do physical activities with the same ease they could in their youth. Or, a sudden diagnosis of a chronic disease like diabetes can lead to abrupt lifestyle changes to manage the condition.

Professionally, an understanding of Physical Surprise is essential, particularly in fields like physical training, healthcare, and human resources. For example, trainers and coaches might be amazed at an athlete's sudden improvement in performance due to a change in technique. HR professionals must account for the Physical Surprise employees might face, such as the onset of a health condition, and facilitate accommodations to ensure a supportive work environment.

Physical Surprise, therefore, offers a window into our bodies' remarkable abilities and adaptability. By understanding and acknowledging this, we can better appreciate our physical selves, push our boundaries, and adapt to change with resilience and grace.

As a parent, you encounter Physical Surprise often as you observe your child grow and develop. The first time your baby takes a solo step, the stunning strength of your toddler's grip, or the agility of your teen on the soccer field - all these can take you by Surprise.

Parents can actively foster and respond to Physical Surprises in their children's lives. Here are a few ways to engage with these moments:

**Nurture Exploration** - Encourage your child to try different physical activities, such as various sports, dance, yoga, or even simple playground play, supporting their physical development but also allowing them to discover their unique physical abilities and interests.

**Celebrate Milestones** - Each new physical achievement, whether a baby's first steps, a child learning to ride a bike, or a teenager scoring their first goal in a game, is an opportunity to celebrate the accomplishment and effort. These moments reinforce a child's confidence in their physical capabilities and motivate them to explore further.

**Discuss Changes** - As children grow, their bodies undergo numerous changes, particularly during puberty. These changes can often be surprising and even scary for children. As a parent, proactively discussing these changes and reassuring them that these are normal parts of growing up can alleviate their anxieties.

**Be Observant** - Children might not always express when they're feeling uncomfortable or when there's a sudden change in their physical capabilities. Regular observation can help you catch any signs of discomfort, illness, or development delays early, allowing for timely intervention.

**Promote Healthy Habits** - Healthy eating and regular physical activity play a critical role in a child's physical development. Encouraging these habits from early on can lead to surprising improvements in a child's physical health and stamina.

**Model Resilience** - Your reaction to your own Physical Surprise (like aging or illness) can significantly influence your child's perception of their physical self. Modeling a positive and resilient attitude can teach them to view their physical surprises as opportunities for growth and learning. It's also a parental game-changer when most of your child's reality is being served in pixels from an unknown source. Model resilience and let them know they have it too.

Your experiences and reactions can serve as valuable models for your children, teaching them to value their physical health and resilience and leading to better futures.

Physical Surprise reminds us of the remarkable capabilities and adaptability of the human body. They inspire us to respect, care for, and challenge our physical selves, enhancing our understanding of what our bodies can endure and achieve.

## SELF SURPRISE
*Unveiling the Unseen Corners of Your Identity*

Self Surprise refers to the sudden realizations, discoveries, or transformations in our self-perception, behavior, beliefs, or capabilities. These moments could range from realizing a hidden talent or changing a long-held belief to Surprising yourself with an unanticipated reaction or resilience in a challenging situation.

Self Surprise can manifest as unexpected resilience during challenging projects, discovering a knack for a skill you'd never tried before, or realizing that you enjoy a task you used to dread.

Each of the following examples illustrates individuals who, when faced with unexpected challenges or opportunities, come to discover latent skills, passions, or perspectives within themselves. These "Self Surprise" moments are pivotal, often leading to profound personal and professional growth.

**Athletics** - Many athletes undergo rigorous training to enhance their physical prowess. Yet, often, it's a mental hurdle that stands as the most formidable. Consider the marathon runner who, hitting "the wall" at mile 20, believes they cannot continue. Pushing through this barrier, they often find a reserve of strength they didn't know they possessed, leading them to finish the race with renewed vigor.

**Education** - Students frequently enter university or college with a fixed mindset about their capabilities. An engineering student might think they're "just not good at writing." However, after taking a mandatory literature course and receiving positive feedback, they could be happy to find a latent passion and skill for literary analysis.

**Healthcare** - Medical professionals, especially those in high-stress roles like nurses or emergency room doctors, might believe they're cut out for the technical aspects but not the emotional ones. Yet, a particularly poignant interaction with a patient or their family can unearth a depth of compassion and empathy they hadn't previously recognized in themselves.

**Artistry** - A classically trained musician, accustomed to the structures and discipline of symphonies, might attend a jazz improvisation session on a whim. To their whammy, they could find they have a natural aptitude for improvisation, revealing a more spontaneous side to their musical personality.

**Parenthood**: New parents often operate under the assumption that they'll be perfect caregivers, following every recommendation to the letter. However, faced with the unpredictable nature of child-rearing, many recognize and embrace their improvisational skills, learning to trust their intuition in ways they hadn't expected.

You will likely experience numerous Self Surprise as a Parent. Perhaps you find unexpected patience when dealing with your child's tantrums, discover a hidden talent for storytelling, or realize your capacity to love and care beyond what you thought was possible.

Self Surprises prompt introspection, personal growth and often lead to transformative life changes. They highlight our identities' multifaceted and evolving nature, reminding us that no matter how well we think we know ourselves, there's always more to discover. They invite us to remain open, curious, and accepting of our continuous journey of self-discovery. So do.

Self Surprise can be valuable catalysts for personal growth and understanding. They shed light on our capabilities, attitudes, and potential that we might have been previously unaware of.

Learning from these surprises can develop a more accurate, nuanced understanding of ourselves. This enriched self-knowledge is essential for communicating authentically and effectively with others.

## Understanding Your Strengths and Weaknesses

In the journey of self-discovery, Self Surprise often illuminates hidden talents or areas awaiting improvement.

Harnessing these insights allows us to refine our communication, amplifying strengths and addressing the areas we're growing in.

For instance, realizing a knack for empathetic conversations can deepen our bonds with colleagues or clients.

Moreover, these personal revelations enhance our authenticity in communication, ensuring our words reflect our genuine essence.

Feeling empowered by these newfound strengths or after navigating unforeseen challenges naturally boosts our confidence, enriching our communication's impact.

Such adaptability, born from embracing change and understanding, is invaluable in our ever-evolving professional world, allowing us to tailor our message to various situations and audiences.

As we turn the page on this chapter, let's carry these insights forward, for they are the key to truly effective and heartfelt communication.

## SENSORY SURPRISE
*When Your Senses Present an Unexpected Show*

Sensory Surprise refers to the unexpected sensations, perceptions, or experiences that arise through our sensory systems - sight, hearing, taste, touch, and smell. These Surprises can occur when our senses are stimulated in unforeseen ways or when they reveal information that challenges our expectations.

This type of Surprise is at the core of Brain-centric's Challenge Wheel neurogogic model, ensuring all senses interact with the concept to be deeply understood.

When we can see the **concept**, touch it, play with it, smell it, hear its sound, and see it from a distance, we begin to understand it.

Substitute the word **concept** in the previous sentence with the concept you need to communicate, and the framework always works.

➜ When we can see a **tree**, touch its bark, climb its branches, smell its leaves, hear its wind chimes, and see it from a distance, we understand what a tree is.

➜ We understand what the **product** is when we can see the product, touch its features, play with its benefits, smell its demand, hear its reviews, and see it from a distance.

➜ When we can see a **customer**, touch their needs, play with their wants, smell their loyalty, hear their feedback, and see them from a distance, we understand who the customer is.

Fill in the spaces below, communicate your concept, your Big Idea, and prepare to be Surprised:

**When we can see the _____,
touch its _____,
play with _____,
smell the _____,
hear its _____,
see _____ from a distance,
we begin to understand _____.**

We reiterate the core message about the subject in four distinct ways, four senses, each providing a unique lens, highlighting the individual advantages stemming from your discussion. Then, we give them time to be themselves and process the information, collaborate on meaning with others, and articulate it to others.

The Challenge Wheel spins on emotions, managed by Surprise, embedded in a framework that aligns with how the brain processes new information. By connecting the concept to be understood by your audience to each learning lobe of the brain, the Challenge Wheel helps people engage with the material more meaningfully. They can't help it. It's how the brain works and results in deeper understanding and better material retention.

The' Per Lobe Perspectives' are fun to develop and presented as a possible solution to the Challenge. They're short, novel, with different voices, and come at you like a social media feed…varied and intentional. Nearly everything you experience is presented to you in this manner. Your muse is Everywhere.

**Sight** - You are walking through an art gallery, expecting to see conventional paintings and sculptures. Suddenly, you encounter an installation piece using innovative light projection. This unexpected visual display challenges your preconceived notions of art and creates a Sensory Surprise sending you to a creative solution for an account you've been working on.

**Hearing** - You buy those tickets to a concert by a band you've heard many times before. But this time, they perform a familiar song with a completely different arrangement, turning it into a thrilling acoustic version. This auditory shift provides a fresh appreciation for the band's musical versatility and the realization that you must add other audio to that podcast to make it not so dull.

**Taste** - Picture going to a local restaurant and ordering a dish you've tried elsewhere. But when you take the first bite, the burst of unexpected flavors – a unique blend of spices, a different preparation method – offers a stunning culinary delight. Your sense of taste has been stimulated in an unforeseen way, leading to a Sensory Surprise leading to a conversation with the chef and your new 'signature dish' at family events.

Sensory Surprise manifests in various forms at work too. An unexpected aroma wafting from the office kitchen can pique your curiosity, or the sudden silence after a busy day can offer an incredible moment of peace.

Designers, artists, and marketers often use Sensory Surprises to engage their audience or customers, like a surprising color combination in a design, an unexpected texture in a product, or a unique taste in a culinary creation. Remember your first 'scratch & sniff' moment?

### The Challenge Wheel Spins On Emotion

Imagine the Brain-centric Design Challenge Wheel as a multiplayer video game. In this game, instead of just one path to win, there are multiple strategies and routes to explore. Just like in the game where teaming up with others makes you stronger and more effective, the concept of "Sensory Surprises from Multiple Angles" means that when we learn something from many different directions, it resonates. It's like when characters in a game team up and level up faster because they're working together – that's what our brain cells (neurons) do, based on Hebb's Rule. The more they work together, the stronger their connections become, helping us learn and remember better.

# Why We Lobe

**Occipital Lobe**: Mainly manages vision and image interpretation.

**Temporal Lobe**: Handles sensory input, turning it into memories, understanding language, and connecting emotions.

**Parietal Lobe**: Deals with sensory information from our body, like touch and spatial awareness.

**Prefrontal Cortex (PFC)**: Manages complex thinking, decisions, and social behaviors.

The Brain-centric method engages all these parts using various sensory and cognitive experiences, making learning immersive and the concept understandable. For instance, a learning space might involve a visual presentation (Occipital), a spoken story (Temporal), hands-on activities (Parietal), and challenging puzzles (PFC). This all-around approach suits various learners and strengthens brain connections, making learning more effective. To demonstrate, and since we've all been onboarded at one time or another, I'll use the concept of 'onboarding' new employees using lobes.

**Occipital** (Visual) - Start with a captivating video showcasing the company's culture, people, and activities. It sets the tone for what the company stands for.

**Temporal** (Auditory) - Follow with a spoken story about the company's journey, goals, and ambitions—perhaps a chat with a senior employee to give a personal touch.

**Parietal** (Tactile) - Introduce hands-on experiences—maybe a facility tour or role-playing customer interactions, familiarizing them with the company's offerings and clients.

**PFC** (Critical Thinking) - End with problem-solving activities, like brainstorming strategies or pinpointing product improvements, sharpening their thinking and creativity concerning the company.

By employing all four lobes, you appeal to various brain functions, making the onboarding experience more effective and memorable for the new hires.

This approach, filled with Sensory Surprise, captures attention and makes learning exciting. It's engaging with the concept they are to understand actively, turning the vague idea of 'learning' into a practical and delightful journey of uncovering and discovery with each element intentional and deliberate at the right time, for the right reason, and in the right amount.

## SITUATIONAL SURPRISE
*When Life Throws An Unexpected Curveball*

Situational Surprise refers to the unexpected events, changes, or circumstances we encounter in our lives. These can range from sudden plan changes to unforeseen outcomes or developments in a given situation.

Situational Example: Move from 'reading' this book to 'impersonating Jerry Seinfeld in this book.'

GO.

Your boss walks in, the one that reminds you of Jerry Seinfeld, and he's facilitating a class on Influence.

*(Now, imagine Seinfeld's voice and characteristic humor)*

"Okay, so we're here today to talk about Situational Surprise. No, not like when you find out your favorite coffee shop started putting cinnamon in their cappuccino without telling you. This is more about those moments when things at work take a sudden turn. You're all businesspeople, right? You've been in situations where you expected one thing, and then - bam! - something completely different happens."

*(Pauses for chuckles, looks around the room)*

"So, let's take an example. You're working on a big project, something you've been chipping away at for months. It's the 'Mother of Projects' - you have to get it right or you're not getting dinner. One day you're told there's going to be a big meeting - everyone's going to be there - the bosses, your colleagues, maybe even the intern who's always taking two donuts when clearly the universal rule is one donut per person."

*(Chuckles under his breath)*

"You're sweating, preparing for this meeting, rehearsing your presentation in the mirror. But then, you walk into that meeting room and instead of the grueling grill session, your boss announces, 'Great job on the project! It's a hit. We're all going out for lunch to celebrate.' Now that's a Situational Surprise!"

*(More chuckles)*

"These Surprises are all around us in the business world. Deals that fall through at the last minute, clients that change their mind out of the blue, projects that take a sudden turn. And I'm telling you folks, these Surprises, they're like a playlist on shuffle. You never know which song plays next!"

"But that's the beauty of it. It's in these moments of Surprise, where the script goes off the rails, that the real opportunities lie. It's where relationships are tested and built. It's when we have to improvise, adapt, communicate in new ways, just like when your stand-up set gets interrupted by a heckler. You learn more about yourself, your team, and your clients in these moments of Situational Surprise than in the routine day-to-day of business. It's why we play golf!"

"So remember, the next time you encounter a Situational Surprise, don't panic, don't run away. Look for the opportunity, and who knows, you might just end up getting dinner!"

*(Laughs and acceptance)*

"And remember, folks, if you're taking two donuts, at least act a little guilty."

*(Ends with a Seinfeld grin and another round of appreciation)*

Situational Surprise might manifest as unforeseen changes in project requirements, unexpected business opportunities, or sudden shifts in market trends. For instance, the rapid rise of remote work amid the COVID-19 pandemic was a Situational Surprise for many businesses, requiring them to adapt quickly to a new operational model.

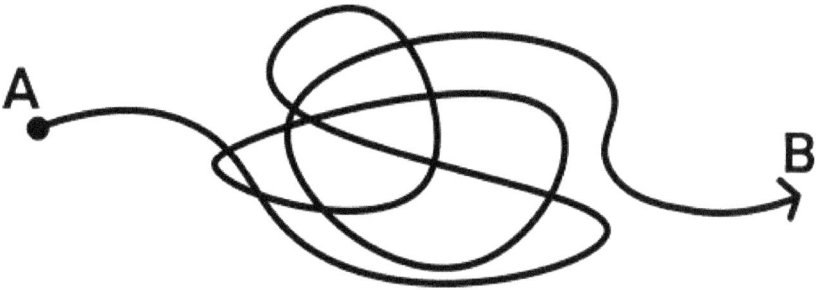

Situational Surprise aren't just about the drastic changes that force you to rethink your business strategies. Sometimes, they can be smaller, more subtle moments that change the conversation or meeting dynamics. For example, imagine you're in a sales pitch, laying out your points perfectly, and your prospective client throws a curveball question at you. That's a Situational Surprise.

Or imagine you're leading a team meeting, anticipating resistance to your proposed changes, and you find unexpected support from the most unlikely team member. These moments, too, are Situational Surprise. They challenge our assumptions, stretch our adaptability, and provide opportunities to improvise and demonstrate our capability to navigate the unexpected.

As a parent, you encounter Situational Surprise regularly. A sudden school closure, an unplanned family trip, or your child making an unexpected friend requires adaptability and often leads to memorable experiences.

These school systems Situational Surprise led me to home-school my children.

Situational Surprise serve as reminders of the unpredictable nature of life. While they can sometimes cause stress or discomfort, they also open doors to new experiences, learning, and growth. Embracing Situational Surprise can lead to a more flexible, adaptable, and enriching life journey.

### Leveraging Situational Surprise

**Creating Conversational Interest** - Situational Surprise makes for engaging stories. By sharing Surprising situations you've experienced, you can spark interest, provoke thought, and generate lively conversation.

**Provoking Thought** - Situational Surprise can also challenge people's assumptions and provoke them to think deeply. For instance, if you're leading a workshop or meeting, you might present a Surprising case study or scenario that forces your team to think creatively.

**Facilitating Learning** - Situational Surprise can stimulate curiosity and facilitate learning in educational or training contexts. Unexpected outcomes or surprising facts can engage students' attention and make the learning experience more exciting and memorable.

**Inspiring Action** - Situational Surprise can whack people out of complacency. If you're trying to inspire change or action, a Surprising situation or fact can highlight the urgency or importance of the issue in a compelling way.

**Building Connection** - Sharing personal Surprise experiences can help build connection and empathy. Sharing these vulnerable moments can facilitate a more profound understanding and create a shared experience.

## Real Beauty Sketches campaign, Dove, 2013

The campaign was based on a Surprising situation: an FBI-trained forensic artist drew women based on their self-descriptions, then drew them again based on descriptions by strangers.

The Surprising outcome?

The sketches based on strangers' descriptions were more attractive and accurate, revealing a significant gap in self-perception and how others perceive us.

The campaign generated colossal engagement and went viral. Within a month of its release, it became the most-watched ad on YouTube at that time, garnering more than 114 million views from over 110 countries. The campaign resonated with audiences because it addressed the universal issue of self-esteem in a novel and surprising way. It led to a massive spike in Dove's sales and solidified its position as a brand that champions real beauty. This campaign is a testament to the power of well-constructed Situational Surprises in capturing attention, driving engagement, and fostering a deep emotional connection with the audience.

The goal of using any Surprise isn't just to shock or disorient - it's to engage, inspire, and create meaningful interactions. I'll repeat this often.

## Step-By-Step: Crafting The Situational Surprise

A successful Situational Surprise is not just the element of the unexpected but its relevance and ability to make a lasting impression. It should serve a purpose: to convey a message, teach a lesson, or create memorable perspectives.

**Understand the Context** - Before anything, you must deeply understand the situation or context. Who are the participants? What are their expectations? What's the "normal" course of things in this situation?

**Identify Expectations** - People always have certain expectations based on previous experiences, knowledge, or cultural influences. Pinpoint what these expectations are in the given situation.

**Devise a Twist** - Consider how you can turn these expectations on their head. Your goal is to do something that is not just unexpected but also relevant and meaningful.

**Ensure Relevance** - The Surprise should not just be for shock value. It should be tied to the message or experience you're trying to convey. If the surprise seems out of place, it could confuse or alienate your audience.

**Test and Refine** - If possible, test your Situational Surprise on a smaller audience or group to gauge reactions. Depending on the feedback, you may need to refine your approach to make it more effective.

**Execution** - When ready, execute the surprise in your chosen context. Make sure to observe reactions. The immediate response of surprise will be evident, but the long-lasting impact will be seen over time.

**Reflect and Learn**: After the situation has unfolded, take time to reflect. How did people react? Did the Surprise have the desired effect? What could be improved for next time.

# TEMPORAL SURPRISE
*When Time Plays Its Own Unpredicted Tricks*

Temporal Surprise is a cognitive phenomenon that occurs when we are presented with unexpected or surprising information. Not to be confused with the Temporal Lobe, Temporal Surprise is the type of Surprise that happens because of *unexpected timing*, like a jack-in-the-box popping out when you least expect it, even if you knew it was going to pop out eventually.

This Surprise can be caused by a variety of factors, such as a sudden noise, an unexpected event, or a new piece of information that contradicts our existing beliefs. When we experience Temporal Surprise, our brains have to quickly update our understanding of the world. This can lead to a variety of cognitive effects, such as increased attention, increased memory, and increased creativity.

Temporal Surprise can be cunning tricksters that appear out of the blue, altering project schedules or disrupting our routines. They may arrive as tidal waves of productivity that have you surfing the crest, accomplishing tasks at light speed. Or, they may drag you into the sluggish undertow of a slow day, where time stretches out like a languid river, your tasks floating lazily on its surface.

Perhaps the most enlightening Temporal Surprise though are those moments when the past and the present collide, revealing insights about past decisions that cast a new, illuminating light on your current predicaments. These are like flashbacks in a film, a sudden shift in perspective that gives depth and meaning to the narrative.

With the advent of remote and hybrid work environments, it is even more important to keep your team engaged and foster a sense of community. Temporal Surprise in this context could come in many exciting forms.

One way to create Temporal Surprise could be with impromptu virtual team-building exercises. For instance, unexpectedly replacing a standard team meeting with an online escape room challenge can not only build camaraderie but also foster problem-solving skills. The novelty and excitement of these Surprise activities will engage your team and may even increase their productivity and job satisfaction.

Or, why not arrange a surprise guest speaker for a team meeting? Inviting an industry expert or an inspirational speaker to share their insights and experiences can be an exciting diversion from the daily work routine. The new perspective could spark fresh ideas, inspire your team, and even provide useful professional development.

Temporal Surprise, when handled skillfully, can invigorate your team, making them feel valued and engaged. They introduce an element of fun into the workday and demonstrate your investment in their well-being and professional growth. As a result, they can help you cultivate a flexible, responsive, and motivated team that's better equipped to handle the ebb and flow of business Surprise.

Being a parent is like being on a rollercoaster ride through a time warp. Temporal Surprise, those unexpected shifts and jumps in the timeline of your child's life, can catch you off guard in the most extraordinary ways. One moment, you're cradling a newborn, and the next, you're waving off a teenager on their first solo drive. It can feel like someone hit the fast-forward button on your life's remote control.

Yet, within these accelerated leaps, Temporal Surprise can also usher in moments of profound connection and joy. Picture this - amidst the relentless whirlwind of a busy day, you hit the pause button. You sit down, take a deep breath, and devote an hour of undistracted attention to your child. You might play a board game, read a story, or simply chat about their day. This unexpected oasis of calm and connection in the desert of a busy day can lead to heartwarming bonding experiences that both of you will cherish.

To engage your kids with Temporal Surprise, make a habit of introducing spontaneous moments of fun or learning in their routine. Surprise them with an unplanned picnic on a sunny day, or a Surprise quiz night that tests their knowledge and wit. In doing so, you're not only creating memorable experiences but also teaching them to welcome and adapt to life's Temporal Surprise. These lessons will serve them well as they navigate the ebbs and flows of their own life journey.

Such spontaneous activities teach your kids to adapt to sudden changes and appreciate the thrill of the unexpected. By creating these Temporal Surprise, you're fostering a flexible and adventurous mindset that encourages them to make the most of life's surprises. These are invaluable lessons that they'll carry into their adult lives, helping them navigate the unpredictable currents of their own journey with grace and resilience.

Temporal Surprises invite us to reflect on our relationship with time. They remind us that time is not just a linear sequence of moments, but a complex dimension filled with Surprises, insights, and opportunities for growth. They encourage us to stay present, mindful, and adaptable in our journey through time. They can help us to appreciate the present moment. When we are caught up in the hustle and bustle of everyday life, it can be easy to forget to appreciate the present moment. Temporal Surprise can help us to slow down and to savor the moment.

## UNEXPECTED OUTCOME SURPRISE
*When Results Defy Your Best Predictions*

Unexpected Outcome Surprise refers to instances where the results or outcomes of an action, event, or process significantly diverge from what was anticipated, ranging from a science experiment with unexpected results to a business strategy leading to unforeseen consequences or a child reacting in a way you didn't expect.

In a professional setting, Unexpected Outcome Surprise might surface as an innovative solution failing to solve a problem as predicted, a marketing strategy resonating differently with the target audience, or a seemingly promising investment not generating the expected returns.

A classic example of Unexpected Surprise is the story of 3M scientist Spencer Silver, who, in the 1960s, set out to develop a super-strong adhesive but instead created a low-tack, reusable, pressure-sensitive adhesive. This Unexpected Outcome Surprise eventually led to the invention of the Post-it Notes.

Unexpected Outcome Surprise remind us of the uncertainty inherent in any action or process. They underscore the complexity of cause-effect relationships and the role of unknown or overlooked factors. These surprises invite us to remain open to the unexpected, learn from Surprising outcomes, and continually adapt our strategies based on new insights.

The world is filled with Unexpected Outcome Surprise, which often add that much-needed dash of humor and life lessons. Let's venture into a few examples.

Take, for instance, the classic tale of my neighbor, Mike. Mike, ever the aspiring handyman, decides to fix a leaky faucet himself. He confidently declares, "Who needs a plumber? A couple of twists here, a turn there, and voila!" Armed with a wrench and a YouTube tutorial, he dives in. An hour later, Mike's house has unintentionally been transformed into a mini indoor water park, and guess who's swimming in the living room? "I didn't expect the great flood in my living room." Ah, the Surprise outcome of DIY plumbing!

Let's talk about introverts, Melissa. When the boss unexpectedly falls sick, she's asked to lead the team meeting. Everyone's thinking, "Sweet Melissa? The one who barely speaks above a whisper?" To everyone's Surprise, Melissa doesn't just talk, she practically transforms into a powerhouse, guiding the team through the agenda with clarity and confidence. The room is stunned into silence and then into applause. She became the girl with the pen, an alter ego she always yearned to be.

**Step-By-Step: Crafting the Unexpected Outcome Surprise**

**Identify your Objective** - Before crafting Surprise, it's crucial to be clear about your objective, your Big Idea. Are you aiming to make a particular point more memorable, stimulate critical thinking, or capture your audience's attention? Your objective will guide your choice of Surprise.

**Understand your Audience** - Not all surprises are appropriate or effective for all audiences. Understand who your audience is, their preconceptions, and what might genuinely surprise them.

**Choose the Surprise Element** - Choose a piece of information, a story, a statistic, or an example that contradicts common belief or is counterintuitive. This Surprise element should be closely linked to your objective and meaningful to your audience.

**Build Suspense** - For maximum impact, don't reveal the Surprise immediately. Instead, build suspense by presenting related information first and leading your audience in a particular direction.

**Deliver the Surprise** - Unveil the Surprise at a high-impact moment. The Surprise can be a twist in a story you're telling, an unexpected result in a demonstration, or a shocking fact or statistic.

**Explain the Surprise** - After revealing the surprise, explain why it's Surprising and how it relates to the topic at hand, facilitating understanding and deepening learning.

**Engage in Discussion**: Use the Surprise as a springboard for discussion. Ask your audience what they thought was Surprising and what they already knew and now see differently, encouraging active engagement and critical thinking.

**Reflect and Connect**: Help your audience reflect on the surprise and connect it with their existing knowledge. Enhance retention and integration of new knowledge in this gift of time.

**Reinforce the Surprise**: Repeat the surprising information or concept at later points to reinforce it. Repetition can strengthen memory traces and enhance recall.

**Evaluate Impact**: After your session, assess the impact of the surprise. Did it achieve the intended objective? Did it engage the audience as you'd hoped? Use this feedback to refine your future surprises.

## Apply It

**Maintain Interest and Engagement** - Unexpected Outcomes attract attention and interest, making the content more memorable and engaging in a learning context. Presenting an unexpected fact or counterintuitive research at the beginning of a lecture can pique learners' curiosity and keep them engaged throughout the session.

**Facilitate Active Learning** - Critical thinking and active learning transpires when learners encounter a Surprising outcome, they may be motivated to understand why it was unexpected, prompting them to engage with the material actively.

**Promote Adaptability** - In our rapidly changing world, adaptability is a crucial skill. Teaching through Unexpected Outcome Surprise can help learners become more comfortable with ambiguity and change, preparing them to adapt quickly in real-life situations.

**Enhance Retention** - Our brains are wired to remember Surprising events. Hence, incorporating Surprising outcomes in your communication or teaching can enhance the retention of information. This can be particularly useful when remembering key facts and figures is essential.

**Encourage Innovation**: Stimulating creativity and innovation with an Unexpected Outcome can prompt us to think differently, consider various perspectives, and develop innovative solutions. For instance, imagine you're conducting a workshop on problem-solving skills. You present a problem and ask the participants to devise a solution. Then, you reveal that the problem was a decoy - the real challenge is to come up with ways to solve the problem under a Surprising constraint. This Unexpected Outcome Surprise keeps the participants engaged and pushes them to think creatively and adapt to unexpected changes.

The effectiveness of Surprise depends on their unexpectedness. Keep refreshing your bank of Surprises to maintain the element of Surprise. And always remember - the aim is not to trick your audience but to engage them, foster learning, and encourage critical thinking.

# THE ELEMENTS OF SURPRISE

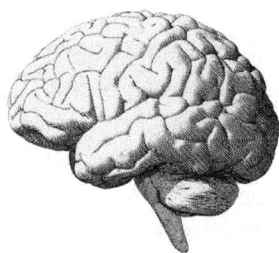

# THE ELEMENTS & ART OF SURPRISE

Our mission with *Surprised* is for you to deeply understand that the elements of Surprise can be managed for a predictable outcome, for a measured Big Idea. Said conversationally, I want you to strategically place Surprise in your communications so your audience engages with, absorbs and assimilates your content.

We both want our audience to 'get it' and to 'use it.'

As a communicator, to communicate, it is critical you understand what you are communicating and what success looks like for that communication. Before you craft your communication answer the following two questions in ten words or less.

1. **Big Idea** - What will my audience walk away with deeply understanding?
2. **Measurement** - How will I measure the success of this communication?

Only after the two anchoring elements of our communication are articulated do we actually begin planning and building a communication of consequence.

1. **Big Idea** - Surprise is incredibly flexible and it's a powerhouse for engagement!
2. **Measurement** - Communicators use this technique, Surprisation, in their communications.

It's always all about the audience. Not you or your presentation or the flashy slides. It's vital to be clear on the key takeaway for your audience and how you'll know if you've successfully conveyed that. Otherwise, you're just passing on information without ensuring understanding. You would just be narrating, not educating. A teller, not a teacher. If you aren't aiming for genuine understanding, you're merely filling the air, hoping the message sticks.

Looking at the big picture: The Elements of Surprise aren't just fleeting moments, but universal components of the emotion of Surprise. They can be seasoned to achieve the desired impact, aligning perfectly with the anticipated outcome of your core message.

## Plan For Successful Communication

Crafting impactful communication hinges on the mastery of the art of Surprise, knowing precisely where and when to unleash its power. Surprisation isn't a happy accident. It's a meticulously planned strategy, a pivotal shift in the narrative that grabs and keeps attention when you most want it. It shatters the mundane, steers your audience toward the Big Idea, and evolves into the X-factor you've been hunting for.

Results. They heard it, understood it, and assimilated it.

The foundational elements of the Surprise Experience are Expectation, Novelty, Suddenness, Incongruity, Emotional Reaction, Valence, Intensity, Uncertainty Reduction, Sense-Making & Adjustment.

Each Surprise follows a pathway, from the spark of anticipation to the satisfaction of understanding. It's a rich tapestry woven in mere moments, all thanks to the intricate network of neurons in our brains which this process uncovers.

Consider this your roadmap to navigating the twists and turns of this momentary jaunt. As you zip down this path repeatedly, it becomes second nature, giving you the insights to accelerate, decelerate, or anticipate the unexpected.

## The Elements of Surprise

**Expectation** sets the stage
**Novelty** fuels curiosity
**Suddenness** strikes like lightning, arresting attention
**Incongruity** challenges the mind with the unexpected
**Emotional Reaction** deepens the connection
**Valence** colors the experience
**Intensity** amplifies the impact
**Uncertainty Reduction** brings clarity
**Sense Making** transforms chaos into understanding
**Adjustment** ensures enduring influence

In this learning space, Surprise is the golden ticket. Those who truly grasp its intricacies wield the power to mold thoughts, ignite passions, and leave a lasting impression from every direction - inside out, top to bottom, and beyond.

It's time to lay out the blueprint of this dynamic path, the master guide that equips you to craft communication that does more than just talk—it resonates, persuades, and triumphs.

The intricate dance of these Surprise elements are yours to choreograph. Dive in, engage, and immerse yourself in its depths. Equip yourself with a writing tool, this journey is interactive. My overarching aim with this guide is to showcase the immense versatility of Surprise and its unparalleled prowess in fostering engagement. And as you flourish using these techniques, I eagerly await tales of your triumphs.

# EXPECTATION

# EXPECTATION

### Expectation sets the stage
Novelty fuels curiosity
Suddenness strikes like lightning, arresting attention
Incongruity challenges the mind with the unexpected
Emotional Reaction deepens the connection
Valence colors the experience
Intensity amplifies the impact
Uncertainty Reduction brings clarity
Sense Making transforms chaos into understanding
Adjustment ensures enduring influence

**Expectation** - The baseline against which the Surprise is measured. The more an outcome diverges from what was expected, the more Surprising it becomes.

Expectation forms the foundation of Surprise, serving as the measuring stick against which Surprise is assessed. It molds our perceptions and anticipations, and Surprise emerges when those expectations are disrupted.

Expectation is pivotal in our daily existence, influencing our actions and shaping our understanding of the world. It encompasses many scenarios, from common daily routines to significant life events.

Imagine starting your day and expecting your usual cup of coffee, only to discover that you've run out of coffee beans.

Your unwritten but self-understood ritual suddenly wasn't available. This minor deviation from your expected routine triggers a mild Surprise, prompting you to adapt and explore alternatives.

Humor often exploits our expectations to create Surprising moments that bring laughter. Jokes frequently involve setting up an expectation and then subverting it with a punchline that challenges our assumptions.

Why don't skeletons fight each other?
They don't have the guts!

This joke relies on the expectation that skeletons engage in combat, but the punchline subverts that expectation with a play on words, generating Surprise and amusement.

### Emotions are ESSENTIAL.

Expectation influences our emotional reactions to Surprise. When a Surprise aligns with our optimistic expectations, it can elicit delight, satisfaction, and happiness. Conversely, when a Surprise contradicts our negative expectations, it may trigger emotions such as shock, disappointment, or frustration. The intensity of our emotional responses often correlates with the extent of deviation from our expectations.

Think about your anticipation surrounding the release of a highly anticipated movie. You may have lofty expectations based on trailers, interviews, and previous installments. If the film surpasses those expectations by delivering an exceptional storyline and stunning visuals, it generates a sense of delight and excitement. In opposition, if the movie falls short of expectations, it can lead to disappointment and dissatisfaction.

Expectation is a pivotal element in the Surprise experience, providing a baseline for evaluating Surprise. It shapes our perceptions, actions, and emotional responses.

Understanding the role of expectation helps us appreciate the profound impactSurprises can have on our lives, fostering adaptability and opening us up to new possibilities.

# EXPECTATION IN ACTION

Understanding and managing expectations is essential in various roles and contexts. By aligning expectations with reality, communicating effectively, and leveraging Surprise, you can enhance experiences, build relationships, and achieve desired outcomes. Picture yourself in the following situations.

**Salesperson** - As a salesperson, understanding and managing customer expectations is crucial. By setting realistic expectations and effectively communicating a product's or service's benefits and features, you can align customer expectations with what you can deliver. This helps create a positive experience, fosters trust and increases customer satisfaction. You can generate Surprise and delight by exceeding customer expectations, leading to repeat business and positive word-of-mouth recommendations.

**Communicator** - In any form of communication, whether it's a presentation, conversation, or written message, understanding the expectations of your audience is essential. By considering their prior knowledge, interests, and needs, you can tailor your message to resonate with them effectively. Addressing and surpassing their expectations can capture their attention, engage them more deeply, and create a memorable impact.

**Parent** - Expectation management is also relevant in parenting. Setting clear expectations with your children helps establish boundaries, promotes positive behavior, and fosters a sense of responsibility. Communicating expectations and consistently following through with consequences and rewards creates a structured environment that supports healthy development and mutual respect.

**Learning & Development** - In Learning & Development, managing expectations is vital for practical training and educational programs. Communicating the learning objectives, content, and anticipated outcomes to participants sets the stage for a successful learning experience. When learners have clear expectations about what they will gain from the program, they are more motivated and engaged, which enhances the overall learning process and increases knowledge retention.

Additionally, leveraging the element of Surprise in learning experiences can be impactful. Introducing unexpected features, interactive activities, or novel approaches captures learners' attention, stimulates curiosity, and enhances knowledge acquisition. Surprises can create a memorable and engaging learning environment that encourages active participation and supports long-term retention.

## BRAIN LIB: EXPECTATION
*Unleash Your Creative Surprise!*

Throughout *Surprised* I am thrilled to unveil Brain Libs! Unleash your imagination and embrace the unexpected as you engage in this thrilling wordplay adventure. Brain Libs is an interactive game that invites you to fill in the blanks with a wide range of words, from nouns and verbs to adjectives and beyond from your world. The choice of words is entirely up to you, no matter how whimsical or outrageous they may be!

The rules of Brain Libs are simple: Each blank space indicates the type of word required, and it's your chance to let your creativity run wild. Whether you choose a quirky noun, a zany verb, or a captivating adjective, the power is in your hands to shape the story with your unique choices.

This first one is all about you! Read it out loud to somebody close to you. Have fun!

### BRAIN LIB: [Name's] Expectation

In the lively heart of Insightsville, there lived a [adjective] salesperson named [Name]. Their [adjective] shoes clicked with purpose and in their eyes shone an [adjective] spark, known around town for turning any sales pitch into a [noun]-filled escapade.

On a [adjective] morning, the phone [verb], announcing a golden opportunity with [Client Name]. The challenge? [noun]! Armed with [emotion] and their trusty [noun], [Name] embarked on a quest to [idiom] and soar beyond the stars.

Stepping into [Client Name]'s [adjective] office, [Name] greeted with a [adjective] smile. The atmosphere was [adverb] charged. Launching into their pitch, they painted [noun] of success, each word dripping with [adjective] allure. Yet, [Name] sensed [Client Name]'s [adjective] hesitance. Time for a [adjective] twist!

With a [adverb] [verb], [Name] unfurled their ace: a [noun] so [adjective] it could only be magic. [Client Name]'s eyes [verb] in Surprise. Addressing the last-minute jitters, [Name] [verb] through concerns, their solutions as [adjective] as a [noun].

As they [verb] hands to seal the deal, Insightsville buzzed about [Name]'s legendary [noun] dance, a blend of [adjective] storytelling and the power of Surprise.

## TALES OF INSIGHTSVILLE

Journey to the heart of Insightsville, where every narrative thread is intricately woven around the brain's delicate dance with 'Surprise,' our most powerful emotion. As you delve into each tale, you'll explore the fundamental elements of Surprise, understanding how they shape our reactions and resilience.

"Tales of Insightsville" is nine interwoven short stories, each echoing a different element of Surprise, converging into a singular narrative arc that exemplifies how our minds grapple with, adjust to, and flourish amidst unpredictability.

From the thrill of defying expectations to the clarity that emerges from unveiling long-hidden truths, each tale offers a unique prism to view the multifaceted world of Surprise. So, step in and let the enchantment of Insightsville envelop you, revealing its myriad secrets one story at a time.

# INSIGHTSVILLE

## Tales of Insightsville: Element One
## UNEXPECTED HORSEPOWER

*When Lyle's version of Evansiano's purpose alters the expectations of Insightsville, residents are enamored by his elevation of their original assumptions.*

At the heart of Insightsville, a town rich with stories, stood 'Evansiano's Jewelers.' Celebrated for its exquisite craftsmanship, the store was a beacon for those seeking true artistry in their jewelry.

Lyle Evansiano, the seasoned jeweler, was the genius behind its allure. With deft hands, he would weave tales of love, ambition, and legacy into every gemstone. But while Lyle was devoted to jewels, his son, Jesse, was enchanted by something different: the roar and rhythm of diesel engines.

Even so, duty anchored Jesse to the family store, assisting with delicate creations. But amidst the shimmer and shine, his thoughts would drift to powerful engines and gleaming machinery. Lyle's unexpected accident, due to an old nerve injury, suddenly placed the store's future in Jesse's hands.

The town watched; their hopes as radiant as the gems Lyle once molded.

Jesse, to put it plainly, was a guy more fascinated by the mechanics of a diesel engine than the sparkle of a diamond. The weight of the town's expectations felt like the downstroke of a piston in its cylinder—a relentless pressure.

As eyes turned to him, filled with unspoken questions, he couldn't help but wonder: Could he really step into his father's jeweler's apron and continue the legacy?

The question haunted him, ticking away in his mind like

the second hand of the wall clock in his father's shop. Jesse found his own kind of music in the rev of an engine, the interplay of pistons, and the satisfying grunt of horsepower. Meanwhile, the town seemed to want a completely different kind of performance—one featuring a cascade of sparkling gems.

Inside Jesse's head, thoughts and memories stirred in a whirlwind. He thought about his father's practiced hands, gently holding tiny gemstones as if they were delicate flowers. Then his mind switched to his own hands, more at home gripping a wrench than a jeweler's torch.

These two worlds—one of gems and one of gears—started to blend in his mind, creating a dissonant yet compelling kind of harmony.

His heart felt more in sync with the beat of a diesel engine than the soft chime of a jeweler's bell. "You're a mechanic, Jesse," his heart seemed to say, its rhythm unmistakable. Yet a recollection of his father's words floated back to him: " Anyone can build their future, buddy."

So, there he stood, caught at a crossroads between a family legacy and his personal passion. But then a surprising lightbulb moment struck: his father's meticulous craftsmanship and his own love for engines weren't all that different. Both required a painstaking attention to detail and an undying dedication to the craft.

Suddenly, he saw it—a diesel engine, unhidden and proud, each component fashioned with the meticulous care his father would give to a ring or necklace. At that revelation, his heart skipped a beat. An idea, bold yet touchingly familiar, began to crystallize in his mind.

In the hands of Jesse's father, uncut gems were transformed into art. Now, Jesse wondered, couldn't he sculpt his future from a humble diesel engine? He'd forge a statement piece—a blend of mechanic's grit and jeweler's finesse. Through it, Insightsville would see him: both the reflection of his father and a man carving his own path.

The town, rife with anticipation, watched as the gears in Jesse's mind shifted into high gear. Fired by imagination and fueled by enthusiasm, like a diesel engine gaining momentum, Jesse was on the move.

Soon, the once-silent interior of Evansiano's Jewelers roared to life, its ambiance dramatically reshaped.

Jesse's project?

An old-world engine, revamped with a jeweler's touch and a mechanic's spirit. The result was an unparalleled fusion of horsepower and meticulous artistry.

Dubbed the 'Unexpected Horsepower', this creation bridged worlds previously thought incompatible. A diesel engine, buffed to mirror-like brilliance, embodying the essences of both father and son.

Upon its unveiling, a wave of astonishment swept over Insightsville. The townspeople had anticipated another gem-laden marvel, another chapter of Lyle's illustrious story. Instead, Jesse delivered a symphony of engine roars—a piece that paid homage to both his passion and his lineage.

The 'Unexpected Horsepower' didn't just extend the Evansiano legacy; it redefined it. Seamlessly melding jewel-like perfection with the raw power of diesel, the town's initial shock transformed into an overwhelming ovation. Evansiano's Jewelers was in a renaissance, headed in a direction that was both exciting and utterly unexpected.

The town's astonishment was a testament to the beauty of redefined boundaries.

Expectations, they realized, were malleable, much like a

gem being sculpted by an artisan. Or a diesel engine tweaked by a mechanic's expert touch. Our anticipations can evolve, grow, and even be reimagined. With 'Unexpected Horsepower', Jesse hadn't merely satisfied their hopes—he'd turbocharged them.

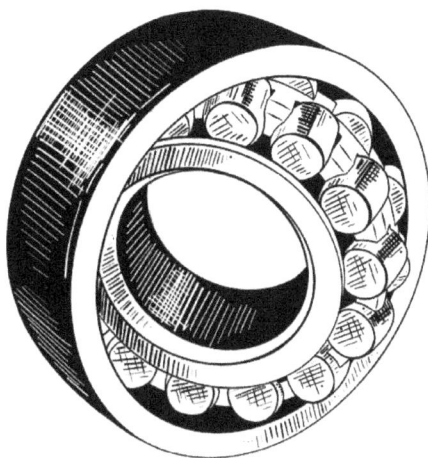

# NOVELTY

# NOVELTY

Expectation sets the stage
**Novelty fuels curiosity**
Suddenness strikes like lightning, arresting attention
Incongruity challenges the mind with the unexpected
Emotional Reaction deepens the connection
Valence colors the experience
Intensity amplifies the impact
Uncertainty Reduction brings clarity
Sense Making transforms chaos into understanding
Adjustment ensures enduring influence

**Novelty** - A Surprise must involve something new or unexpected. This could be a unique situation, new insight, new information, and so on.

Novelty is the beating heart of Surprise, infusing it with freshness, excitement, and uncharted territories. Let's explore the novelty concept further, drawing inspiration that underscores its importance in crafting memorable Surprise experiences.

Imagine walking through a bustling city and stumbling upon a hidden gem—a charming café tucked away in an alley. The unfamiliar aroma, the unique decor, and the unexpected flavors of the food Surprise and delight your senses. This novelty sparks curiosity and creates a memorable experience that lingers in your mind.

Think about attending a live concert where an up-and-coming artist takes the stage. The unfamiliarity of their name doesn't deter you. As they perform, their raw talent, unique sound, and passionate energy captivate the audience. The novelty of this discovery leaves a lasting impression, igniting a newfound appreciation for their artistry.

Across various domains, novelty plays a pivotal role in Surprise experiences. It sparks curiosity, captures attention, and leaves a lasting impact on our lives. We open ourselves to new knowledge, fresh perspectives, and personal growth by embracing the unfamiliar sparked by novelty.

You embrace the unknown, seek out new experiences, and are open to the Surprise life offers without even realizing it. Now you do realize it. Novelty.

### Seven Ways To Inject Novelty

Novelty is the shimmering thread that brings vibrancy and allure. It is the spark that adds depth, turning the everyday into a series of remarkable excursions. By embracing new experiences, we not only enrich our journey, adding layers of profoundness, but also broaden our horizons, welcoming a myriad of cultures, ideas, and revolutionary perspectives. Beyond the mere thrill of the unknown, novelty has the power to ignite an insatiable passion for the extraordinary, pushing us beyond the commonplace into the realms of the awe-inspiring.

As we navigate the waters of Surprise, ensuring it remains exhilarating and fresh is paramount. And what better way to do so than by intertwining it with the unexpected? Discover seven exceptional methods, or ideas to get you thinking, on how to weave novelty into every Surprise.

1. **Change the Environment** - Often, a change in setting or environment can enhance the element of Surprise. This could mean setting up a surprise in a place the recipient wouldn't expect.

2. **Merge Different Cultural Elements** - Introduce facets from various cultures, like a unique dish from a different cuisine or a tradition from another country.

3. **Utilize Technology** - Use virtual reality, augmented reality, or even simple smartphone apps to elevate the experience. For example, an augmented reality scavenger hunt.

4. **Incorporate the Arts** - Introducing elements like live music, a dance performance, or an interactive art piece can add a novel touch.

5. **Personalization** - Tailor the Surprise specifically for the individual. This could involve deep diving into their likes, dislikes, and past experiences to offer something they've never encountered but will surely love.

6. **Educational Twist** - Make the Surprise a learning experience by incorporating something new they can learn, be it a workshop, a DIY kit, or an educational game.

7. **Involve Nature in Unexpected Ways** - This could be a surprise midnight stargazing trip, a surprise encounter with an exotic animal, or planting a garden with plants they've never seen.

Remember, the goal is to ensure the Surprise isn't just unexpected but also fresh and novel, adding more depth to the experience.

# NOVELTY IN ACTION

By infusing novelty into their interactions, these personas leverage the power of surprise to captivate, engage, and leave a lasting impression, ultimately achieving their desired communication effects.

For each, we'll utilize the Brain-centric framework focusing on a Big Idea (what the audience understands after your communication) and then deliver ideas to get you started, warm up your thought processing, and inspire in your world.

### Coaching

**Big Idea** - Introducing unique and unexpected training methods.

**Thought Starter 1** - A soccer coach surprises their team by incorporating circus skills training, such as juggling and acrobatics, into regular practice sessions. This novelty not only adds an element of fun but also enhances players' coordination, balance, and teamwork.

**Thought Starter 2** - A life coach organizes a Surprise outdoor retreat where clients face wilderness survival challenges. This unconventional approach sparks personal growth, resilience, and self-discovery, as individuals step out of their comfort zones and conquer unexpected obstacles.

### Communicators

**Big Idea** - Utilizing unconventional storytelling techniques.

**Thought Starter 1** - Public speakers Surprise their audience by opening their presentation with a captivating magic trick that symbolizes the main message. This unexpected and novel approach immediately captures attention, creating an engaging experience for the audience.

**Thought Starter 2** - A podcaster Surprises listeners by integrating interactive elements into their episodes, such as live polls, audience participation, or guest interviews. This novelty fosters a sense of connection and involvement, keeping the audience intrigued and eager to tune in for more.

### Educators

**Big Idea** - Incorporating innovative teaching methods.

**Thought Starter 1** - A science teacher Surprises their students by conducting a "reverse" classroom, where students are given a scientific challenge to solve before any formal instruction. This novel approach sparks students' curiosity, critical thinking, and collaborative problem-solving.

**Thought Starter 2** - An art teacher surprises their class by organizing a pop-up exhibition where students' artwork is displayed publicly, catching passersby off guard. This novelty boosts students' confidence and pride and creates a unique opportunity for artistic expression and community engagement.

### Management

**Big Idea** - Implementing unexpected rewards and recognition.

**Thought Starter 1** - A team manager Surprises their employees by hosting impromptu "Thank You" lunches, where they serve a special meal to the team, expressing gratitude for their hard work. This unexpected gesture fosters a positive work environment, boosts morale, and strengthens team camaraderie.

**Thought Starter 2** - A project manager surprises their team by organizing a surprise day off after completing a challenging project. This unexpected reward acknowledges their dedication, promotes work-life balance, and motivates the team for future endeavors.

## Parenting

**Big Idea** - Creating memorable and unconventional family experiences.

**Thought Starter 1** - Surprise your children of any age with a spontaneous "Indoor Camping Night," transforming the living room into a cozy campground with tents, sleeping bags, and a pretend campfire. This novelty sparks the imagination and family bonding and creates lasting memories.

**Thought Starter 2** - Parents surprise your teenager with a Surprise day trip to a nearby city, exploring hidden gems, trying new cuisine, and immersing themselves in local culture. This unexpected adventure cultivates a sense of exploration, fosters meaningful connections, and strengthens the parent-child relationship.

## Sales

**Big Idea** - Personalizing the sales experience.

**Thought Starter 1** - A salesperson Surprises a potential client by sending a handwritten note expressing genuine appreciation and highlighting a unique conversation aspect. This unexpected gesture demonstrates attentiveness, builds rapport, and sets the stage for a meaningful business relationship.

**Thought Starter 2** - A sales representative Surprises a prospect by creating a personalized video presentation showcasing how their product or service explicitly addresses the prospect's unique needs and challenges. This novel approach captures attention, highlights the value proposition, and differentiates the sales pitch from competitors.

# NOVELTY REWIRE

### Instructions
Read the example sentence. Embrace your creative powers to rewrite the sentence, transforming it into a new communication. Let your imagination run wild as you infuse the rewritten sentence with the essence of surprise and novelty.

Challenge yourself to craft a sentence that elicits a sense of wonder, captivation, or unexpectedness. Enjoy the process of reshaping language and exploring the realms of surprise through the power of words.

### Practice Sentence
"Novelty sparks curiosity and fosters growth."

### Rewritten Practice Sentence
"Surprise ignites the flames of wonder and cultivates transformative evolution."

In the above example, the original sentence focusing on novelty transforms into a rewritten sentence emphasizing Surprise as the catalyst for sparking wonder and enabling profound personal growth. Unlock your creative potential and discover novel ways to communicate the essence of surprise in your unique style.

Now it's your turn to rewrite the following sentence on a separate piece of paper, infusing it with a sense of novelty and Surprise. If you'd like, email me at pfc@brain-centric, I'd love to read it :-)

**The novelty of the unexpected brings joy to our lives.**

## Tales of Insightsville: Element Two
# RICCO'S REVOLUTION

*New to town and effortlessly supported, Ricco initiates an artistic movement, infusing the town with a fresh perspective and birthing a newfound appreciation for the unexpected.*

The winds of change blew through Insightsville, and at its forefront was Ricco, a beacon of unpredictability and originality.

As a fresh face in town, Ricco was a whirlwind of artistic brilliance. His unorthodox persona and groundbreaking art were the talk of the town almost overnight.

For Ricco, art wasn't confined to a canvas or a lump of clay—it was his life's rhythm. He had an uncanny knack for breathing vibrancy into the mundane, turning the ordinary into awe-inspiring art installations.

At first, his creations seemed outlandish, bordering on whimsy.

Yet, beneath the surface, they pulsed with deep insights, challenging one's perspective.

With the belief that our perceptions were the grandest canvases, Ricco painted using novelty as his medium. He jolted static viewpoints, making everyday objects rethink their existence, from spatulas pondering their roles to toasters introspecting their daily grind.

Ricco's artistry had an unfettered reach, transforming the prosaic into the wondrous, stretching the conventional definitions of art.

His charm wasn't just in his works, but also in his quirkiness. Everything around him had a name—the old fir became "Big Doug," the chirping robin was "Karen," and that nimble squirrel? That was "Vickie."

In the canvas of Ricco's universe, names became

stories, transforming the mundane and the living into actors in his unfolding drama.

For Ricco, the kitchen wasn't just a space but an amphitheater of artistry, alive with audacious combinations and broad strokes of culinary imagination. His recipes weren't mere guidelines; they were narratives steeped in mystery, each with a tale behind its curious title.

In both his culinary endeavors and artistic expressions, Ricco was a maestro of the unexpected. Each dish he whipped up, every piece he showcased, narrated tales of metamorphosis and adaptability, beckoning the observer to probe, journey, and exult in the avant-garde.

For Ricco, creativity wasn't just birthing novelties—it was an excavation of the sublime from the mundane, viewing the habitual with ceaseless wonder.

In Ricco's space, art wasn't hemmed into frames or static behind velvet ropes. He aimed to shatter norms, redefine vision, and reshape the world—one daring artwork at a time.

His innovative tactics and fiery enthusiasm made individuals reconsider the paradigms of art, appeal, and originality.

Then came a day when Insightsville's square became Ricco's canvas. On a whim, he orchestrated a spontaneous showcase of his ingenuity. At the square's heart, he masterfully positioned everyday household objects - kettles, ladles, and vacuum cleaners - fusing them into a grand sculpture echoing daily existence's chaos and charm.

The spectacle instantly piqued curiosity.

For those who wandered through Ricco's creations, astonishment and contemplation awaited. His masterworks weren't mere visual delights; they uncovered tales gesturing to the onlooker to become an integral part of the tale.

"It's a reflection, isn't it? Of us..."

"It's more than aesthetic—it's a beacon of optimism."

"The ebb and flow as one... our life in its raw, nuanced glory."

Every uttered word, each hushed appreciation, serenaded Ricco's spirit. The visceral responses of his spectators weren't merely endorsements of his craftsmanship; they epitomized its triumph. Every drawn breath of wonder, the subtle nod of realization, and the soft exclamations were a tribute to his art's inherent potency - its ability to spark, to challenge, and to stir souls in a melody uniquely Ricco's.

The town square buzzed with animated chatter, eyes darting and minds whirling. Jesse Evansiano, often ensconced in his mechanical pursuits, found himself irresistibly drawn in. Even the astute Aaron Castle, known for sealing business deals, was pulled into the magnetic force of Ricco's display. There was an infectious energy about Ricco's creations that enkindled a delightful blend of wonder and introspection.

Lyle Evansiano, the master jeweler with a seasoned eye for detail, pondered the intricate installations. "It's like peering into the whirlpool of existence, our daily dance and dalliances. You've taken the humdrum and painted it with strokes of magnificence," he mused.

Ricco's silent nod acknowledged the depth of Lyle's insight. His creations were mirrors reflecting the everyday but tinted with hues of surprise and enchantment. This wasn't merely about capturing attention or trending online; it was about reshaping perspectives and introducing Insightsville to an unfamiliar prism.

As whispers of Ricco's genius permeated beyond town limits, intrigued visitors began to converge on Insightsville, desiring to witness the maestro's craftsmanship for themselves.

Ricco's Revolution, as the locals came to call it, marked a new era of novelty and innovation in Insightsville. His art stirred emotions, thoughts, and conversations, pushing the boundaries of expectation, transforming the ordinary into extraordinary, and always surprising those who engaged with his creations.

# SUDDENNESS

# SUDDENNESS

Expectation sets the stage
Novelty fuels curiosity
**Suddenness strikes like lightning, arresting attention**
Incongruity challenges the mind with the unexpected
Emotional Reaction deepens the connection
Valence colors the experience
Intensity amplifies the impact
Uncertainty Reduction brings clarity
Sense Making transforms chaos into understanding
Adjustment ensures enduring influence

**Suddenness**: Surprises often occur suddenly, without much warning. The abruptness of the Surprise can enhance its impact.

Of all the things we experience as humans, , "suddenness" is that unexpected thread that pulls your eye, forcing you to look, to listen, to be present. Picture this: a world that moves in predictable rhythms, like the tick-tock of a grandfather clock. It's comfortable, yes, but therein lies the danger - the danger of monotony, of attention waning, of the magic of life slowly ebbing away.

Enter suddenness.

It's the crackle of a firework in a quiet night sky. The unanticipated chord changes in a familiar tune. It's that unpredictable twist in the plot, yanking you from the brink of boredom and thrusting you, heart racing, back into the story. But why, you ask, do we need to understand this? Ah, it's not just for the thrill, though that's part of its charm. The mastery of suddenness is the mastery of the human heart and mind. Our brains, magnificent as they are, are designed to notice the unexpected, to prepare for the unseen, to engage with the unknown. That's the survival instinct in its finest attire.

In the empire of engagement, whether you're penning an advertisement, weaving a tale, or simply telling your grandkid a bedtime story, the power of suddenness cannot be understated. Sure, it's about capturing attention, but it's more about holding it, making a mark so deep, it lingers long after the moment has passed. When you infuse suddenness into your narrative, you're not just whispering; you're echoing in the vast canyons of memory.

The world today is noisier than it's ever been. Yet, it's the sudden, the unexpected, the startling that cuts through that noise. Suddenness is the unexpected note that makes the heart flutter and the soul dance. So, if you wish to truly engage, to resonate, to be heard and felt, harness the power of suddenness and watch as the world stops, listens, and remembers.

**Step-By-Step: Mastering Suddenness:**

> **Break the Pattern** - A presentation often follows a particular flow or pattern. To incorporate suddenness, break this flow. Introduce an abrupt shift in your narrative or a sudden change in your visuals. This unexpected change would engage your audience's attention, making the presentation more memorable. Think of it like a plot twist in a movie - the sudden, dramatic turn that keeps viewers on the edge of their seats.

> **Use Shocking Statistics or Statement** - One of the ways to create suddenness is through your content. Use shocking statistics, statements, or facts your audience wouldn't see coming. The sudden realization or revelation can make a powerful impact.

**Embrace Multimedia** - The sudden introduction of a video, an audio clip, or an interactive game can effectively disrupt the presentation flow, causing a Surprise. What's more, multimedia engages multiple senses, making the Surprise more potent.

**Unconventional Start or End** - Begin or end your presentation on an unexpected note. This could be a thought-provoking question, a bold statement, or a Surprising fact. The suddenness of this incredible start or end can capture your audience's attention immediately or leave them with a memorable ending.

**Interactive Surprises** - Include sudden interactive elements, like a quick poll, a pop quiz, or an on-the-spot activity. The abruptness of the task would Surprise your audience and also encourage participation.

**Master Your Delivery** - Suddenness is not just about what you present but how you present it. Your tone, your body language, your pace - these can be tools to create suddenness. A sudden change in tone, a deliberate pause, and a swift shift in a topic can Surprise your audience and keep them engaged.

Be mindful of the fact that the key is to disrupt the expected and introduce elements your audience wouldn't see coming. Plan deliberately, execute confidently and watch as the magic of suddenness amplifies your impact.

## SUDDENNESS IN ACTION

A letter from a Brain-centric Instructional Designer (BcID) recalls 'Suddenness.'

"I vividly recall the day we ran for the Leadership Group. A collection of some of the company's brightest and most ambitious minds, their collective energy was nearly palpable. The Big Idea was simple yet challenging: elevating their communication for engagement via Brain-centric Design's Challenge Wheel.

"Alright, folks," I began, looking at the expectant faces. "We're not here to tell you about the Challenge Wheel, we're going to show you, and you won't see it coming."

Giggles, light as a feather, danced around. Leaders, versed in the usual cadence of such meetings, expected routine. Ah, but this melody was set to Surprise. This one, they'd soon realize, was anything but predictable.

As we waded into the frameworks of Brain-centric, we suddenly veered off into what seemed like an unrelated topic. I started discussing the history of chess, the strategic depth, and the masters of the game. There was an element of Surprise, of humor, as the group found themselves engaging in an animated discussion about grandmasters and gambits in what was supposed to be a session about cognitive communications.

But then, as swiftly as the detour had started, we steered back on track. I unveiled the Challenge Wheel on the screen, now uncovering the phases of the cognitive learning process in the discussion we just had but I had them bring it to light because as I walked around the room, I placed an index card upside down on each table.

"Table One! One of you turn that index card over, read it out loud to us all and inform us of the first step in understanding!"

"Attention!" chirped a younger executive. "This is the first phase of the learning process, where you focus on the concept you're trying to learn."

"Table Two...same directions!"

The room began to murmur in enthusiasm. "Encoding." said the stately woman reading from the card. "This is where you take in new information and store it in your memory."

"Table Three!"

"Storage...This is where you keep the information you've encoded in your memory."

"Table Four!"

"Retrieval! This is where you bring the information you've stored in your memory back to mind."

"Table Five!"

"Application, This is where you use the information you've learned to solve problems or complete tasks."

"Think of the chess history as information," I explained, "You were curious, we provided information, you discussed it, practiced a bit of strategic thinking, and now you can transfer that knowledge, telling someone else about the dynamics of chess."

The suddenness of the diversion and its tie-in to our main topic had caught them off guard. There was a brief silence before the room erupted into appreciative laughter and applause. We had planned and executed suddenness to perfection, transforming a simple training session into a memorable learning experience.

Their feedback was gratifying. They appreciated the effectiveness of Brain-centric and the value of experiencing it together as leaders. The shared experience forged a sense of unity, a common understanding that would echo in their leadership voices, instantly Greenhousing the environment in the organization."

## Apply It

## Educator

Educators have the constant challenge of maintaining students' attention and interest. As an educator, introduce suddenness into your lesson planning by incorporating unexpected elements.

Imagine you're teaching a history lesson which usually involves a textbook and discussion. On a day when the topic is particularly dense, project a gripping documentary on the subject instead of turning to the usual page.

The sudden shift in teaching medium will engage the students, break the monotony, and make the lesson more memorable.

## Sales

In sales, capturing your client's interest is paramount. Use suddenness to your advantage by revealing a problem they weren't aware of.

In your next meeting with a potential client, after you've outlined the benefits of your product or service, drop the bombshell - bring up an issue or challenge their company faces that they haven't noticed, one your product can solve.

The suddenness of the problem's revelation, followed by the relief of having a solution at hand, could lead to a significant boost in perceived product value and sales closure rates.

## Manager

As a manager, you must constantly keep your team engaged and motivated. Use a sudden dose of Foreshadowed Surprise to achieve this.

In a team meeting, hint towards an upcoming project or policy change without giving too many details.

When nurtured over a period, this seed of anticipation can

lead to a more enthusiastic and engaged response when you finally unveil the full details.

### Coach

A coach ensures their team is always adaptable and ready to tackle new challenges. Suddenness can be incorporated into training sessions to achieve this.

In the middle of a session, without prior warning, introduce a new strategy you co-create as a perspective.

The abrupt shift from routine will engage them, enhancing their adaptability and responsiveness.

### Communicator

Communicators aim to captivate their audience and leave a lasting impact.

To incorporate suddenness, unveil a surprising fact or a staggering statistic related to your topic during your next presentation or speech seemingly 'out of nowhere.'

The unexpected reveal not only hooks the audience's attention but also deepens their understanding of your message, making your communication more powerful and impactful.

# SUDDENNESS GRID

A quick change of pace, a sudden shift from our intellectual discourse, and we plunge into a game.

Yes, a crossword puzzle!

This isn't just any crossword puzzle, however. It's a collection of terms, concepts, and hints that we've navigated together in our exploration of the concept of 'suddenness.'

How fitting, to encounter a Surprise in a book about Surprise!

We invite you to pick up your pen (or pencil if you prefer), and test your recall of our shared journey so far. See if you can crack the clues, fill the squares, and relive our exploration of suddenness.

Take your time, enjoy the shift in pace, and let the sudden surprise of a crossword puzzle enhance your engagement with the material. The answers you fill in might just serve as a spark for your next Surprising presentation, negotiation, or learning experience.

The activities, templates, and 'To-Dos' in this book are conveniently available for you online at
**https://surprised.brain-centric.com**

# Suddenness Grid

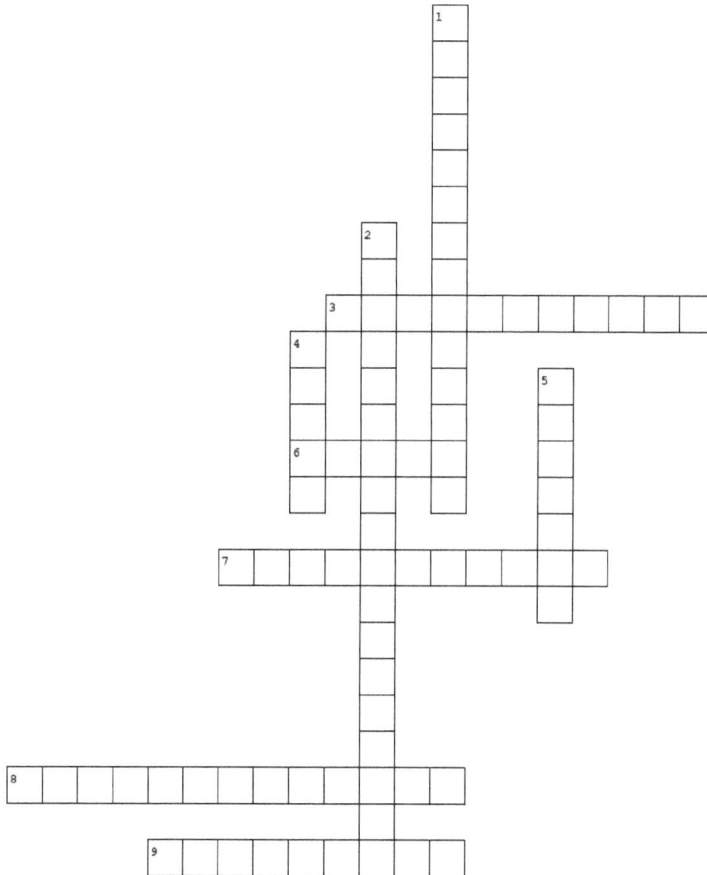

## Across

3. Professionals who use strategies and plans in the business world
6. The game used as a metaphor in a training session
7. Unpredictable element used in training or lessons
8. The technique of giving a hint about an upcoming surprise
9. A wheel associated with the cognitive learning process

## Down

1. Unpredictable element used in training or lessons
2. Framework prioritizing whole-brain, learner-centric communications
4. A sports leader who can use suddenness in training drills
5. The feeling often elicited by a surprise

## Suddenness Grid Answers

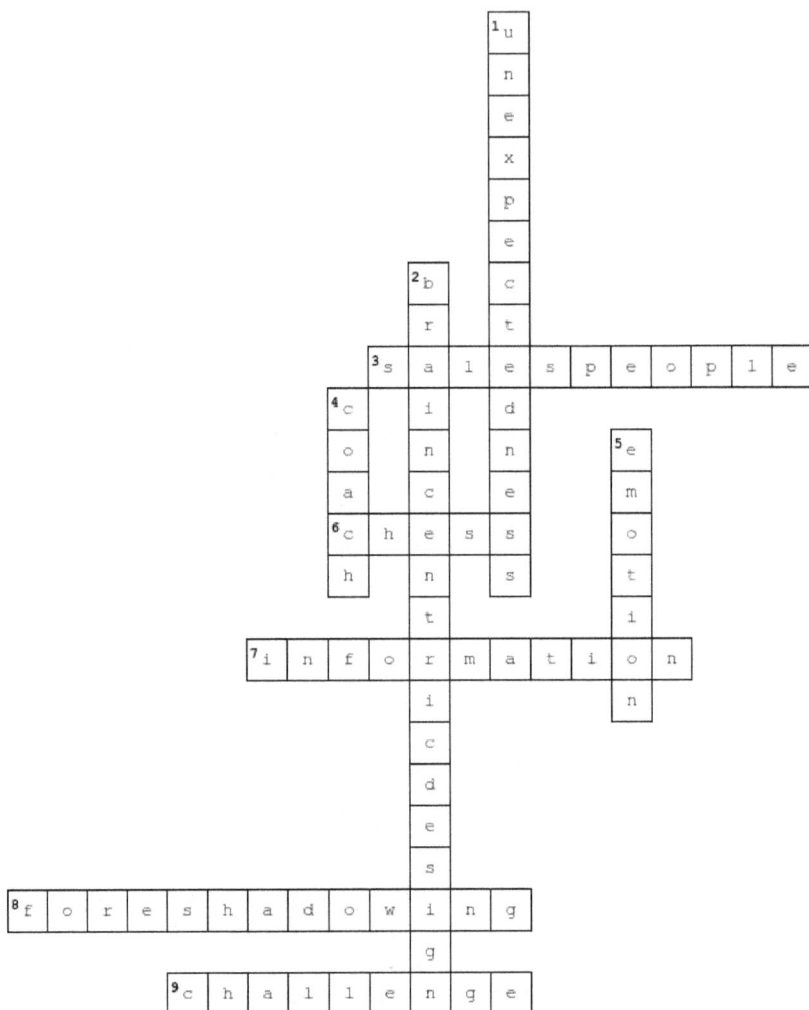

Crossword grid answers:

1. (Down) unexpectedness
2. (Down) braincideness — b r a i n c i d e s g g
3. (Across) salespeople
4. (Down) coach
5. (Down) emotion
6. (Across) chess
7. (Across) information
8. (Across) foreshadowing
9. (Across) challenge

## Suddenness Grid Word Bank

BraincentricDesign • Challenge • Chess • Coach •
Emotion • Foreshadowing • Information • Salespeople •
Unexpectedness

# Tales of Insightsville: Element Three
## GEMS FROM BENEATH

*A sudden series of natural events leads to Jesse unearthing radiant gems, their sudden appearance becoming a symbol of Insightsville's untapped potential.*

Insightsville, where life moved to its steady beat, found itself on the edge of an epochal event. Beneath the town's surface, the earth hid a profound secret, soon to be unveiled within its mining core. This revelation promised change and excitement, especially for Lyle and young Jesse.

The jewelry store of Lyle and Jesse has since become a sanctum of 'precision'. Their showcases brim with elaborate designs crafted from local semi-precious gems. Lyle, the seasoned jeweler with tales of time etched across his features, once took pride in crafting these delicate masterpieces. Meanwhile, Jesse, always the innovator, took charge of the store's operations. Simultaneously, he channeled his passion for diesel mechanics into creating pieces inspired by the intricacies of engine parts.

Holding up a pendant towards the sunlight, Jesse declared, "This one's named Combustion. Feel its warmth as it dances with the rays."

The shop, their shared domain, was bathed in an array of gemstones, their many faces reflecting a vibrant spectrum upon the walls. The gentle song of the wind chimes played in the background, their melodies made you smile just because of their perfect pitch and unchained melody.

With his gaze fixed on the horizon, Jesse started, "Dad, I've been thinking..."

Raising an eyebrow, Lyle teased, "Sounds risky, kid."

Shaking his head, Jesse replied with a chuckle, "Bear with me. I've been reflecting on the similarities between our precious jewels and the diesel engine of our vintage truck."

Caught off-guard, Lyle let out a hearty laugh, "Jewels and our rugged engine? Now that's a first!"

"Sounds odd, I know," Jesse acknowledged. "But you often discuss the nuances in both."

Nodding, Lyle mused, "Yup. Jewelry, like an engine, is a collaboration of elements. A brilliantly cut diamond, shimmering just so, resembles a piston at its prime, and the gentle curve of a gold band, it's reminiscent of the crankshaft, channeling power into motion."

"And the chandelier earrings displayed upfront," Jesse chimed in, "they sway like valves, modulating the flow, governing the engine's heartbeat."

Laughing, Lyle exclaimed, "That's a reach, but I hear you! Who would've imagined finding allure amidst the grime of a diesel engine? Next time there's a query about my fondness for that vintage beauty, I'll draw parallels with a fine jewel."

Jesse, shaking his head in amusement, remarked, "I'd love to see that!" Their shared laughter resounded, two souls connecting over the unlikeliest of comparisons.

As the day unfolded, a sudden earth-shaking revelation rocked the very core of Insightsville.

A profound vibration, oddly soothing, rattled teacups on their saucers, caused fences to quiver, and threw the town's fauna into animated disarray.

An earthquake? A landslide in the foothills?

The ground of Insightsville, typically steadfast, now whispered secrets only discerned by a privileged few.

It was soon apparent that a treasure trove of jewels lay concealed beneath the town's facade. Not just any jewels, but an array of unique gems that had taken eons to form, silently waiting for their grand debut.

Word of this discovery raced through the region, setting hearts aflame with anticipation. Every conversation at Yohan's

Diner was dominated by the remarkable find.

"Just think, all this time, right below us!" a waitress marveled.

"It's like we've landed a jackpot, only with gems!" an elderly miner mused, hope gleaming in his eyes.

The revelation infused Insightsville with renewed vitality.

The once-quiet mine transformed into a hive of activity, with diligent miners extracting the jewels with reverence.

The town's financial prospects soared, and tourists thronged to witness the newly christened "Gem Town." For Lyle and Jesse, this turn of events promised an unforeseen evolution in their trade.

The influx of precious stones elevated their creations. With materials ranging from amethysts to sapphires and rubies to emeralds, their artistry shone brighter. Lyle ventured into territories he'd only imagined, crafting gems of legends. Meanwhile, Jesse unearthed a fresh synergy between the sturdy gemstones and the process of sculpting them.

Gazing at the jewels, Lyle mused, "Jesse, it's as if we're in a crystallized rainbow."

Chuckling, Jesse replied, "All along, I believed rainbows led to pots of gold, not heaps of precious stones."

With a grin, Lyle responded, "But these 'stones' are priceless, more than any gold, my boy."

With the heart of an engineer, Jesse held up a radiant sapphire, inspecting it. "It's crazy, Dad. One moment, we're fashioning quartz, and now, sapphires adorn our workshop. We've stepped into a world of charm."

Lyle nodded, sharing the sentiment, "It's like shifting gears seamlessly, coasting into a new realm. What a journey it's been."

As Jesse let a gem play with sunlight, he remarked, "Given that we're now in the universe's most opulent workshop, there's no room for complaints."

The town's gem renaissance altered not just its visual tapestry but also its emotional fabric.

A newfound euphoria embraced its inhabitants, transforming the commonplace into a destination, the routine into the exciting. Insightsville, mirroring its underground treasures, was poised to dazzle.

# INCONGRUITY

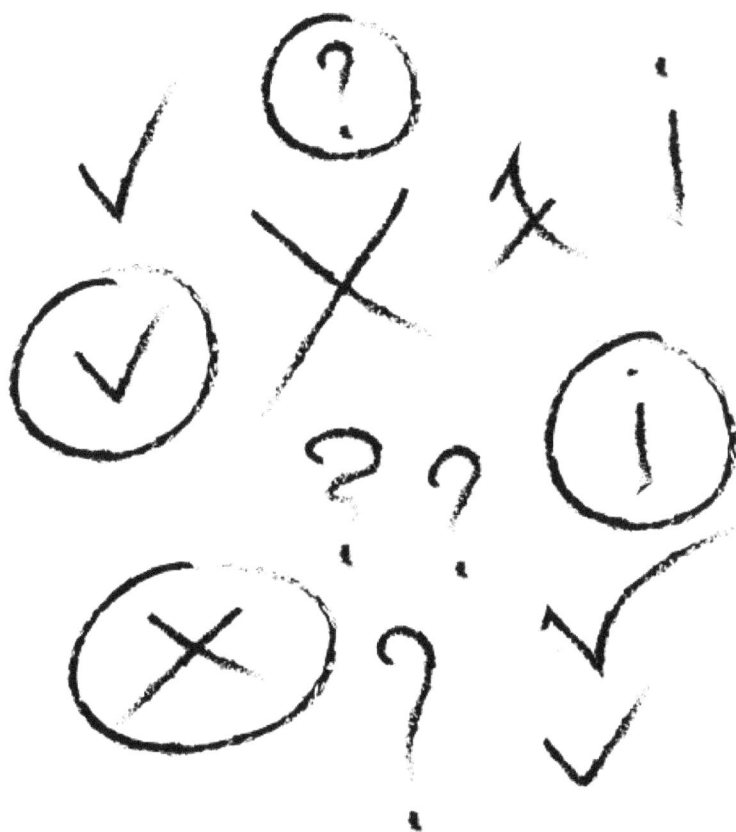

# INCONGRUITY

Expectation sets the stage
Novelty fuels curiosity
Suddenness strikes like lightning, arresting attention
**Incongruity challenges the mind with the unexpected**
Emotional Reaction deepens the connection
Valence colors the experience
Intensity amplifies the impact
Uncertainty Reduction brings clarity
Sense Making transforms chaos into understanding
Adjustment ensures enduring influence

**Incongruity**: A crucial part of the Surprise involves a clash between what is expected and what happens. This Incongruity can be minor (*like a surprise party*) or major (*like an unexpected natural disaster*).

The eloquence of the acronym "WTF" lies in its candid portrayal of the human brain's reaction to incongruity. At its core, incongruity is about the unexpected; it's those moments when what's unfolding before our eyes doesn't quite match the patterns we've come to expect. And when we encounter these mismatches, our brain — in its raw, unfiltered manner — reacts with a resounding "WTF."

Initially, our brains identify this incongruity almost instantaneously, recognizing something is amiss. This is swiftly followed by the juxtaposition of what we know and expect — the "W" for "What" — against this novel and bewildering input, represented by the colorful exclamation encapsulated in the "TF."

But it's not just about a recognition of difference; "WTF" is disruptive. It's not a gentle query, but a potent, forceful proclamation of confusion. The very essence of incongruity is about disruption, breaking away from our neatly constructed schemas of the world.

Yet, as forceful as this initial reaction might be, it also paves the way for curiosity and the desire for resolution. After that initial wallop of Surprise, our brains aren't content to simply leave the incongruity hanging. There's a drive, an innate need to dig deeper, to explore and understand the roots of this unexpected divergence.

In this dance of recognition, disruption, and eventual resolution, "WTF" becomes more than a casual slang. It becomes a reflection of our innate human response to life's incongruities. Embracing this response, understanding its nuances, offers a powerful lens through which we can engage, provoke thought, and even surprise those around us.

As you navigate your personal and professional engagements, remember the potency of Incongruity. Use it to capture attention, evoke curiosity, and imprint memorable experiences. It's your paintbrush for creating the unexpected, your chisel for sculpting Surprise, your pen for authoring engagement.

Harness its power, and transform the world around you into a canvas of endless possibilities.

Incongruence is the muse of visual art. We can't help but be entranced by the surreal - think of a towering elephant on spindly insect-like legs, or a room where furniture is suspended upside down from the ceiling. These seducing scenes defy our everyday logic, toss aside our neatly packed perceptions, and Surprise us with their departure from reality. This is the mesmerizing power of Incongruity – a delightful mismatch between our expectations and reality that shakes us awake, makes our eyebrows shoot up, and has us leaning in for a closer look.

Imagine you're poised to give a talk on data privacy. The crowd is shuffling in their seats, bracing for the predictable spiel on encryption and cyber safety. But what if you took a sharp left turn, recounting instead the tale of the legendary Trojan Horse, a symbol of deceptive triumph from ancient times? The room is suddenly all ears. As you artfully weave connections between this historic ruse and modern-day data breaches, portraying our personal data as the coveted treasure inside the horse and hackers as the cunning Greeks, you've spun an entirely unexpected narrative on a familiar topic. That's the enchanting spell of Incongruity.

Now, let's play with this in the world of sales. Imagine you're a sales rep, showcasing a product that, quite frankly, most have seen in various avatars. The prospects are mentally rolling their eyes, prepped for the clichéd spiel.

But what if, instead of launching straight into the product specs and benefits, you commence with a story about a trip to the Amazon rainforest and your encounter with a captivating bird species, the Resplendent Quetzal?

WTF?

Suddenly, your audience is hooked, their interest is ignited, and their expectations are subverted. They want to know more. How does this relate to your product? How does this story connect to them?

The answer comes in the form of your product, designed to help businesses stand out in the market, much like the Resplendent Quetzal in the heart of the Amazon rainforest.

You've turned an expected sales pitch into an engaging narrative, an incongruous blend of storytelling and salesmanship.

A vital part of the Surprise involves a clash between what is expected and what happens. This Incongruity can be minor or major.

# INCONGRUITY IN ACTION

Have you ever found yourself purposely mismatching your socks to shake things up? Or maybe you've decided to paint your office an outrageous shade of burnt orange to break the monotony of beige?

This is the charm of incongruity.

It impacts us, tickles our senses, and flips the switch on what's expected.

Let's bring this playful yet powerful concept into different professional settings focusing on this fourth element of Surprise.

### Executive Coach

You're an Executive Coach, and instead of starting with your qualifications, the history of whatever you're talking about today, you hand your client a mosaic tile.

You tell them that over your sessions, you'll build a beautiful, colorful mosaic that represents their leadership journey. It's unexpected and metaphorically rich.

Incorporate this into your practice: Start your next coaching session with a physical object that symbolizes your client's goals. It's a memorable and engaging way to set the tone for your work together. If you work remotely, sending it online with a Surprising note is easy to cement your relationship and prime the next session. Better still, spend a few moments handwriting that note on a card, place it in an envelope, address it to them, add postage and mail it. The romance of receiving a written message in the mail like this is so incredibly powerful and Surprising in any profession.

Write a note to somebody and mail it to them. The effects are immediate, long-lasting, and truly incongruent in the best of ways.

## Sales Manager

Imagine you're a Sales Manager at a software company. At the next team meeting, instead of pushing for higher sales targets, you start with a compelling narrative of how your software helped a small business thrive during a global pandemic.

It's an incongruous approach in a typically numbers-focused meeting, but it reminds your team of the real-world impact of their work.

Incorporate this into your work. Use storytelling to highlight the value of your product. It breaks the monotony of the sales pitch and offers a more human connection to your potential customers.

## Parenting

Picture this: You're a parent, it's your child's bedtime, and your child insists that TV needs to stay on!

Instead of the usual 'no,' you propose they plan a home-theater night where they decide on the movie, and you provide the popcorn.

It's an incongruous approach, turning a no into a different, yes, but it also teaches them planning and negotiation skills.

Try the *'yes, and'* technique with your child's subsequent request. It leads to creative solutions that both of you enjoy.

## Facilitator

Now, you're a facilitator for a strategy workshop.

Instead of hosting a traditional round-table discussion, you organize a walking brainstorm around the office park.

It's incongruous for a business setting yet encourages creative thinking and sparks unexpected ideas.

Incorporate this into your sessions and experiment with different physical setups for your meetings. An unusual setting might lead to those breakthrough moments.

# DOODLE SWAP

Even in a world of words, sometimes the most incongruous thing you can do is use none. Let us toss aside our language for a moment and engage in a different form of expression you probably do all the time. When we think Brain-centric, we transform this seemingly innocuous activity into cognitive gold.

Here's your task: Grab your trusty pen or coveted PALOMINO Blackwing 602 Original Soft Pencil, and let's have a Doodle Swap.

**Step 1:** Consider a personal experience with incongruity, something unexpected or out-of-place.

Instead of writing about it, I want you to doodle it. That's right, put pen to paper and create a simple, non-verbal representation of your story.

**Step 2:** Now for the 'swap' part. Imagine you're handing your doodle to someone else, someone who knows nothing about your experience.

How would they interpret your doodle?

Write a brief, whimsical story about what they might think your doodle represents.

Done right, this exercise isn't just about taking a creative detour from the traditional text path. It's about immersing ourselves in the heart of incongruity. It's about acknowledging how different perspectives can make sense of the same thing wonderfully differently. And above all, it's about embracing the Surprises that such incongruity can gift us.

# Tales of Insightsville: Element Four
## DARIAN'S PARADOX

*Darian Rae, intrigued by Jesse's gems, creates a machine that reproduces them, sparking a debate on authenticity versus imitation, and highlighting the town's evolving values.*

Darian Rae was an enigma wrapped in the familiar. On the surface, she was a doting mother to joyful children Ava and Giovanni and a loving partner to Chris. Yet, beneath her nurturing facade was a mind that treads the fine line between brilliance and chaos and a spirit that defied the ordinary.

Insightsville buzzed with tales of Darian, the unconventional inventor. Legend had it that she could see the wonder every day and spin the impossible into reality. Like her kids, her inventions were adored and debated but never dismissed.

This time, Darian had unveiled a creation that left Insightsville both amazed and perplexed: a device capable of replicating gemstones. The town was torn between admiration and skepticism.

Nestled in her workshop among strewn schematics and neglected microchips, the gemstone replicator pulsed with a mysterious vitality. It was a tangible emblem of Darian's unique essence: wonder wrapped in the ordinary.

"Unbelievable, Darian," Aaron Castle managed, eyes wide as he beheld the contraption. Lured by the town's fiery gossip, he now stood amidst Darian's unbelievable invention.

She beamed, her excitement unmistakable, "Surprising, isn't it? To think that precious stones could spring from circuits and silicon."

She motioned Aaron closer. The machine was a marvel of artistry, an intricate weave of colorful wires, gleaming indicators, and potent microprocessors housed within a metallic skeleton. As a hobby mechanic, Aaron was riveted by the detailed craftsmanship, tracing the circuitry that sprawled across the device like lifelines.

Darian pointed to a chamber filled with an ordinary gray substance. "This, silicon carbide, is commonplace in electronics. Yet here, it births wonders."

With deft movements, she activated the machine. It sprung to life, emitting an opus of beeps and hums, filling the space with electric tension. Aaron, infected by Darian's intensity, waited with bated breath.

Then, as if conjured from thin air, a gleaming gem emerged—a flawless diamond replica, born from the most unassuming origins. The sheer improbability of it struck Aaron.

"Darian," he breathed, awe evident in his voice, "you've just charted a new frontier for us."

Her laughter, light, and tingling merged with the ambient hum of her invention. "Oh, Aaron, Insightsville always has a card up its sleeve. And this?" She gestured at her creation, her eyes reflecting its shimmer, "This is just the tip of the iceberg."

The news of the replicator sent ripples of anticipation, excitement, and apprehension across Insightsville.

Over at Evansiano's, Lyle and Jesse exchanged worried glances. Their blooming business could either skyrocket or crumble under the weight of this revelation.

"Pop, we need to talk to her," Jesse suggested one afternoon, a severe look on his face.

"I know, buddy. We need to understand what this means for us," Lyle agreed, concern etched on his face.

"Insightsville is on the edge of change," Ricco said to himself. " In this space, I perceive harmony and dissonance, as if contradictions have found a canvas to coexist.

"We're stepping into a world of incongruity, and Darian's leading the way!" he said as he imitated a game show announcer and scurried down the sidewalk.

The challenge to adapt, evolve, and rethink their values and lifestyles was now on everyone's doorstep.

Darian Rae had given Insightsville its newest paradox, a riddle they would have to solve together.

# EMOTIONAL REACTION

# EMOTIONAL REACTION

Expectation sets the stage
Novelty fuels curiosity
Suddenness strikes like lightning, arresting attention
Incongruity challenges the mind with the unexpected
**Emotional Reaction deepens the connection**
Valence colors the experience
Intensity amplifies the impact
Uncertainty Reduction brings clarity
Sense Making transforms chaos into understanding
Adjustment ensures enduring influence

**Emotional Reaction:** Surprises are often accompanied by a strong emotional reaction, such as positive (fun, delight, joy, wonder) or negative (shock, fear, disgust), depending on the nature of the surprise.

A momentous revelation awaits us in this chapter as we navigate the terrain of Emotional Reaction, the fifth element of Surprise. Here, in this intricate tapestry of feelings and responses, the power of surprise truly takes flight.

Consider the thrill of joy as a long-anticipated reunion suddenly unfolds or the instinctive intake of breath when a surprising twist transpires in your beloved mystery novel.

In its various manifestations, Surprise often acts as a portal to deep-seated emotional reactions. It can guide us swiftly across our emotional terrain, moving us from the pits of boredom or anxiety to a heightened state of receptivity.

**Surprise is a cognitive circuit-breaker,
resetting our emotional state in a heartbeat.**

Drawing from the groundbreaking insights of premier neuroscientists and cognitive psychologists, we unravel the potency of Surprise in counteracting emotional turbulence. When we're gripped by an emotional whirlwind, often referred to as an 'amygdala hijack', our focus narrows sharply to potential dangers, overshadowing opportunities for growth and learning. This tunnel vision not only drowns out positivity but also stifles our brain's knack for knitting new neural pathways, jeopardizing our long-term ability to learn.

Enter our golden-yellow bridge from the unengaged emotions to the engaged: Surprise. This sudden jolt has the power to recalibrate our emotional compass, shifting us from apprehension to awe and curiosity. And in that magic moment, we've unlocked the door to true engagement.

Let's breathe life into this rich repository of empirical wisdom. It's time we employ it, without hesitation. Grasping the nuances of emotional states is paramount in the Brain-centric engagement model, where Surprise isn't merely sprinkled in but is architecturally woven into its fabric. This innovative approach births the notion of the Emotional Mood Ring, an evocative portrayal of our ever-changing emotional canvas.

Resonating with Robert Plutchik's profound Wheel of Emotions, the Emotional Mood Ring expands upon this, articulating, with great simplicity, our emotional ebb and flow. Influenced by the dynamic dance of our daily interactions and experiences, this ring beautifully showcases the pivotal 'golden-yellow bridge of engagement' through Surprise, demystifying the transition between states of deep engagement and passive indifference.

We're on the cusp of delving into this illuminating mental paradigm of emotions, so brace yourself for an enlightening journey as we move forward.

## The Emotional Mood Ring

*A deep-dive into the Emotional Mood Ring is waiting for you online at https://surprised.brain-centric.com in the form of training, templates, and applications!*

⌗OBJ⌗

©Brain-centric

Again, the goal is not merely to surprise but to maintain that engagement by keeping our audience bathed in the radiance of 'Fun' and its correlative emotional states: Happy, Contentment, Peace, Love, Gratitude, and Optimism.

The Emotional Mood Ring illustrates why I implore, "If we're not having fun, we're doing something wrong."

Why so? The answer lies in the intricate weave of our cognitive and emotional processes.

In a world saturated with fleeting joys, it's not enough to merely feel. It's the depth, the authenticity of these feelings that counts. Imagine strolling down life's path, indulging in fleeting moments of elation, only to confront an abyss of emptiness and inauthenticity. Such is the fate of those who chase basic happiness, divorced from genuine character.

When we speak of an audience or learner swathed in a cocoon of genuine positive emotions, we're talking about engagement that's undeniable. Their minds become dynamos, charged up and ready to go. Their focus sharpens, and their hearts and minds are poised to receive. Yet, it's more than just heightened alertness; it's about truly immersing oneself in all the elements of the experience.

Consider happiness as a golden key, unlocking doors to profound presence, insatiable curiosity, and meaningful connection. When draped in these sunlit emotional cloaks, individuals aren't merely passive onlookers but are spirited adventurers, primed to delve deep, question relentlessly, and grasp profoundly.

True happiness does more than just lift our spirits; it elevates our very thought processes. It ushers in an expansiveness of mind, a flexibility of thought. Specifically, in this sunlit kingdom, there's an inherent sense of safety, an environment conducive for profound learning. With walls down and hearts open, new ideas find a place and take root.

Picture an environment – a veritable 'Greenhouse' if you will – where intellect and emotion, reason and passion, all thrive in harmonious tandem. This is where every thought, be it as resilient as a dandelion or as delicate as an orchid, finds its place under the sun. Herein lies the magic of Engagement: using Surprise to captivate and then nurturing that very engagement to sustain an enriching state of joy.

The Surprising shift? Marrying the shock value of Surprise with the desired emotional response, thereby enhancing the overall reception of the message at hand. It's truly simpler than it seems.

To masterfully harness the might of Surprise, we must keenly discern the emotional pulse of our audience, letting it light the way. Let's choreograph this intricate ballet between the raw power of emotion and the artful allure of Surprise.

# EMOTIONAL REACTION IN ACTION

Tapping into emotional reactions can be a powerful tool for fostering engagement and creating memorable experiences across various roles and contexts. Anybody can and does foster deep connections by evoking emotions, resonating with the core feelings, creating positive emotional connections, building lasting relationships, and driving outcomes.

What separates hacks from the adept is understanding how to move an individual from the red emotions to green emotions of 'happy' and how to manage the recovery period that follows.

### Salesperson

For a salesperson, evoking a strong emotional reaction can differentiate a transactional interaction from a transformative one. Instead of merely explaining the benefits of a product or service, connect with the customer's emotional needs and aspirations. For instance, selling a home isn't just about the number of rooms or amenities; it's about creating memories, building a future, or finding a sanctuary. By tapping into these emotional reactions, a salesperson can make a stronger bond with customers, leading to loyalty and, often, further recommendations.

### Communicator

A communicator should not just relay information but also evoke emotions. Storytelling is a potent tool in this regard. By incorporating personal stories, real-life examples, or emotionally charged anecdotes, communicators can capture the audience's heart, making the message more relatable and impactful. The difference between a forgettable speech and a moving one is often the emotional reaction it elicits.

## Parent

Emotional reactions play a pivotal role in parenting. Celebrating successes, empathizing during challenges, or sharing in the joy of a new experience strengthens the parent-child bond and instills values and emotional intelligence. A child remembers the times their emotions were validated, understood, and shared, and it contributes significantly to their emotional and psychological development.

## Learning & Development

In Learning & Development, emotional reactions can enhance the learning experience. Learners can relate more deeply when a topic is related to an emotional experience or a personal journey. For example, instead of explaining the consequences of workplace safety violations with statistics, sharing a poignant story of a worker's experience can create a more profound emotional connection to the topic. Emotional engagement enhances memory retention and encourages proactive behavior.

Additionally, leveraging emotional reactions during learning can lead to transformative experiences. I suggest incorporating emotional triggers to engage learners. Emotionally charged content, be it through multimedia, real-life testimonials, or powerful narratives, can create an environment where learners absorb information and deeply connect with it.

To chase the proverbial squirrel, think 'Empathy and Resonance' to encompass the depth of human interaction and connection, especially when aiming for genuine engagement. While distinct, the two elements are interconnected and represent the science and art of engagement. Let's break down these elements and explore their significance:

## Empathy

Empathy, at its core, is the ability to understand and share the feelings of another. It is rooted in our neurobiology; the brain's mirror neurons activate when we perform an action and see someone else perform that action. This neural basis enables us to feel connected to others, even if we haven't personally experienced what they're going through.

In the context of engagement:

1. **Listening Actively:** Engagement begins with listening to another person's perspective, concerns, or feelings. We demonstrate our willingness to understand and relate to their experience through active listening.
2. **Personalization:** Whether tailoring a learning module to a specific audience or customizing a sales pitch, empathy allows professionals to tap into individual needs and preferences.
3. **Building Trust:** Authentic empathy fosters an environment of trust. When individuals feel understood, they are more likely to engage genuinely and openly.

## Resonance

Resonance is the harmonious alignment of emotions, often resulting in a deep emotional connection. When something resonates, it strikes a chord emotionally, mentally, or spiritually. It goes beyond understanding (empathy) to create a shared emotional experience.

In the context of engagement:

1. **Storytelling**: Narratives have the power to resonate deeply because they often encapsulate shared human experiences. A well-told story can evoke emotions and create a lasting impact, making it a powerful tool for engagement.

2. **Shared Values and Beliefs**: Resonance can be achieved when individuals discover shared values, beliefs, or passions. This common ground establishes a deeper emotional connection, often leading to sustained engagement.

3. **Feedback Loop**: Resonance is mutual. Engagers should be receptive to feedback, allowing the relationship or interaction to evolve dynamically. The engagement becomes more potent when both parties feel a sense of resonance.

## Linking Empathy and Resonance in Engagement

To truly engage with another, it's crucial to understand them (empathy) and connect with them emotionally (resonance). The science lies in understanding empathy's biological and psychological mechanisms, while the art is crafting experiences, narratives, and environments that resonate deeply with the audience.

SURPRISED encapsulates a holistic approach to engagement, urging you to harness both the cognitive understanding and the emotional depth of human connection.

When empathy and resonance converge, they craft a genuine and memorable engagement experience.

## Disney Deals It

A universally recognized scene that encapsulates this convergence of empathy and resonance is the reunion of Simba and Nala in "The Lion King."

When Simba, believed to be dead by his kingdom and friends, encounters Nala after years, the initial Temporal Surprise of recognition is unmistakable. Nala's disbelief and joy upon discovering Simba is alive, and Simba's mixture of happiness and anxiety at meeting his childhood friend, evokes empathy. We feel for them, understanding their complex emotions of joy, nostalgia, and the looming responsibility of saving the Pride Lands.

The resonance is felt deeply when they romp around and play just as they did as cubs, set to the backdrop of the song "Can You Feel the Love Tonight?" It's a moment that tugs at viewers' heartstrings, reminding them of lost friendships, reconnections, and the simplicity of childhood amidst the complexities of adulthood.

This scene is memorable because it captures the reunion's emotional intensity, driven by empathy (understanding their feelings) and resonance (feeling deeply connected to the emotions on display).

**FUN FACT**: When Nala and Simba encounter each other, it's at a moment (in terms of the narrative's timing) that's unexpected to the audience, creating a Temporal Surprise. The audience knows that Nala is looking for help, but they don't anticipate her running into Simba, especially given the prevalent belief that he's dead. The Surprise is rooted in the timing of their reunion in the storyline.

We love watching this stuff. Now, imagine you doing it with deft skill. How would your life change if you could manage emotional reactions like Disney?

Think about that for sixty seconds. Seriously.

# THE EMOTIONAL MOOD RING

When I first stumbled upon Robert Plutchik's Wheel of Emotions, it struck me deep, like a midnight chime in an empty cathedral. The brilliance, complexity, and depth - it was all there, laid out in a scholarly format that, while insightful, wasn't exactly bread and butter for the everyday soul.

And that was the problem. There was groundbreaking work, but it was trapped in an academic echo chamber, its full potential untapped.

This goldmine of human emotions and their intricacies needed context and application and to be placed in the hands of everybody who communicates to others for a result.

### Cognitively Control Your Environment

We live in a world where salespeople, teachers, business coaches, or even that random guy at the bar can tap into the pulse of their audience's feelings and ride that wave for the thrill of 'rocking your boat.'

You are different. You long for a world where talking to someone isn't just about saying a bunch of facts. Instead, you want everyone to understand the message and know what to do next.

Enter the Emotional Mood Ring.

Taking inspiration from those quirky mood rings of the '70s - the ones that supposedly changed colors with your emotions, I gave Plutchik's work a makeover. A dynamic, fluid representation, constantly shifting and adapting to our moods.

Every interaction, new piece of information, and every twist in our day influences this dance of displayed moods and emotions, affecting those around us. Instead of randomly coloring moods and emotions for visual separation, I grouped them into three colors we all understand–Red, Yellow, and

Green–because they mean Stop, Yield, and Go in any language.

We know Stop is Stop and Go is Go, but did you know Yield means prepare to receive something unexpected?

And the real kicker?

When I applied the learning sciences in cognitive neuroscience to this visual representation of 'What must our state of mind be to absorb and assimilate new information effectively?', the 'bridge of engagement' was marked by none other than Surprise! An emotion so powerful, so visceral, that it could make or break an experience.

With it, I wanted to communicate something profoundly meaningful that makes a difference by organically changing how we connect, present, and engage.

The Emotional Mood Ring is an instrument and a symbol. A symbol that emotions aren't just some touchy-feely thing you shove in a corner. They're at the core of our experiences. And if you are ready to master that, strap in because you're in for one hell of a short ride.

Short because the Emotional Mood Ring is so easy to understand: Surprise (Yellow) causes people to become engaged (Green) when they are unengaged (Red).

For those who said emotions had no place in serious discourse? Surprise.

# THE EMOTIONAL MOOD RING

[OBJ]

©Brain-centric, LLC

## Decoding the Emotional Mood Ring

The neuroscience of the Emotional Mood Ring is crafted around the seven foundational emotions at the center of the ring which I've relabeled as "Moods." The distinction? Moods are observable, something we intuitively perceive in others. In contrast, emotions often remain a profoundly personal and internal journey.

**Innermost Circle**: Represents the central foundational mood.
**Middle Circle**: Expands on the myriad of emotions that characterize this main mood.
**Outermost Circle**: Excavates the finer nuances, providing a richer understanding of the main mood.

Assigning universal colors—Red, Yellow, and Green—to these moods isn't just visually appealing; it carries a profound significance.

### RED

Emotions in the Red zone, such as Boredom, Stress, Worry, Concern, and Entrapment, correlate with the amygdala's heightened response. Scientifically, when 'in the red', one's ability to process new information diminishes. It's a state where engagement is stifled.

### YELLOW

Yellow signifies Surprise, signaling anticipation of the novel. It heralds feelings of Excitement, Awe, and Eagerness. Brace yourself for the unexpected.

### GREEN

Green captures the essence of happiness and fun, pivotal forces driving engagement.

Why? Let's further articulate the beauty of the brain and why we engage.

Our brains are like bustling metropolises...such as the meta-narrative of *Surprised*, Insightsville, for instance. Here's a city where joy is the currency, and this currency doesn't merely rest in a vault; it courses through the streets, ushering in a golden age of discovery and connection.

When we experience joy, our brain becomes an alchemist, conjuring dopamine and endorphins. These molecules are nature's elixirs, giving our spirits a lift, sharpening our focus, and engraving memories with the chisel of clarity. With them, our souls are irresistibly drawn, like moths to a flame, to pursuits that stoke these very emotions.

But the story doesn't end there. When we indulge in activities that tickle our fancy, a fire is lit within. This isn't a flame born of obligation but of passion. An insatiable desire propelling us deeper into realms where mere duty would never tread.

And oh, the fun. The sheer joy of exploration breaks down the walls we so cautiously build, inviting in new experiences and fresh vantage points. In places colored by happiness, there's an unspoken pact – a pact that paints them as sanctuaries, brimming with safety. In these havens, creativity isn't just alive; it dances.

Yet, what of life's shadows, those stresses that loom large? Here's the beauty of joy: it has a knack for dialing down the stress symphony, reigning in the cacophony of cortisol. In its wake, attention finds its muse, no longer fragmented by anxiety.

Now, imagine the resonance of shared laughter, the collective euphoria of a group basking in mutual delight. It's infectious. It's the kind of joy that doesn't just linger; it binds, knitting individuals into a tapestry of camaraderie.

Nature, in its infinite wisdom, ensured we're creatures of habit. And joy? It's the siren song we can't resist, always pulling us back for yet another encore. Time and again, we return, hungry for the familiar thrill, eager for continued immersion.

This is the dance of the mind, the alchemy of joy, and the art of engagement. Stick around, for the ballet has just begun.

### 'Out of The Red & Into The Green'

Science stresses that happiness and fun are powerful engagement catalysts. They align with our neural preferences, echoing our innate pursuit of positivity, making them influential anchors for profound engagement.

## Tales of Insightsville: Element Five
## CASTLE'S GAMBIT

*In the face of the town's rapid changes, Aaron Castle emerges with a game that challenges Insightsville's emotional mettle, uniting them in ways they hadn't foreseen.*

Insightsville wasn't just another town; it was a beacon of ambition, a hub where innovation thrived. From this bustling metropolis, Aaron Castle emerged, not just as an industry leader but as a visionary.

Castle's reputation was multifaceted: he was known as a formidable negotiator and a connoisseur of classic vinyl records, an unexpected twist to his professional demeanor. Time and again, his strategies transformed dwindling businesses into industry front-runners.

His secret? Recognizing the power of positive emotions like Joy, Gratitude, and Optimism in the people he did business with. Anybody really. Castle believed these emotions were the lubricants keeping the machinery of business running seamlessly. His mantra was simple yet profound, "Stay in the green. That's where happiness and success merge."

On the horizon was his next negotiation challenge: Jake Hardknock of Hardknock Industries. Hardknock was self-made, resilient, and commanded respect with his formidable presence. Castle realized that to reach Hardknock, traditional tactics wouldn't suffice.

In preparation, Castle dug deeper. He didn't just prepare business data; he invested time understanding Hardknock 'as a person,' from humble beginnings to industry prominence. Castle aimed to resonate with Hardknock's personal achievements and challenges, believing in the power of emotional connection.

This episode in Castle's journey underscored the significance of the Brain-centric approach in business negotiations. His triumphs weren't just about eloquence or charm; they stemmed from understanding the 'humans', tapping into emotional states, and cultivating genuine connections.

The step-by-step recount of his strategy can be applied to many situations or needs:

1. **Identify Emotional Drivers** - Aaron recognized pivotal emotions - Joy, Contentment, Gratitude, and Optimism. Such emotions activate the prefrontal cortex, essential for decision-making and cognitive behavior. Engaging these states leads to increased creativity and receptivity.

2. **Research the Stakeholder** - Dedication to understanding Jake Hardknock was paramount. Guesswork doesn't apply here. Comprehensive background checks revealed Hardknock's past challenges and successes, offering a deeper grasp of his emotional backdrop.

3. **Establish Emotional Alignment** - With this insight, Aaron constructed a narrative echoing Hardknock's journey. Instead of traditional business pitches, Aaron emphasized shared challenges, growth, and realized ambitions, ensuring the conversation resonated with Hardknock.

4. **Promote Positive Emotions** - Through his carefully chosen approach, Aaron activated beneficial 'green' emotions in Hardknock. He highlighted the fulfillment in building an enterprise, the satisfaction of a realized vision, and the stability of growth.

5.  **Encourage Forward-Thinking** - Aaron ended by instilling a sense of optimism. He envisioned a future characterized by joint growth and aligned objectives, ensuring Hardknock left the discussion with a positive outlook.

6.  **Sustain the Connection** - Throughout the discussion, Aaron anchored back to themes of determination and achievement, ensuring Hardknock remained in a state of emotional openness, helping cooperation.

Utilizing the principles of Brain-centric frameworks, Aaron Castle transformed a challenging negotiation into an emotionally-charged dialogue. The result? A profound connection with his counterpart that paved the way for success. Think about integrating these steps into your interactions, realizing that genuine engagement is the element of Surprise as an initiator and a sustainer and using these instruments in forging a deep, emotional bond.

As negotiations with Hardknock began, Castle was met with the anticipated cold demeanor. But Aaron was prepared to pivot. Instead of lingering on financial metrics and corporate speak, he chose a different path, chatting about stories of ambition and accomplishment, stories that mirrored Hardknock's own rise in the business world.

Castle highlighted the joy in creating a company, the fulfillment of watching a vision come alive, and the shared bonds and stability that come with business growth. He expressed thanks for the inroads Hardknock Industries had made, changing lives and inspiring future leaders. Concluding with a vision of a shared thriving future, he framed it as a trek of combined ambitions and mutual growth.

By the time Aaron finished, a transformation was evident. The once cold atmosphere had turned into a fertile environment for collaboration. Hardknock's demeanor warmed up, clearly affected by Castle's heartfelt narrative. The once rigid tycoon was now engaged, even excited.

"Castle," Hardknock began, his tone gentler, "Today, you did more than present numbers. You spoke to my journey, my experiences. Let's do this...

And, is that a first pressing Elvis RCA on the wall?"

**The Power of Emotion**: Aaron Castle's strategy showcased the profound impact of connecting on an emotional level. His approach wasn't about the shock factor, but the essence of understanding and aligning with one's audience. By tapping into positive emotions, he was able to create a genuine connection, demonstrating the true potential of emotionally-charged interactions in the world of business.

# VALENCE

# VALENCE

Expectation sets the stage
Novelty fuels curiosity
Suddenness strikes like lightning, arresting attention
Incongruity challenges the mind with the unexpected
Emotional Reaction deepens the connection
**Valence colors the experience**
Intensity amplifies the impact
Uncertainty Reduction brings clarity
Sense Making transforms chaos into understanding
Adjustment ensures enduring influence

In human interaction, few players hold the transformative power that Surprise does. Surprise, akin to a wildcard in a deck of cards, can upend the game or steer it in entirely unexpected directions. But its real magic lies not just in its arrival, but in its interpretation: the Valence.

### Now Playing: When Surprise Meets Perception

Valence is, in essence, the emotional value we assign to an experience. It's that gut reaction, the immediate sentiment that washes over us when confronted with the unexpected. Picture it as the critical review after a movie premiere, the audience's immediate response that can cast the film into stardom or sink it into obscurity.

*"I walked out of that theater either feeling like my soul had been touched or like I'd just wasted two hours of my life."*

*"It's that split second when the lights come back on, and I instantly know if I've witnessed magic or if I've been robbed of my dreams."*

To emphasize, all Surprises are not born equal. The masterful storytellers — whether they're filmmakers, novelists, or speechwriters — understand this well.

It's about crafting a Surprise that resonates, but it's equally about how it's perceived.

Think about the Apple iPod reveal in 2001. The tech world was awash with MP3 players. Yet, when Steve Jobs unveiled that sleek, white device, it was a revelatory moment. But why? Because the Valence was overwhelmingly positive. The design, the simplicity, the sheer audacity of "1,000 songs in your pocket." It wasn't just another MP3 player – it was a revolution in a pocket-sized rectangle. The Surprise wasn't the product, it was the promise.

On the flip side, appraise the introduction of New Coke in the mid-80s. Coca-Cola, in a bid to revitalize its brand and compete with Pepsi, reformulated its classic drink. The announcement was a surprise, no doubt. But the Valence? Bitterly negative. The company had underestimated the deep emotional connection people had with the original drink. The backlash was swift and merciless, making it clear that not all Surprises are greeted with open arms.

Now, to sprinkle a little Pulp Fiction into the mix: It's like you're in one of those dimly lit, grungy bars. A stranger walks in, slams a mysterious briefcase on the table. Everyone's eyes are glued to it, hearts racing. That briefcase? It's the Surprise. But what's inside — the gold glow or a ticking bomb — determines the Valence. It's that twist, the revelation that turns the narrative on its head, that drives the story home, making it memorable, powerful, and in some cases, legendary.

When we're talking about leveraging Surprise in communications, it's not just the shock value we're after. It's the aftertaste, the lingering sentiment, the Valence.

With your attention on Valence, Surprise is the flash and bang that yanks the audience from slumber and the resonant hum that remains long after the curtain falls. It's about that taste it leaves on the mind's palate – that essence we call Valence.

As you are beginning to understand, when you orchestrate a Surprise with finesse, you're shaping an emotional journey. Instead of casting a stone into a pond in hopes of a few skips, you're meticulously sculpting the ripples that follow. Whether you're weaving the story for your audience or painting the vision of your next grand venture, always bear in mind: the magic lies in the subtleties.

The craft of Surprise, therefore, is the revelation AND the echoes of what follows. Get the Valence just right – that delicate balance of sentiment – and you do more than just snag their gaze. You enthrall their very souls. So when you unleash your next Surprise, remember, it's the initial splash and the waves it creates.

# VALENCE IN ACTION

Recognizing and influencing valence — the positive or negative evaluation of an experience — is a potent tool across diverse roles and situations. Professionals can mold reactions, drive decisions, and encourage specific outcomes by understanding and steering the emotional impact in the desired direction.

Recognizing and influencing valence — how good or bad someone feels about an experience — is a powerful skill that applies to many jobs and situations. Think of it like adjusting the temperature on a thermostat. If it's too cold (negative), you warm it up (make it positive). And if it's too warm (overly positive), you might want to cool it down a bit to make things just right. By tapping into people's feelings and adjusting the "emotional temperature," professionals can guide how others react and their choices and even inspire them to take particular actions. It's like being a conductor, guiding the orchestra of emotions to play your desired tune.

### Salesperson

A customer's emotional response to a product or service is paramount for salespeople. A product eliciting positive valence boosts the likelihood of purchase and recommendation. For example, introducing a bonus feature or unexpected perk can transform customers' ambivalence into enthusiasm, swinging their valence from neutral or negative to decidedly positive.

### Communicator

The art of communication thrives on the emotional undertones of the message. A communicator can guide the audience's valence by anchoring key points with emotive content. For instance, a public speaker telling an inspiring personal anecdote can convert a skeptical audience into believers, shifting the room's valence in favor of the speaker's agenda.

### Parent

With parenting, understanding and influencing valence can help nurture a child's development. Recognizing what elicits joy, fear, or sadness in a child allows for more effective communication. Turning a child's negative valence from fear of the dark into a positive one by introducing a fun "night-guard" toy can make bedtime an event to look forward to.

Imagine your 17-year-old has just obtained their driver's license. The freedom to drive represents a new level of independence and responsibility. As a parent, you're both excited for them and anxious about the potential risks. Here's where understanding and influencing valence becomes pivotal.

Before handing over the keys, you sit down with your teen. You discuss the significance of this new responsibility: the privilege of driving is more than just getting from point A to B—it embodies trust, maturity, and accountability. You express your pride in their achievement, setting a positive emotional tone (positive valence) for the conversation.

Then, you set clear expectations: avoiding distractions while driving, not speeding, and never drinking and driving. You discuss the potential negative outcomes (negative valence) not to instill fear but to emphasize the weight of their responsibility.

You then introduce a challenge. If they can demonstrate responsible driving habits over the next month—perhaps by checking in with you when they reach their destination, keeping the car clean and fueled, and adhering to traffic rules—you'll consider helping with some of the costs associated with the vehicle, like fuel or insurance, creating a clear positive incentive (positive valence) tied to responsibility.

Fast forward a month. If your teenager upholds their end of the bargain, you commend them on their maturity and acknowledge their sense of duty, cementing the positive valence. This positive reinforcement will likely encourage them to continue acting responsibly.

However, if they fall short, rather than severe reprimand, you have a constructive conversation, focusing on the areas they need to improve. This way, they associate responsibility not with punishment but with personal growth and the natural consequences of their actions.

By skillfully steering the valence of the situation, you mold your teen's perception of responsibility, guiding them toward making mature, thoughtful decisions on the road and in life.

### Learning & Development

Valence plays a significant role in educational contexts. Suppose learners associate positive emotions with the learning experience, their engagement and retention skyrocket. An instructor can use multimedia, storytelling, or gamification to introduce a fun element in the session. A dull topic suddenly becomes an exciting adventure, making the valence swing towards the positive end and fostering a conducive learning atmosphere.

Harnessing valence means wielding the power of emotional resonance.

When leveraged correctly, it's like hitting the sweet spot in human interactions, creating moments that stick and decisions that align with your intent.

# The Surprise Valence Scale

*Understand the emotional value (valence) of different Surprises by gauging immediate reactions.*

**Materials**: A notebook or piece of paper, a pen or pencil.

**Instructions**:

**Brainstorm Surprises**: List down five unexpected moments or surprises you've experienced in the past. It could range from surprise parties to unexpected news.

**Emotional Response**: Next to each surprise, jot down your immediate emotional reaction. Was it happiness, shock, disappointment, excitement, or something else?

**Scale of Valence**: On a scale of -5 to +5, where -5 is extremely negative, +5 is extremely positive, and 0 is neutral, rate each of your surprises based on your emotional response.

For example:
- Surprise puppy as a gift might be +5.
- Missing the bus might be -3.
- Receiving a neutral letter in the mail might be 0.

**Reflect**: Looking at your ratings, can you identify any patterns or factors that influence whether a Surprise has a positive or negative valence for you?

**Wrap-up**: Just as moviegoers' reactions can shape the fate of a film, our personal 'valence ratings' determine how we remember and respond to Surprises. Knowing this can help us better understand our own reactions and those of others.

## Tales of Insightsville: Element Six
# DR. ANNEMARIE'S HAPPINESS CENTER

*Building on unity, residents embrace Dr. AnneMarie's Happiness Center promoting well-being, tapping into the town's positive energy, and underlining the significance of collective joy.*

In most towns, a distinctive structure stands tall – a grand town hall or an age-old church. Yet, in Insightsville, it wasn't historical charm or architectural marvel that caught one's attention. It was Dr. AnneMarie's Happiness Center, a beacon of positive vibes and emotional well-being.

Dr. AnneMarie, with her infectious smile and compassionate eyes, was a pillar in Insightsville. Her expertise lay not just in her academic knowledge but in her ability to navigate the intricate web of emotions connecting people together. Think of her as a mind maestro, with every emotion as her note and the townspeople her orchestra.

Her Happiness Center wasn't just about feel-good sessions. It combined cognitive therapy, mindfulness, and emotional intelligence in a way that made mental well-being accessible...she called it 'Greenhousing' because she lovingly called her own business The Greenhouse, an environment for all to thrive. And her signature? Quick, three-minute educational videos, each demystifying a facet of emotions, making them engaging and actionable that became an online global sensation on YouTube at www.youtube.com/@Brain-centric.

People didn't just come to attend her live sessions in 'The Greenhouse'; they emerged transformed, with heightened self-awareness and a clearer emotional roadmap. Like they emerged with directions for their brain; how it functioned, how to make it function better for you and those around you.

One day, amid her regular review, Dr. AnneMarie spotted something astonishing. Insightsville's happiness quotient wasn't just above average; it was chart-topping. This wasn't just individual contentment but a town-wide phenomenon. Intrigued, she embarked on a mission to decode this communal euphoria.

Her explorative journey was revealing. Insightsville's happiness wasn't a single thread, but a textile of tales. Ricco's innovative take on art, the community's shared and vibey bond, Lyle & Jesse's newfound success, and the marvel of Darian's gem creation — each was a chapter in this narrative of joy.

For Dr. AnneMarie, this was an epiphany.

The core of Insightsville's happiness was intricate. It was a collection of distinct emotional moments, discoveries, and interactions, all meticulously stitched into the community's day-to-day life...the perfect recipe to be yourself around others who did the same, all aligned on a common goal.

Dr. AnneMarie, her eyes beaming at this data defined, watched Ricco walk into the Happiness Center, when she felt a rush of excitement. Holding the freshly printed results of the town's happiness survey, she approached him eagerly.

"Ricco!" She greeted him with intense animation. "There's something remarkable I need to share."

Ricco's smile met hers, an eyebrow playfully raised. "You always have something up your sleeve, AnneMarie. What's the grand revelation today?"

She motioned him to her office, and as they settled down, she began, "The happiness index of Insightsville? It's surpassing all expectations, notably higher than the national norm. But there's more."

His interest piqued, Ricco leaned in, "I'm all ears."

Dr. AnneMarie dove deeper, "It's not mere serendipity. It's an orchestrated flock of emotions. Your art, Aaron's shrewd business strategies, Darian's innovative contributions - all these stories infuse happiness throughout Insightsville. This is epigenetics, Ricco! Scientific proof that what we do and where we do it – social context - can cause changes that affect the way our genes work."

Ricco mulled over her words. "So, our collective joy is like an evolving artwork. Every piece, every narrative, symbolizes an individual's touch to Insightsville's shared masterpiece?"

She nodded in agreement. "Exactly. And the elevation in happiness helps people be themselves, share thoughts and ideas, share in the excitement of being there. It fosters a setting ripe for growth, creativity, and innovation. For everybody!"

As he processed her words, Ricco grasped the deeper essence of his creations and every individual's role in Insightsville. It wasn't about just introducing novelty. It was about curating an emotional ambiance that ignited engagement, innovation, and contentment.

Dr. AnneMarie, reflecting on their discussion, remarked, "You know, Ricco, it all aligns with Insightsville's foundational ethos."

He looked at her, curious. "Go on."

She continued, "Our town has always championed individual uniqueness and diverse contributions. It's not just a slogan; it's our lived reality."

Absorbing her words, Ricco responded, "Yup, every resident, be it an artist, a scientist, or a diesel mechanic, adds their distinctive shade to Insightsville's mosaic. That's the magic of this place, our Greenhouse!"

Dr. AnneMarie's smile radiated warmth. "But it's more than just happiness, Ricco. When people experience acceptance and feel welcomed, when they are celebrated for whatever makes them 'them' and feel their efforts are appreciated and that they are heard, there's an innate surge of joy. This joy is contagious, creating ripples of happiness throughout."

Ricco paused, processing her words. "It's a revelation, AnneMarie. Our creed isn't solely about celebrating individualism but more about fostering a pervasive sense of joy. And each one of us is a cog in this happiness machine."

Her eyes sparkled in agreement. "Precisely, Ricco. It's the very essence that we must always uphold. Our shared euphoria, this emotional sweet spot, is the lifeblood of Insightsville. Happiness is the sweet spot."

As their conversation drew to a close, Ricco, on his way out, reflected, "You blow my mind, AnneMarie. We're not just contributing to a place but to a shared emotion, a collective sentiment. And that, in itself, is magical."

Striding out of the Happiness Center, Ricco felt a surge of inspiration, the town's ethos resonating deeply within him. He breathed deeply and with intent. It was a reminder that his artistry wasn't solely about introducing novelty but about adding to communal bliss. And, who doesn't want that?

Whistling a tune to himself, he mused with determination as he walked to the beat of his thoughts back into town.

# INTENSITY

# INTENSITY

Expectation sets the stage
Novelty fuels curiosity
Suddenness strikes like lightning, arresting attention
Incongruity challenges the mind with the unexpected
Emotional Reaction deepens the connection
Valence colors the experience
**Intensity amplifies the impact**
Uncertainty Reduction brings clarity
Sense Making transforms chaos into understanding
Adjustment ensures enduring influence

Of all our emotions, Surprise is undeniably magnetic. Its power, however, is measured in its presence and its magnitude: the Intensity. Comparable to a crescendo in a harmonious melody, the amplification of the Surprise truly resonates.

Intensity measures how powerful a Surprise is. It's the difference between the soft fluttering of a butterfly's wings and the commanding swoop of an eagle. Picture it as the audience's reaction to a breathtaking art piece. Was it a subtle nod of appreciation or a wide-eyed wonderment?

Understand this distinction whether they're managers, painters, writers, or inventors. The emphasis isn't just on evoking Surprise but modulating its volume.

Reflect upon the release of an innovative tech gadget that revolutionized its sector. The world had its share of innovations. But the buzz was palpable when a breakthrough defied conventions and promised to reshape daily routines. The Intensity of the event, amplified by unique features and unexpected capabilities, made it an instant sensation.

Conversely, think of the release of a movie that, while highly anticipated, ends up feeling too familiar, rehashing old plots. The element of Surprise might exist, but its Intensity is diminished. Without a robust emotional charge, such narratives might fade amidst more vital, impactful stories.

To conjure an analogy, imagine being at a dramatic theater performance. An actor takes the stage, capturing everyone's attention. The Surprise is there. But the Intensity? It's determined whether he delivers a monologue that's comfortably familiar or challenges every notion, leaving the audience spellbound. The story's highs and lows trajectory relies heavily on this.

Recognizing and playing with Intensity is pivotal in weaving any narrative or introducing a product. It's not just the unexpected twist that matters but the force with which it is delivered.

Perfect the Intensity of your Surprise, calibrate its depth, and you don't just engage your audience; you enthrall them. Whether you're designing a product, unveiling a masterpiece, or crafting a story, one principle stands tall: it's not just the Surprise that counts; it's the weight it carries.

# INTENSITY IN ACTION

The power of Surprise delivery is about more than just the surprise itself - it's about the intensity with which it's delivered. Professionals across various fields can create unforgettable experiences and ignite action by mastering the art of amplifying this intensity.

In all these domains, amplifying the intensity of Surprise delivery can turn ordinary into extraordinary, making experiences more memorable and impactful.

### Salesperson

For salespeople, the unexpected introduction of a game-changing product feature should be as thrilling as the feature itself. Amplifying the intensity - perhaps through a live demonstration or a dramatic reveal - can make the moment unforgettable, enhancing the value proposition and sealing the deal.

### Communicator

As a communicator, unexpected twists and revelations in your narrative can resonate powerfully, especially when delivered with intensity. Think of dramatic pauses, shifts in tone, or even changes in medium - these techniques heighten the surprise and make your message stick.

### Parent

For parents, intensifying the delivery of Surprise can turn simple moments into cherished memories. An elaborate setup for a Surprise birthday party or a dramatic reveal of a family vacation can amplify the Surprise, strengthening bonds and creating impactful experiences.

### Learning & Development

In education, intensifying the delivery of unexpected challenges, collaborations, or interactive elements can make lessons unforgettable. Imagine revealing the answer to a complex problem through an interactive game or Surprising students with a pop quiz hidden within a virtual reality experience.

### Athlete

For athletes, a Surprising strategy or move can be amplified by the intensity of its execution. A sudden, powerful sprint to the finish line or a breathtakingly precise goal can awe the audience and competitors.

### Artist

In art, the intensity of Surprise delivery can make all the difference. An unexpected twist in a storyline revealed with dramatic flair or a surprising note in a musical piece, introduced with amplified emotion, can deeply move the audience.

# BRAIN LIBS: INTENSITY

*Now, it's your turn! Grab a pen and let your imagination run free! How would you fill in the blanks? The story's intensity is in your hands! Write your answers in the spaces provided and have some fun :-)*

## BRAIN LIBS: Intense Corporate Training!

We're about to embark on an adventure of [adjective] proportions! Our new program focuses on the very heart of teamwork: psychological safety.

In the bustling city of [noun], a CEO named [proper noun] realized that while his employees were brilliant at their tasks, there was a missing ingredient. The room lacked that [adjective] aura of trust and open communication.

The CEO brought in an expert known far and wide for their unique [adverb] approach. Dr. [proper noun] had once turned a team of [plural noun] into a choir, emphasizing the need for psychological safety. Dr. [proper noun] believed that for teams to excel truly, each member had to feel safe enough to sing their own [noun].

The first exercise was called "Trust or [verb]." Each team member was asked to [verb] a [noun] while blindfolded, emphasizing the need to rely on each other. It was an intense sight to behold!

Next up was the "Open Mic [noun]," where participants could voice their [plural noun], all while dodging [plural noun]. It was intense, fun, and immensely beneficial.

By the end of Dr. [proper noun]'s session, the room was [verb ending in -ing] with energy. The team wasn't just a group of individuals anymore. They were a united front, ready to face challenges with [noun] and [adverb].

From that day on, psychological safety wasn't just a [noun] in the company. It was the thread that held everyone together, making work productive and intensely [adjective].

# Tales of Insightsville: Element Seven
# EMBERS OF UNITY

*The firefighter's heroics during a fire further fuel the town's intense spirit, showcasing the unwavering bonds forged in the face of adversity.*

Glowing specks dotted the night canvas, painting an urgent picture for Insightsville. A wildfire, birthed unexpectedly at the town's edge, visible flames on the foothills leading to town, unsettling the once-calm atmosphere.

Television and radio from neighboring Biasedtown broadcasted tales of heightened terror, pouring oil on the fires of concern already beating in Insightsville's heart. Terms like 'Inferno Tsunami' and 'Combustion Vortex' underscored with scary music, theatrical in their dramatic descriptions. The reportage was dense with alarming descriptors: 'encroaching nemesis' and 'relentless conflagration,' sentiments aimed to incite panic.

Ricco, ears tuned to the radio waves, frowned. "'Inferno Tsunami'? Really now?" He was bound towards his sanctuary, his studio, where his brushes and colors became his voice. The palette he chose voiced the resilience and solidarity of Insightsville, a vivid contrast to the fiery hyperbole flowing from Biasedtown.

Elsewhere, Darian Rae, amidst her lab's blinking lights, caught a broadcast terming the fire a "Furious Flame Phantom." Concern not just for her invention, but also for the soul of the town, tugged at her. Glancing at her children, Ava and Giovanni, she voiced strength, "Remember, kids, there's always another side to a story. I'm turning this theater off."

Within the calming walls of the Happiness Center, as Dr. AnneMarie conducted a therapy session, a screen in the welcome room blared: "Inferno Invades Innocent Insightsville." The reaction was instant; faces clouded with anxiety. Calmly, she muted the intrusive broadcast, "Fear might knock, but it's our choice to open the door. We have the strength of unity. We face this as one."

At the shimmering jewelry store, Jesse and Lyle, eyebrows raised, processed another exaggerated headline: "Perilous Firestorm Engulfs Peaceful Town." Jesse quipped, "Feels like someone's writing a thriller, Pop." Recognizing the negative impact of the sensational stories, they chose action over anxiety – safeguarding their gems and reaching out to the community.

Though the sensationalist tales from Biasedtown persisted, the heart of Insightsville beat with determination. Tired of the dramatic narratives and the anxious undertones, they anchored their trust in unity and mutual support as they always had, drawing strength from their local luminaries and the unwavering spirit of their community.

Amidst the orchestrated turmoil of flame and smoke, Lance Delgado, Insightsville's stalwart fire chief, moved with purpose. He appeared almost ethereal, illuminated by the fierce firelight, a symbol of undeterred resolve in turbulent times.

"All hands on deck!" he cried, his voice booming over the fire's growl. "This isn't only the flames we face; it's a measure of our spirit, our unity. Tonight, we're guarding more than houses; we're safeguarding the very heartbeat of our town."

Everest and Samantha Spencer, the newest additions to Lance's brigade, shared a fleeting glance, their youthful faces a canvas of trepidation and determination. Raised on stories of Insightsville's indomitable spirit, tonight was their crucible. Samantha's voice, unwavering, broke their silent pact, "You heard him, Everest. Tonight, we defend our town's legacy. This is real."

Everest, ever the silent storm in contrast to his sister's vivacity, nodded. Few words ever passed his lips, but when they did, they carried weight. Adjusting his gear, he affirmed, "I'm here. Let's roll."

Old-timer Tyler, with battles against flames etched into his memory, respected Lance's rallying call. Through the veils of smoke, he cast an approving glance at the Spencer twins, silently commending their mettle.

Sara, often playfully dubbed the brigade's heart, felt a wave of emotion at Lance's declaration. The trust vested in them by Insightsville residents fortified her resolve. "OK Insightsville...here we go," she whispered, stepping in line with her comrades.

In this furnace-like scenario, their unity was radiant, exemplifying Insightsville's essence. They weren't firefighters but guardians of the town's ethos, ready to brave tempests for its honor. United, they faced the blaze head on.

Lance felt the gravity of the situation; the crisis either united communities or tore them apart. He saw not just worry on the faces of the town's people but a steely resolve, a profound devotion to their community's well-being.

A familiar silhouette dashed his way. Darian Rae, distress evident in her eyes, spoke hurriedly, "Lance, my gemstone replicator—it's still in the lab. We can't lose it..."

Gently, Lance reassured, "Darian, we've got you. We'll protect your life's work." The relief in her gaze reinforced his resolve; Insightsville's spirit was indomitable.

As darkness held its reign, the town showcased heroism throughout. Jesse and Lyle, ensuring the safety of their precious store, also aided their neighbors. Ricco, ever the artist, painted whimsical messages of hope across the pavements: "Through Night, Hope Shines Bright," "Together, We Ascend," and "Unity is Our Stronghold," each captioned with a delightful stick-figure rabbit, bringing smiles amid the soot.

By dawn, as the flames bowed to their collective will and Lance's tenacious leadership, a redefined Insightsville emerged. A town that had weathered the storm, their spirit only glowing fiercer against adversity.

Gazing at the dawning day, Dr. AnneMarie mused to Lance, "Such adversities, and yet the town finds strength in unity."

Lance, eyes forward, responded, "It's not the ordeal, AnneMarie. It's our response to it. It's what we do."

Insightsville was reborn. More than recovery; it was a transformation. The town had found a renewed sense of camaraderie, a sturdier spirit. Central to this rejuvenation was Lance, whose valor sparked a flame of unity that would forever shine in Insightsville.

# UNCERTAINTY REDUCTION

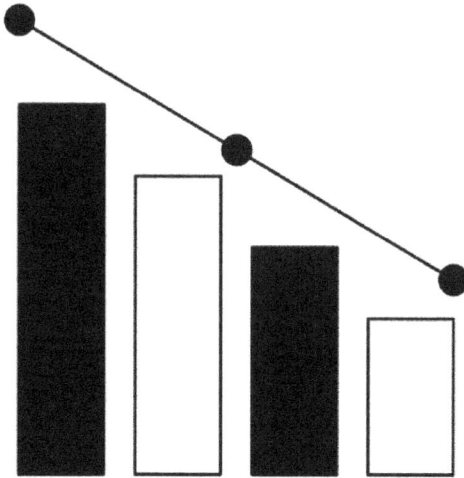

# UNCERTAINTY REDUCTION

Expectation sets the stage
Novelty fuels curiosity
Suddenness strikes like lightning, arresting attention
Incongruity challenges the mind with the unexpected
Emotional Reaction deepens the connection
Valence colors the experience
Intensity amplifies the impact
**Uncertainty Reduction brings clarity**
Sense Making transforms chaos into understanding
Adjustment ensures enduring influence

Picture this: You're on a hike, and suddenly you find yourself at a fork in the trail that wasn't on your map. Two paths lie ahead, one winds into a dense, dark forest, and the other opens onto a sunny meadow. At this moment, you're engulfed with uncertainty. Which way should you go? What lies down each path? Will one of them take you back to your starting point?

Uncertainty feels like standing at that fork, not knowing which path to take. It's the fluttering in your stomach, the hesitancy in choosing a direction. And when Surprise comes our way, it often brings this crossroad moment along with it, making us yearn for clarity.

We humans, by our very nature, have an innate desire to comprehend the world around us. So, when we face a Surprise, our first instinct is to reduce our uncertainty. Think of a time you received a Surprise letter in the mail. The very act of quickly tearing it open is an act of Uncertainty Reduction. We want to know - Who is it from? What does it say? Why did I receive this?

Imagine going to the doctor and receiving unexpected health news. Your first reaction might be shock or disbelief.

But soon after, you'd likely seek more details. What does the diagnosis mean? What are the next steps? What will your future look like? This quest for more information, for understanding, is Uncertainty Reduction in action.

Say, you've been suddenly promoted to a role you hadn't anticipated. The news is thrilling but also, bewildering. You might find yourself diving into job descriptions, reaching out to predecessors, or seeking mentorship. All of these actions are geared towards understanding your new role better and, in essence, reducing uncertainty.

You receive a surprise gift without a tag. While the joy of a gift is undeniable, the immediate question is, "Who sent this?" Asking around, checking for any missed messages, or thinking of recent conversations where someone might have hinted at it - all these are your ways of reducing uncertainty about the gift's origins.

Surprises, by nature, shake our understanding and present us with unknowns. Uncertainty Reduction is our way of navigating these Surprises. It's like turning on a flashlight in a dark, unfamiliar room. Piece by piece, as we gather more information and insights, the room becomes clearer, less intimidating, and we start to find our way.

# UNCERTAINTY REDUCTION IN ACTION

Uncertainty Reduction, the process of seeking clarity amidst ambiguity, is akin to navigating through fog. Imagine driving on a foggy night; you'd naturally slow down, turn on your fog lights, and perhaps use your GPS to guide you safely to your destination. Similarly, in various roles and situations, reducing uncertainty means gathering more information, asking questions, or relying on tools and expertise to make clearer, informed decisions amidst ambiguity.

### HR Manager

For an HR manager, hiring a new employee is a journey filled with uncertainty. Resumes and interviews only provide a glimpse of the candidate. To reduce uncertainty, they might conduct reference checks, skill assessments, or trial periods. This not only ensures a better fit for the company but also eases the transition for the new employee, setting a foundation for success from the onset.

### Instructional Designer

Crafting a new curriculum or training module comes with its own set of unknowns. How will learners respond? Is the content pitched at the right difficulty level? To reduce this uncertainty, an instructional designer might pilot the module with a small group, gather feedback, and make refinements. By doing this, they ensure that when the training is rolled out widely, it's effective and meets learners' needs.

### Radiology Technician

While interpreting medical images, a radiology technician deals with the critical task of identifying abnormalities or diseases. Any uncertainty could have serious implications. To reduce this, they might cross-reference with previous scans, consult with peers, or use advanced imaging techniques. Their goal is to provide the most accurate information possible to the medical team and the patient, ensuring the best care pathway.

### IT Engineer

In the world of IT, uncertainty often arises when troubleshooting system issues or implementing new solutions. An engineer might encounter a problem they've never seen before. To reduce uncertainty, they could refer to online forums, consult with colleagues, or run diagnostic tests. By systematically narrowing down the root cause and potential solutions, they can restore systems to optimal functioning, ensuring minimal disruption and maximum efficiency for end-users.

Mastering Uncertainty Reduction in each of these contexts allows professionals to navigate challenges with confidence, ensuring more predictable, effective outcomes even when faced with the unknown.

## TRY IT - Predict the Pattern

*We often find ourselves seeking patterns, harmonies, and rhythms that make sense. This quest for clarity in the midst of chaos is what we call Uncertainty Reduction.*

## Materials Needed
- A coin
- A small notebook or piece of paper
- A pen

## Instructions

**Predict the Flip**: Sit comfortably and take your coin. Before you flip it, write down your prediction: Heads or Tails.

**Flip the Coin**: Flip the coin 10 times, and after each flip, jot down the result next to your prediction.

**Analyze the Outcome**: After 10 flips, count how many times your prediction was correct.

**Uncertainty Reduction in Action**: Now, for the next 10 flips, instead of just guessing, try to look closely at the coin's starting position, the force of your flip, and any other factors. Does paying closer attention to these elements improve your predictive accuracy?

**Reflection**: What strategies did you employ to reduce uncertainty and make more accurate predictions? Were there times when, despite your best analysis, the result was still unpredictable?

**Debrief**: Life, much like the coin flips, is full of unexpected turns. While we naturally try to gather information and look for patterns to reduce uncertainty and predict outcomes, there are still moments that catch us by Surprise. Recognizing the balance between what we can predict and what remains uncertain is essential for navigating the world with a curious and adaptive mindset.

# Tales of Insightsville: Element Eight
## SEAN'S REVELATION

*Detective Sean Sparks unravels Insightsville's greatest mystery, the Lost Mosaic, bridging the town's past and present and reducing its veil of uncertainty.*

Detective Sean Sparks sat in his office; eyes focused on the details of the aged documents about The Tale of the Lost Mosaic. This wasn't just an academic curiosity; it was a personal journey into a story that had been shared across generations in Insightsville.

Legend held that the mosaic was crafted by the founders of Insightsville, capturing the unique spirit and values of the town of its first settlers. Multiple interpretations had sprung up over time. Was it a coded map? Did it hide the essence of the town's happiness? A talented child's hobby?

When Sean needed a break from the hustle of detective work, Lake Kya was his sanctuary. On one such visit, an unusual pattern of pebbles on the shore caught his eye. They seemed to echo a design from the mosaic's description. His heart raced. Retrieving the mosaic's sketch from his bag, he cross-referenced the two. The resemblance was more than just coincidental.

This breakthrough was not only about unraveling Insightsville's history but also reconnecting with the tales Sean had grown up with. The legacy of the mosaic and the legacy of his family might be intertwined more than he had ever realized.

"I think I'm onto something," Sean murmured to himself, a wave of anticipation washing over him. This was more than just a fishing trip now; it was the beginning of an adventure he had been expecting all his life. Little did he know that the Lost Mosaic was about to reveal secrets that connected everyone in Insightsville, each character of our tales, in a tapestry of shared history and collective purpose.

He sat back, taking a moment to absorb the implications. His mind was on fire with the potential connections to the characters that inhabited Insightsville. His eyes widened as he pieced together the stories - Ricco's art, Darian Rae's machine, Dr. AnneMarie's Happiness Center, the firefighter's acts of heroism during the recent fire.

On a hunch, he decided to visit Ricco first, knowing his knack for finding beauty and meaning in unexpected places. "Ricco," he said, showing him the worn-out map, "I believe this leads to the Lost Mosaic. But I need your artist's eye to decipher the clues hidden in these symbols."

Ricco, known for his curiosity, leaned in closer, letting the hints of the map speak to him. "It's not just about finding a mosaic, Sean. It's about connecting our stories."

As Sean examined deeper, he uncovered connections that were far-reaching. Darian Rae's gem replication machine had a motif that echoed patterns from the mosaic. Dr. AnneMarie's 'Greenhouse,' revered by many, held symbols uncannily like those on a dusty, ancient scroll he'd come across. The word 'Felicitas' was hastily added, making Sean wonder about its significance.

But the most unexpected link was the mark left behind after Samantha and Everest's heroic actions during the fire while cutting, scraping, and digging a Fireline with hand tools—unearthing a clue pointing to the mosaic's possible location.

In solving the old mystery, Sean did more than just reduce uncertainty. He uncovered an intricate web that tied together the people of this town, their actions and passions, in ways they could never have imagined.

Through his revelation, Insightsville's residents came to understand that their shared history was more complex and interconnected than they ever knew. And as Sean peered deeper into the mosaic's mystery, Insightsville began to see itself not just as a town, but as a living, breathing testament to unity and purpose.

# SENSE MAKING & ADJUSTMENT

# SENSE MAKING & ADJUSTMENT

Expectation sets the stage
Novelty fuels curiosity
Suddenness strikes like lightning, arresting attention
Incongruity challenges the mind with the unexpected
Emotional Reaction deepens the connection
Valence colors the experience
Intensity amplifies the impact
Uncertainty Reduction brings clarity
**Sense Making transforms chaos into understanding**
**Adjustment ensures enduring influence**

When we talk about Surprise, we often think of the initial KAPOW! – that immediate emotional reaction. But Surprise is more than just a fleeting moment; it's an experience that unfolds over time. One of the most critical phases in this unfolding is Sense Making & Adjustment.

**Sense Making**: Think of this as the puzzle-solving phase. Imagine you've been given a jigsaw puzzle without the picture on the box. The moment you see the jumbled pieces is Surprising. Your brain starts to ask questions: What is this supposed to be? How do these pieces fit together? This process of figuring out and understanding the unexpected event is Sense Making.

**Adjustment**: Once you've made sense of the puzzle and have an idea of the bigger picture, you start placing the pieces together. In real life, after understanding an unexpected event, we start to change or adjust our behavior, expectations, or thoughts to accommodate this new information. This phase is all about adapting to the newfound understanding.

Remember getting a Surprise test in school? At first, you're shocked (the initial Surprise). Then, you try to recall what you've studied and how it might be relevant to the test (Sense Making). Finally, you adjust by deciding which sections to tackle first or recalling strategies that help you in such situations (Adjustment).

Sense Making & Adjustment might seem like simple steps, but they are crucial. They help us understand the world around us better and equip us to deal with unexpected twists and turns more effectively. Without them, the experience of Surprise would remain just a brief emotional spike without any deeper understanding or learning. It's like having a puzzle without ever putting the pieces together.

Picturing a puzzle put back together is an easy mental picture.

## Recognize & Measuring Sense Making & Adjustment

### Reflective Thought and Inquiry

One of the first indicators of Sense Making is the act of questioning or reflective thought. When faced with an unexpected event or information, if an individual starts asking questions like "Why did this happen?", "What does this mean?", or "How does this fit with what I already know?", it's a clear sign that Sense Making is in process.

### Measurement

Survey or feedback tools can be used to gauge the number and depth of questions individuals have after a Surprising event. Higher levels of inquiry suggest deeper engagement with the Sense Making process.

———————————

## Change in Behavior or Strategy

Adjustment, on the other hand, becomes evident when there's a noticeable change in behavior or strategy post the surprising event. This could be an immediate shift, like adapting a new technique after a surprise training session, or it could be a longer-term behavioral change, like adopting a new daily routine after a surprising health diagnosis.

### Measurement

Observational techniques, before-and-after assessments, or even self-reports can help measure these changes in behavior or strategy.

———————————

## Integration into Existing Knowledge

Once an individual starts integrating the new information into their existing knowledge base, it suggests that Sense Making has occurred. For example, after a Surprising historical fact is revealed, a student connects it with other events from the same era they already know about.

### Measurement

Qualitative and Quantitative measurements that require individuals to connect new information to pre-existing knowledge can indicate successful Sense Making.

———————————

## Emotional Stability

Surprising events often come with heightened emotions. Once these emotions stabilize and an individual feels more grounded, it can be a sign that they've made sense of the event and adjusted accordingly.

### Measurement

Emotional self-assessments or mood tracking tools can monitor emotional fluctuations before, during, and after exposure to the Surprise.

### Consistent Narratives

When individuals can consistently explain the Surprising event or information to others, it's a sign they've made sense of it. The ability to communicate their understanding without confusion or hesitation indicates successful Sense Making.

### Measurement

Conducting interviews or having individuals explain the event to others and assessing the clarity and consistency of their narratives can be revealing.

---

Sense Making & Adjustment isn't always a swift process. For some, it might be almost immediate, while others might take longer, depending on the complexity of the Surprise and individual cognitive styles. The key is to look for these signs and measure them to understand the depth and success of this process that you, too, have come to make sense of and adjust to.

## SENSE MAKING & ADJUSTMENT IN ACTION

The ability to understand new situations and adapt our behavior accordingly — is a vital competency, no matter your role or context. Imagine this process like deciphering a puzzle: first, you identify the new pieces you're given, then you fit them into the existing picture you have in mind. Sometimes, you might even realize you need to rearrange the picture a bit. Master this process and navigate changing circumstances with grace, make informed decisions, and drive desired outcomes with fresh insights into your existing framework.

### Entrepreneur

An entrepreneur's journey is full of unforeseen challenges and opportunities. For instance, market feedback on a new product might be different from expectations. By employing Sense Making, the entrepreneur can decode this feedback, understand the gaps, and adjust the product offering. Perhaps an initial product feature wasn't resonating with customers, but a different feature they hadn't emphasized as much is getting a lot of positive feedback. Now, it's time for Adjustment: the entrepreneur pivots to spotlight and develops that appreciated feature.

### Educator

The education world is dynamic. A teacher might come across a topic that students find difficult to grasp. Using Sense Making, the teacher tries to understand where the disconnect is: Is it the delivery method? The complexity of the topic? Or external distractions? Once pinpointed, Adjustment kicks in. The teacher might introduce a more hands-on approach, use more relatable examples, or provide supplementary materials to bridge the comprehension gap.

## Salesperson

In the ever-evolving world of sales, a salesperson often encounters unexpected objections or concerns from potential clients. Using Sense Making, they try to understand the root of these hesitations. Maybe it's a feature the client feels is missing or a miscommunication about the product's benefits. With this understanding, the Adjustment phase comes in as the salesperson tailors their pitch, offers additional information, or even suggests a modified product package to address the client's concerns.

## Manager

Leaders and managers frequently face unexpected changes — from shifts in company strategy to personnel changes. A good manager uses Sense Making to understand the implications of these changes on their team and workflow. For instance, if a top-performing team member resigns unexpectedly, the manager first assesses the impact on ongoing projects. Then, during Adjustment, they might redistribute tasks, bring in temporary help, or accelerate the training of another team member to fill the gap.

## Parent

With children growing and changing every day, parenting is a continuous journey of Sense Making & Adjustment. When a child brings home an unexpectedly poor grade, a parent first seeks to understand the reasons. Is it a challenge with the subject matter, distractions, or perhaps issues with a classmate? Once identified, Adjustment takes place, which could involve hiring a tutor, setting specific study times, or having a chat with the teacher to gain more insights. This ongoing cycle ensures the child's needs are continuously met as they evolve.

**TRY IT: The Unexpected Path**

*Imagine you're on an expedition. You have a map, and you believe you know the terrain. But suddenly, you encounter an obstacle that wasn't on your map: maybe it's a new river, a dense forest, or even an unexpected bridge. What you do next, how you interpret this new information, and how you change your route is the essence of Sense Making & Adjustment.*

**Materials Needed**:

- A blindfold (a scarf or a handkerchief will do)
- A set of 10-15 random objects (e.g., books, cups, shoes)
- A spacious area (like a living room or backyard)
- A friend or family member

**Instructions**

1.  **Creating the Terrain** - In the spacious area, ask your friend or family member to randomly place the objects around the room to create an "obstacle course." This represents the unknown terrains of life.

2.  **Initial Understanding** -Without the blindfold, walk through the room once to get an understanding of where things are. This is your "map."

3.  **Confronting the Unknown** - Now, put on the blindfold. Try to navigate through the room based on your memory and understanding from your initial walk-through.

4.  **Sense Making in Action** - As you encounter the unexpected objects (the ones you don't remember or didn't notice the first time), try to understand what they might be and decide how to move around or interact with them.

5. **Adjustment** - Once you've made it through the obstacle course, remove the blindfold. Look at the objects you encountered. Were your assumptions correct? How did you adjust your movements based on these Surprises?
6. **Reflection** - Discuss with your friend or family member about the moments you had to pause, make sense of the new "terrain," and how you adjusted your path.

**Debrief** - Life doesn't always go as planned. We often think we have a clear map, but new challenges and unexpected events make us stop, evaluate, and change direction. Just as you navigated the room's unexpected objects, in life, you'll use Sense Making & Adjustment to understand new situations and change your path accordingly.

# Tales of Insightsville: Element Nine
## CASTLE'S GRAND FINALE

*Culminating their shared journey, Aaron Castle hosts a grand event, helping Insightsville make sense of their intertwined tales and adapt to their collective destiny.*

The town square was alive, an undeniable buzz in the air. Everywhere one looked, there were glints of excitement; banners fluttering, announcing "Castle's Grand Finale". The din of chattering people of all ages and from throughout the town created a backdrop of eager expectation.

At the heart of it all was a stage, glistening under lights and garlands. Aaron Castle, Insightsville's pride and famed motivational speaker, stood tall, his presence commanding attention. His voice, powerful and resounding, reached every nook and cranny.

"Good evening, Insightsville," he began, the crowd silencing. "We gather today as one, not just as bearers of individual tales but as curators of our town's legacy."

"Recent events have reshaped us, and today, it's our time to reflect and embrace these changes."

A brief, reflective pause followed.

Faces in the crowd - Ricco's animated gaze, Darian Rae's thoughtful expression, Dr. AnneMarie's hopeful smile, Lyle and Jesse's attentive stance, the firefighters standing together, and Detective Sean's sharp eyes - all mirrored the depth of his sentiment. Their roles had undeniably influenced the evolving tale of Insightsville.

"Our journey," Aaron resumed, "is one of metamorphosis. Through twists and turns, hurdles and breakthroughs, we've grown, rooted in unity and steered by our shared purpose to be ourselves, together."

His pace across the stage mirrored the energy of his speech. Every word, punctuated by his gestures, carried the essence of Insightsville's journey.

"We've lived through the unpredictable and celebrated the victories. All these moments, highs and lows, define us. This is Insightsville's tale," Aaron's voice rang out, filled with conviction. "A tale that keeps evolving. A tale that beautifully underscores our 'We' while remaining 'Me'."

The crowd's response was electric. Cheers and applause rang out, a testament to the shared feeling.

As the evening deepened, and stars peppered the sky, Aaron Castle's Grand Finale wasn't just an event. It became a touchstone, a reminder of Insightsville's spirit - undying resilience, growth, and the beauty of shared stories.

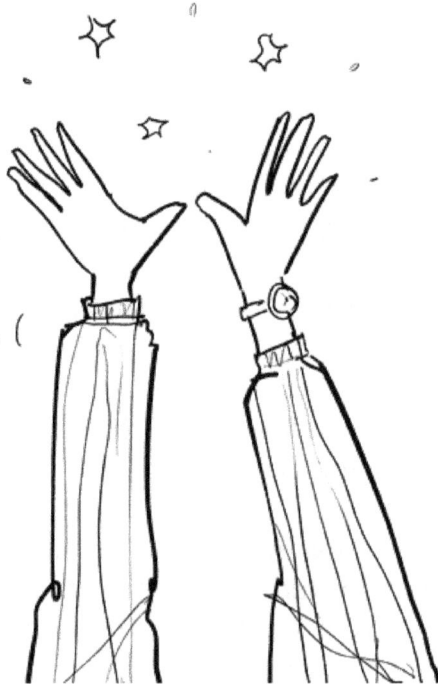

# ENGAGEMENT

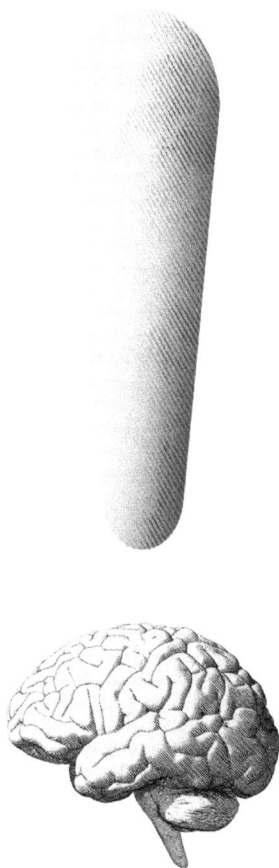

# RECOVERY.

After delivering any well-planned Surprise, what follows is crucial. We call these moments the 'Recovery Period.' This is when we truly begin to internalize, understand and embrace the Surprise, whatever just happened.

Think of this period like a deep reflection after hearing an unexpected piece of news. Our brain kicks into gear, processing this new information and understanding its significance. It's almost as if our brain is rearranging its furniture to make room for this fresh insight.

Why does this matter?

Every Surprise reshapes our thinking in some way. Our brain is incredibly adaptable, always finding ways to adjust and make sense of new information. After a Surprise, it immediately starts forming new connections, helping us understand and remember this new experience.

Our ability to adjust, called cognitive flexibility, allows us to see things from different angles. This is crucial in understanding the full picture. It's recognizing the Surprise and understanding its value and context.

But the real magic? How our brain collaborates. Different parts of our brain come together to piece together the Surprise, ensuring we understand it wholly.

As you now know, grabbing someone's attention with a Surprise is just the start. The true challenge lies in keeping their interest alive.

It's one thing to ignite curiosity, but the real success lies in sustaining that interest.

In any engaging experience, you must first understand the heart of the 'Surprise' element that ignited the spark of interest. Consider for a moment the core of that surprise. Perhaps it was a twist that none saw coming in a tale, catching readers off guard and leaving them yearning for more. Maybe it was an unanticipated feature in a product, something so innovative that it left consumers in awe. Or it could have been a sudden, unforeseen event, jolting everyone and drawing them into its midst.

But the deeper question to ponder is: *Why did this Surprise touch so many souls?* The key lies in comprehending the emotional or intellectual chords it struck. By recognizing these triggers, we gain invaluable insights into crafting strategies to maintain and nourish the interest it generated.

Let me give you an example by telling a story inspired by very similar events.

At The Education Engine, Rhett, an experienced manager, introduced a groundbreaking policy. The reactions were mixed, with some staff showing enthusiasm and others voicing reservations. Recognizing the need for clarity, Rhett organized sessions to explain the underlying research, thought processes, and experiences that inspired this new approach. The staff learned about the policy's origins, its initial testing, and its promise to improve operations.

To further support his initiative, Rhett showcased data from other successful Learning Management Systems, interviews with education experts, and testimonials from staff who had been part of the pilot program. This variety of information transformed the policy from a directive into a compelling narrative of innovation and progress.

But Rhett's most strategic decision was to open ecosystems of communication. He launched forums on The Education Engine's intranet where staff could discuss the policy and express their viewpoints. He also held 'town-hall' meetings, creating a platform for concerns to be aired, questions to be answered, and uncertainties to be clarified using the Nested Egg as a framework to provide clarity to all. Feedback was taken seriously, and the staff felt that their contributions were genuinely valued.

With this foundation of trust and dialogue, the policy became a beacon of progressive change, strengthening the sense of unity and commitment among the employees and cementing Rhett's leadership in the process.

Because engagement isn't a place we go, it's a space we sustain, you need to 'evolve' the content throughout the engagement.

When you want to evolve a Surprise for engagement, imagine it's like your favorite TV show. If every episode ended with the same twist, you'd soon lose interest. Similarly, to keep things engaging, it's essential to introduce fresh elements or features at different times. But here's the catch: while it's crucial to refresh content, becoming too predictable can be counterproductive. If your audience can anticipate every move, then the element of Surprise diminishes. Mastering Surprise takes effort and those that exert that effort are rewarded greatly.

Now, when it comes to educating your audience, think of a situation where you've been handed a unique gadget. The initial reaction might be awe or curiosity. But then, wouldn't you want to know more? How does it work? What's the story behind its creation? Sharing these details can sustain engagement. You need to think like your audience, not for your audience. Offering avenues for learning, like webinars, Q&A

sessions, and YouTube videos can be particularly effective. Even trivia challenges related to your Surprise element can amplify engagement by providing fun interactions.

## Trivia!

*"The concept of cliffhangers in TV shows, where an episode ends with a suspenseful unresolved twist, dates back to the Victorian era. Charles Dickens used this technique in his serialized novels, making readers eagerly await the next installment. Just as TV shows keep viewers hooked with unexpected twists, Dickens mastered the art of engaging his readers with tantalizing plot turns."*

User-Generated Content, often abbreviated as UGC, is another key tool. Picture this: you've experienced something Surprising and delightful. Your first instinct might be to share it with friends or on social media. When you encourage your audience to share their reactions, you're making them feel part of the journey and gathering fresh perspectives. Creating competitions or challenges related to your Surprise can deepen this engagement further, giving your audience an active role in the experience.

In the Challenge Wheel, we ask a Challenge Question after we introduce the concept; ***How would sustaining engagement in my communications benefit me?***

Then let them think without interruption.

The pure genius of this question within the first few minutes of introducing the concept you're about to communicate is that the audience is literally given the opportunity to THINK ABOUT WHAT YOU ARE COMMUNICATING AND HOW IT WILL BENEFIT THEM. Without you talking, without music, without prompting or interruption, sixty seconds so they can think about your concept, and then encode that thinking onto a piece of paper for them, not you, to be able to reflect on without the use of memory.

In a sales pitch, ask the prospect, right after introduction of the concept you are to communicate, your Big Idea, you say, *"Mr. Prospect, take twenty seconds all to yourself and answer this Challenge, "How would (Product/Service) make my life easier?"*

*"Don't tell me your answer, just answer that question for yourself."*

Then let them think without interruption.

By doing this, you are creating a sense of community. By collaborating with one another, you're fostering an environment where they feel they belong to something bigger than themselves. This connection can be amplified from this point on. Through shared experiences, communities, events, or even something as simple as a hashtag. Sustaining engagement requires you to plan your communication from **Blueprint** through **Performance** through **Encore**, outlined in the next chapter. When you do, as you have seen, success happens because it was defined in your plan.

Feedback is another cornerstone. Imagine designing a product without ever asking if people liked it. Communicating is the same thing. To ensure you're on the right track and meeting your audience's expectations, it's crucial to gather feedback every time you introduce something new, good or bad, it is what it is-unfiltered comments that tell you what your audience is feeling and don't take it personally.

Everyone loves being recognized, especially if they've been with you from the start. You want that show of love whether you can express it or not. I'm right there with you. By offering exclusive content, discounts, or perks to your loyal audience, you're not just acknowledging their loyalty but deepening their engagement. We are planning that journey of our Big Idea to the measurement once we get there. If you are not planning, you are winging it.

**Winging It**: *To do something without thorough preparation or planning, often relying on improvisation or making things up as one goes along.*

Everybody 'wings it' on occasion. While acting on the spur of the moment based on one's instincts or experiences often defines the superstar in any setting, they do it within a predetermined plan or script. They know what success looks like and can gauge its success.

While the element of Surprise can draw someone in, staying genuine is what will keep them around. In a world rife with fleeting attractions, authenticity stands out. Always ensure that in your endeavors to Surprise and engage remain true to your core values and genuine in your communication.

Our brain's capability is incredible, but it's up to you to use it effectively.

Go ahead, Engage.

# BLUEPRINT, PERFORMANCE, ENCORE

If you know your Big Idea, how you will measure your success, you are ready to begin building their engagement journey. Crafting engagement with Surprise can be likened to a theatrical performance. Let's break it down further using our three periods: **Blueprint**, **Performance**, and **Encore**.

You are, after all, 'on stage.'

Yet, the pivot in this scenario isn't about you entertaining; it's to foster a profound grasp of the idea or message you're guiding, whether for an individual or a larger group. This presentation centers not on personal accolades, titles, or past achievements. Instead, it's anchored in your Big Idea—the takeaway you desire for your audience—and your Measurement, which defines the parameters of your success of that delivery.

In the **Blueprint** phase, much like a playwright who maps out the plot, you conceptualize your core message, which is your "Big Idea." This is the foundation, the reason behind your communication, what the audience gains from you. It's essential to know what you want to convey, just as a builder needs architectural plans before starting construction. Furthermore, by setting benchmarks on how you'll measure success, whether it's audience reactions, feedback, or tangible outcomes, you're essentially setting up checkpoints for yourself. It's like knowing the critical scenes that will hold your play together.

Moving on to **Performance**. This is the execution of your Blueprint. In a play, this would be the actors taking the stage, delivering their lines with precision, emotion, and intent. For your communication, it's about presenting your Big Idea in a way that not only informs but also engages and resonates with your audience. Here, the Challenge Wheel is your most powerful tool serving like the arc of your communication, introducing the concept, analogizing it, providing disequilibrium, the Challenge Question, multiple perspectives that might solve the Challenge, reflection, collaboration, all keeping the audience on the edge of their seats, eager to know what comes next.

Lastly, the **Encore** is about sustaining that initial engagement. In theater, a performance doesn't end when the curtain drops; the lasting impression it leaves, the discussions it sparks, and the memories it creates all contribute to its legacy. Similarly, after delivering your Brain-centric communication, it's vital to ensure the message continues to engage and resonate. Through follow-up discussions, additional resources, or feedback sessions, there's a myriad of ways today to keep the communication alive. It's about ensuring that the Big Idea lingers and remains relevant.

Understanding these three steps is crucial if you aim to communicate with intent. Just as a play goes through scripting, performing, and post-performance discussions, crafting engaging communication is a continuous process. It's about preparation, presentation, and perpetuation. By focusing on each stage with equal importance, you ensure your message is not only heard but also felt, remembered, and acted upon. You will have delivered the communication and enabled intrinsic motivation that is profoundly personal to the audience, and they'll want to learn more because they see the value in doing so for themselves.

## The Blueprint
*Preparation & Insight*

**Reading the Room** - Grasping the pulse of your audience means gauging their existing knowledge, nuances of their preferences, and even their silent expectations. Who are they? What do they need?

**Feedback as Your Compass** - Before you dive deep, it's crucial to understand where you're headed. Equip yourself with tools such as surveys and interactive sessions to receive real-time audience insights. Ensure the results are anonymous and that your audience knows that...this keeps things psychologically safe.

**Weaving in the Unexpected** - While you've got a sense of your audience's expectations, it's the twist you introduce – the calculated Surprise in your content's design, format, or delivery – that truly captures attention. Always plan for the end and ensure that where you plant Surprise that it will further underscore that Big Idea.

## The Performance
*Delivery & Engagement*

**Crafting Your Masterpiece** - Like an artist, meticulously designing your content, making the Surprise elements its heartbeat. This is where the magic happens, ensuring both education and captivation for the audience. Always trust the Challenge Wheel for the communication of new information to another; It is infinitely malleable.

**Multiple Perspective Approach** - I cannot overemphasize this portion of your communication. While we all have our learning style preferences, the fact is you-and your audience-uses 100% of the brain, all the time. This is science folks. While they might prefer something they visually interpret (Occipital Lobe), you also need to deliver your communication to excite the thinking, audible, and physical movements associated with your content (Prefrontal cortex, Temporal Lobe, Parietal Lobe). In this Brain-centric framework, you 'light up' the brain on the concept you are communicating.

**A Two-Way Street** - Passive listeners rarely transform into engaged participants. Embed active components like the Challenge Question, collaborative activities, co-creation opportunities, reflection and revised thinking making your audience an integral part of the engagement. Half the time you have scheduled for your communication, your audience should be talking...Not You. It is about them understanding the concept, it's not 'your show.'

## The Encore
*Evaluation & Iteration*

**The Engagement Thermometer** - After concluding your communication, did it effectively convey your Big Idea and achieve the success criteria you set out beforehand? To gauge your audience's level of engagement, employ a combination of both qualitative and quantitative approaches. However, I'd advise against anything that feels too much like a formal test. The core aim here is comprehension and application — truly understanding and implementing the knowledge. While remembering the information is valuable, it's merely a part of the process. The ultimate goal of your communication was to impart knowledge or skills. So, the pressing question remains: how can you ascertain that this objective was met?

**Open Channels of Communication**: The journey remains unfinished until its influence is recognized. Make it a habit to gather feedback, honing your approach based on their responses. Encourage this seamlessly by integrating Long Term Potentiation (LTP) at the conclusion of any communication that will lead to further interactions. A detailed introduction to LTP is on the horizon for you.

**Evolution is Key**: Never remain static. With the feedback in hand, be prepared to evolve, refining your approach so that every new interaction is a step above the last. If it helps, what is now known as Brain-centric was once termed 'Legacy Axis' then 'Online Education Design' then 'Brain-centric Design' the Brain-centric :-)

# ENGAGEMENT FOR UNDERSTANDING
*Long Term Potentiation (LTP)*

When Dr. Kieran O'Mahony and I stood before a gathering of over 40 global educators and scientists at Columbia University's Teachers College in 2019, a profound statement was made. Dr. O'Mahony asserted, "Long Term Potentiation occurs in the brain. If you overlook that when teaching, you're missing how students truly learn." This proclamation marked a transformative moment for the worldwide educational realm, pivoting from traditional 'teaching' to 'facilitating understanding.'

The significance of this concept, necessitating the placement of LTP to prime the Encore. It's at this juncture that this groundbreaking neuroscience truly takes the stage — after the initial communication and before the next encounter.

If you search online for 'LTP' or 'Long Term Potentiation,' you'll find a plethora of scientific explanations. Yet, my approach, especially with *Surprised*, is to focus on the practical application of engaging instruments of mind. And in this arena, LTP stands as the formidable force.

Long Term Potentiation (LTP) in a nutshell:

Your presentation concluded.

Prompt your audience to jot down a word, phrase, or even sketch something that struck a chord with them from your communication.

*"It can be anything, there are no wrong answers. Place anything that resonated with you on that paper., simply."*

Don't say anything after that and wait for the feedback to be delivered.

Safeguard this feedback for your next meeting. At that time, present the feedback back to them to start the meeting and ask, "You noted _____. What prompted this choice?

Remain silent and allow them the space to respond.

You might be astounded by the insights your audience derives from your message and the fervor with which they convey it. While I won't delve deep into the intricate cognitive neurosciences backing this within these pages (but do dive deep online), you've essentially given them a platform free from constraints to share what resonated most with them.

They feel acknowledged, valued, and connected to their LTP. Gauge your success based on how closely their feedback aligns with your Big Idea. Does their LTP reflection mirror your initial intent and success markers? Invariably, it does. It's grounded in scientific understanding.

Your audience is highlighting the key takeaways from your prior communication. There were no predefined boundaries, no strict procedural formalities like Robert's Rules of Order, nor constrained response formats. They're empowered to voice their perspectives, drawing from the challenge you presented.

The LTP tool is versatile, adaptable to any setting or medium. I'll showcase how you can seamlessly incorporate it, whether you're interacting with an individual or a group and plan to reconvene or further examine the topic. As you review the upcoming examples, grasp the foundational principle of 'Ask, Reflect, Re-ask' and recognize its cognitive impact on the engagement of what you communicate.

### Salesperson

During a product demonstration for a potential client, the salesperson introduces the unique features of the product. At the end of the presentation, the salesperson asks the client, "From what you've seen today, what resonated most with you?" The client notes down their impression.

In their follow-up meeting, the salesperson presents the note back and inquires, "You mentioned being impressed with _____. Can you elaborate on why that resonated with you?"

*The salesperson can tailor subsequent conversations around the client's specific interests.*

## Parent

After a discussion about responsibilities around the house, a parent asks their child, "What's the thing from our talk that was most interesting to you?" The child writes down their thoughts and you place it on the refrigerator door. The next day, the parent revisits it with the child and asks, "You sketched this doodle about _____. Why do you feel this is important?" *This reinforces the child's voice in family matters and opens doors for more in-depth conversations.*

## Leader

At the end of a team meeting discussing the goals for the next quarter, the leader prompts the team: "What do you believe is the most urgent priority for our group? Write that down on a Post-It note and stick it to the door on the way out." Each team member notes their perspective and sticks it to the office door as they leave.

In the next team huddle, the leader revisits these notes by selecting one and reading it out loud, asking, "Who highlighted _____? Tell us all why that resonated with you most, and then select the next Post-It note so they can share theirs. Let's hear from all of you and collaborate on moving forward."

*This engages the team in actionable steps towards their shared objectives and gets everybody on the same page, high performing on the shared objective.*

## Executive Coach

During a session exploring leadership challenges, the coach asks the executive, *"From our discussion today, what feels most pressing to you?"* The executive jots down their feelings and hands it to the coach who places it in their folder.

In their next session, the coach brings it up, "Last time, you mentioned _____. Why?did this resonate?"

*This centers the coaching around the executive's immediate needs.*

## Online Training

Towards the close of a workshop on a platform such as Zoom or Teams, the facilitator asks participants, *"From today's session, beginning to end, what are you taking home with you? What really resonated personally?"* Participants write down their answers in the Chat box and then leave the meeting.

In the follow-up workshop, the facilitator begins by revisiting these notes, displaying them all like a word cloud on a PowerPoint slide to start the gathering: *"I'm going to select a phrase one of you placed into Chat last time we met. If this is your LTP, please let us know why this is important to you so we all understand this concept from different angles. When finished, you select the next phrase and we'll all learn from each other."*

*This ties back to real-world applicability and ensures the training remains pertinent to participants.*

## Chiropractor

After concluding an adjustment session with a patient, the chiropractor asks, *"Reflecting on today's session, what felt most significant or different for you?"* The patient jots down their sensations or observations.

On the patient's next visit, before beginning the adjustment, the chiropractor revisits the note, stating, *"Last time you mentioned feeling _____. Let's discuss this further before we proceed."*

*This approach not only emphasizes the chiropractor's attentiveness to the patient's experience but also tailors subsequent treatments to address individual concerns or capitalize on positive outcomes.*

As you read over each of these examples, you too were seeing the opportunity of LTP. You felt it. I gave many examples to emphasize the simple point of LTP: Ask the question, let them sleep on it, and let them express the concept as they see it without fear of correction, ridicule or interruption.

In the symphonic realm of communication, where every note carries intent, the art of true engagement often eludes us. Words spoken, wisdom shared, yet are they heard? More importantly, are they felt? Herein lies the enigmatic dance of LTP, a method so deceptively simple, yet strikingly profound.

As an engagement strategy, LTP is a revelation, a bridge between communicator and listener, an echo of the soul's yearning to connect.

Imagine a salesperson, reaching out across the abyss of commercial exchange, seeking not just transaction, but connection. With LTP, the salesperson tunes in, listens, and evolves, evolving the dance to the rhythm of the client's heartbeat. A conversation rooted in genuine interest, where the focus is not on the product but on what the product means to the prospect

I mean, "Damn."

Parents, too, embark on the most sacred of voyages with their children. In the sea of adulting, children seek anchors, affirmations that their voices matter and their choices are valued. LTP, in this context, becomes more than a technique. It is the parent's hand, outstretched, saying, *"I hear you. Tell me more."* The refrigerator door, laden with the child's thoughts, stands testament to the parent's commitment to understanding, not instructing.

In the corporate corridors, leaders wield vast power. But true leadership is born not from authority but from understanding and influence. LTP transforms mundane team meetings into vibrant brainstorming sessions, where each Post-It is not just a task but a team member's heartbeat, an insight into their perspective.

Similarly, the executive coach, with LTP as their compass, navigates the stormy seas of leadership challenges, centering each session around the executive's most pressing need, echoing their aspirations, fears, and hopes. It wasn't about you waxing on in front of a wall of diplomas. It was about them, as it should be.

Online training, a realm often criticized for its impersonal nature, becomes a canvas of shared experiences with LTP. Every chat message, a thread in the intricate web of collective learning, each session a journey of mutual discovery. And the LTP exercise is the absolute best way to start the next meeting. Everybody shares, everybody engages, it becomes fun as the audience feels the psychologically safe learning space. Orchids bloom and Dandelions delight when we get to be ME in a WE.

And in the chiropractor's chamber, amidst the clinical precision of adjustments, LTP introduces a touch of humanity. Each session transformed from a routine adjustment to a voyage into the patient's very essence, their fears, hopes, aspirations and well-being.

LTP is a powerful tool for genuine engagement in all areas of life. It encourages communicators to move beyond routine responses and deeply connect with their audience. At its core, LTP is a commitment to understanding and impactful communication. Remember, effective communication isn't just about words but the emotions they evoke, and LTP is the key to unlocking that depth.

# THE GREENHOUSE ENGAGES

Engagement is about catching someone's eye AND holding their gaze, keeping them intrigued. The first step in this dance is Surprise, serving as the catalyst to draw attention. But attention alone doesn't cement engagement. It's just the introduction, the handshake.

The real conversation starts when Surprise intertwines with personal key elements—curiosity, relatability, and, crucially, a Challenge. When you lace your communications with familiar emotions, humor, or even social dynamics, you further deepen this connection. These tactics are ingredients for a compelling narrative.

This method sidesteps the allure of tangible rewards. Instead, it offers richer, more soul-satisfying prizes: the thrill of autonomy, the pride of mastery, and a sense of purpose.

The Challenge Wheel embodies this philosophy, championing the diversity of thought, often drawn from experts, to enrich its core Challenge.

I've placed training online for you to experience the simplicity. RIght here, right now, let's unravel how it beautifully integrates Hebb's Rule, ensuring engagement isn't just initiated but sustained.

Hebb's Rule, encapsulated by the mantra "neurons that fire together wire together," stands as a pillar in neuroscience and psychology. Donald Hebb introduced this concept in his 1949 work, "The Organization of Behavior." At its core, this rule sheds light on synaptic plasticity—how repeated stimulation of one neuron by another strengthens their connection. In layman's terms, how learning a new concept happens.

Let's break that down. Picture Hebb's Rule as the bond between two pals. Much like how spending more time together strengthens a friendship, frequent interactions between two neurons make their connection more robust.

Within the constructs of neuroscience, psychology, and cognitive science, Hebb's Rule is a cornerstone. It's been instrumental in crafting theories about neural network learning in artificial intelligence and laid the groundwork for numerous neural network algorithms.

The brain's complex structure is divided into different learning lobes, each responsible for unique functions that you can specifically cater to in any presentation of new information to another. Learning and understanding are enhanced when the multiple regions are engaged.

The Frontal Lobe is responsible for decision-making and problem-solving. For instance, when you're making strategic choices in a group setting.

The Parietal Lobe helps with understanding spatial relationships and movement, like comprehending the big picture from a map by navigating its elements.

The Temporal Lobe is crucial for interpreting audio and connecting it to past experience, such as recalling a familiar song or a past story that aids in understanding a concept.

The Occipital Lobe processes visual information. When you look at an infographic, this region helps you interpret and understand the visual data.

Engaging different parts of the brain helps everyone get a clearer, fuller grasp of a topic. Think of it this way: we all have our unique ways of understanding something, similar to walking different paths in a park. And the more we walk those paths, the clearer they become.

Now, speaking of the Challenge Wheel, its strength is making things relatable. It combines the essence of the "Cognitive 3Rs" to promote reflection and growth, and it encourages open dialogue among learners.

What sets the Challenge Wheel apart? It's harmonized with our brain's operations and emphasizes individual input. While it offers a predictable structure, it's also adaptable to different learning styles and environments. Central to its design is ensuring everyone feels supported and valued.

I was fortunate enough to write Brain-centric Design when I spent several months in Italy specifically to pen thoughts where so many innovators have sprung. On a morning walk in the hills of Lerici, I was struck by a peculiar sight: amidst the stone walls of my walkway, adorned with orchids stood a solitary dandelion, defying its mundane reputation and gleaming with a kind of resolute beauty from a crack above the sidewalk about five feet from the ground. This scene reminded me of Thomas Boyce's insightful concept, 'The Dandelion & The Orchid.' In Boyce's eyes, Dandelions are those robust individuals, resilient in the face of change. Orchids, though delicate, have the potential to shine brightest given the right care.

Drawing inspiration from this, the Challenge Wheel is crafted 'for the Orchid,' aiming to nurture even the most sensitive learners. By being attuned to those who perceive environmental subtleties keenly, this approach crafts an ideal learning atmosphere.

For starters, stress isn't a welcome guest here. The Challenge Wheel anticipates and addresses potential anxiety triggers. Its well-defined path ensures that learners always know the way forward, removing any guesswork.

Moreover, when you are Brain-centric you don't believe in dull moments. Our content stays vibrant, kindling the ever-present flame of curiosity. By aligning closely with the learner's interests, we ensure that boredom never finds a seat at the table.

Freedom, in this book, is non-negotiable. Learners are entrusted with autonomy, allowing them to navigate, understand, and absorb at their own pace, in their own style. They have brains and are invited to have fun with them.

In this world, safety isn't an afterthought—it's the foundation. With the Challenge Wheel, learners find solace knowing they're backed by an approach that values their emotional and cognitive wellness.

Lastly, the transfer of new information to another is about forming deep connections. When emotions are in play, the learning is richer. This is the Kieran Principle known as A Before E; Affect Before Effect. Emotional Connection before Business Outcome. So, instead of simply passing on information, we strive to captivate, ensuring that external distractions don't stand a chance.

In this optimized learning space, psychologically safe and tailored for every participant, the collective learning experience reaches new heights. While Dandelions are naturally resilient and adaptable, they too flourish significantly when immersed in such enriching conditions.

The Challenge Wheel, though rooted in principles tailored for the Orchid, casts a wide net, enriching everyone with deep engagement and understanding. Imagine walking into a greenhouse, where each plant, regardless of its origin, thrives. This 'Greenhousing' effect is precisely what the Challenge Wheel aims to emulate. Just as greenhouses offer the best conditions for diverse plants to flourish, the Challenge Wheel ensures every learner, by addressing the Autonomic Nervous System (ANS), feels less stress and more deeply engaged.

Harnessing the power of the 'Greenhousing' approach in business can change the game completely. Think of it as setting up the right environment, like a greenhouse, where every plant, be it an Orchid or a Dandelion, can thrive. When employees are given such an environment, they soak up knowledge faster and implement it with gusto. The result? Job performances skyrocket, fresh ideas sprout, and problem-solving becomes second nature.

But it's not just about individual growth. Training becomes a breeze because this method respects everyone's unique learning curve, making sure no one's left behind. And the best part? Resources aren't wasted in one-size-fits-all methods. With an approach that inherently fosters inclusivity, workplaces become hotbeds for diversity, paving the way for mutual respect and understanding. It's no Surprise then that employees in such environments feel valued, leading to increased job satisfaction and a drop in those dreaded exit interviews.

The benefits don't stop there. This ideal environment primes teams to work in harmony, break down silos, and amp up collaboration across the board. And as employees feel safer and more included, they're more likely to think out of the box, sparking innovations that can catapult a business forward.

Lastly, with the business world always in flux, adaptability is gold. A workforce that can quickly grasp and adapt to new paradigms is invaluable, and the Greenhousing method of presenting information in the Challenge Wheel framework ensures just that.

In essence, the ripple effect of the 'Greenhousing' methodology, inspired by the Challenge Wheel, transforms communications. Elevating every facet of business - from innovation to team dynamics, from inclusivity to lifelong learning - begins with elevating the impact of your communications. Trust the Challenge Wheel

# ENGAGEMENT IN A CHALLENGE WHEEL

Navigating the intricate intricacies of neuroscience might feel like cracking the code to a vaulted treasure, and in many ways, it is. That's where the Challenge Wheel steps in, a tool I've innovated, distilling the complexities into a relatable and actionable framework. Let's dive deep into this innovation and uncover its brilliance.

At its heart, the Challenge Wheel is more than just a structured tool—it's an embodiment of neuroscience tailored for optimal engagement. To help you grasp its intricacies, I've unpacked its elements, laying bare the perfect blend of art and science driving its design. It isn't just about information dissemination; it's about embedding those delightful moments of surprise, aligning seamlessly with how our brains naturally tick. It's the why and how behind making messages stick and resonate.

Ever noticed how we remember and respond best when our emotions are involved? That's not by accident. The Challenge Wheel taps into this fundamental truth of our nature. It harnesses the Kieran Principle, beautifully distilled into the "A Before E" concept. The idea? For any message or content to etch itself into our minds and catalyze action, it first has to tug at our heartstrings. It's like the jingle that gets stuck in your head because it evokes a feeling.

Drawing parallels to Miller's Law, which captures our cognitive bandwidth in the neat '4+/- 2' package, the Challenge Wheel isn't just about sheer volume but strategic content delivery. It intertwines the visceral power of emotions (A Before E), the simplicity of Miller's Law, and the reinforcement magic of Hebb's Rule into a cohesive communication strategy. And that is the secret sauce to compelling communication and deep-rooted understanding.

Imagine a company on the cusp of rolling out a snazzy new software system. Now, if they just dive headfirst into the technical jargon and user manuals, chances are they'll lose half the room before the first slide transition. But enter the Challenge Wheel, and the narrative takes a tantalizing turn.

Picture this: The presentation kicks off with a captivating tale about Jane from accounting, battling late nights due to outdated tools. Everyone nods, relating to her plight, feeling that pang of empathy. There's your emotional hook - the Affect. Riding this wave of connection, the curtain is then lifted on the software, showcasing its top level bells and whistles - the Effect. But that's not all. Throughout this introduction, attendees are sprinkled with delightful tidbits - that the software is like gelatin or a live demo with unexpected results, sprinklings of Surprise and Novelty that keep them on their toes.

And just when you think it can't get any more personal, this audience is nudged to ponder: *"How might this software mean one less sleepless night for me?"* That's the Challenge Question, drawing them into the narrative, making it about their wins.

Follow this up with perspectives whacking every learning lobe with professional insight as to what might solve that Challenge, and then ample time to reflect, revise your thinking with a group of intelligent novices on the subject, just like you, and finally report out to each other about what you just discussed.

The Brain-centric outcome? Not just nodding heads, but hearts and minds won over, all geared up to embrace the new software with open arms.

I've placed a bevy of training online for you to master at your convenience at https://surprised.brain-centric.com

# THE CHALLENGE WHEEL

Let's imagine, for a moment, that the Challenge Wheel is like a revamped, modern clock face. Just as an hour sweeps around a clock, our journey circles the Challenge Wheel.

Our journey starts with a stretch of 5-7 minutes, much like the short hand nudging the first few numbers. This is the time for 'Initial Thoughts', setting the stage for what's to come. As we approach the first quarter, we're invited in personally with the 'Challenge Question', making this concept all about ME.

As the clock hand saunters on, we embark on a Surprising exploration of 'Multiple Perspectives.' Picture this segment as the heart of our hour, lighting up the four cardinal points on our clock, akin to the brain's four learning lobes getting lit up like a Christmas tree.

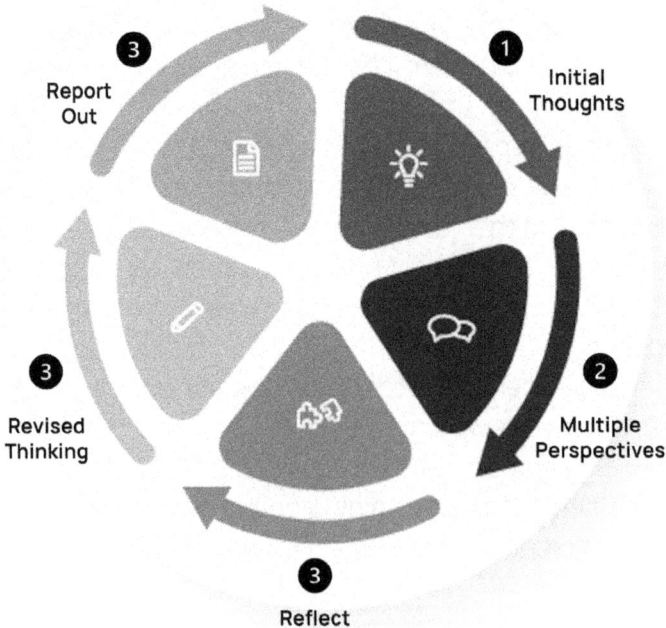

Then, about the half-hour mark, we take a brief pause—two minutes—for a 'Reflect' session. This is that moment when you catch your breath and soak it all in and write down your answers to the Cognitive 3Rs:

What was Surprising?

What did I already know, but now see differently?

What do I still need help with?

Moving forward, the clock's hand lingers around the thirty-two-minute mark, giving us a generous fifteen minutes for the audience to exchange notes, sharing their reflections.

And finally, as we near the close of our hour, groups get a good ten-plus-minute window to showcase their insights. They dive deep into their discussions about the Cognitive 3Rs and share them with all as WE, because throughout the first half of the hour it was all ME. The Challenge Wheel facilitates the shift from Me to We by its very structure.

By the time our hour—or our journey around the Challenge Wheel—wraps up, not only have we traversed an entire gamut of emotions and insights, spent half the time talking, but we're also primed and ready for the next cycle. Just like clockwork!

1. **Initial Thoughts**

   * *Big Idea*: This is the anchor point, the main takeaway. The surprise here is the revelation of a broader concept or idea that the learners might not have considered.

   * *Analogy of the Big Idea*: Analogies often act as unexpected bridges to understanding. Drawing a connection between a familiar concept and the new Big Idea is a surprise that aids comprehension.

   * *Disequilibrium of the Big Idea*: Introducing an element of conflict or imbalance grabs attention. It's like tossing a puzzle piece onto the table – it's surprising because it disrupts the initial understanding and makes learners curious about how to resolve or understand it.

* *Challenge Question*: Framing the Big Idea as a challenge is a strategic surprise. It shifts the learning mode from passive absorption to active engagement. The element of personal effort required to answer the question keeps learners invested.

## 2. Multiple Perspectives

Catering to all four learning lobes means presenting the content in varied formats: auditory, visual, kinesthetic, and analytical. Each design is a surprise for the respective lobe:

* *Auditory*: Maybe a sudden chime, song, or unexpected sound byte is relevant to the Big Idea.

* *Visual*: A startling image, a vibrant infographic, or a compelling video.

* *Kinesthetic*: An interactive activity or a tactile experience related to the Big Idea.

* *Analytical*: A thought-provoking statistic or a mind-bending puzzle.

The unpredictability of which perspective comes next and what format ensures sustained engagement. The brain thrives on variety, and with each new perspective presented differently, the learner is constantly kept on their toes.

## 3. Cognitive 3Rs:

* *Reflect*: Reflection can bring surprises as learners might discover connections or insights they hadn't previously considered. In this case, the Reflection is both timed, and its questions are specifically designed to bring the new concept in the same way the brain processes information:

- What was Surprising?
- What did I already know but now see differently?
- What do I still need help with?

* *Revised Thinking*: Encouraging learners to adjust their thought processes introduces the surprise element of change. As learners identify and rectify misconceptions, the feeling of having an "aha" moment can be invigorating. Here, learners discuss the three questions' answers with each other to gain a deeper understanding and have time to process the information while staying on task.

* *Report Out*: Going back over the learned material, especially with others, yields unexpected connections or deeper understandings, especially when learners are now armed with a more holistic view of the Big Idea and, in Report Out, are invited to articulate their findings to another. Here we share what was discovered due to the scaffolded Reflection and Revised Thinking.

We just read how Ken Yohan developed his course. Now, let's use another scenario: Rae Lyn, an electrical engineer, is going to use the Challenge Wheel to present a one hour course to students centered around basic electricity, with her Big Idea of wanting the students to deeply understand why knowing what a grounded circuit is is imperative to their chosen profession. Her measurement of success will be in the responses she hears at the end of the class during the Cognitive 3Rs demonstrating their understanding in Report Out.

Rae Lyn, a masterful electrical engineer, harnesses the Challenge Wheel for her teaching endeavor.

Picture this: A dark room suddenly lights up, not just with electricity, but with the spark of curiosity. Rae Lyn stands at the forefront, ready to embark on an hour to illuminate young minds about the very essence of basic electricity.

Her guiding star? A singular Big Idea. She doesn't wish for her students to memorize facts and figures. No, Rae Lyn's ambition is loftier. She desires that each student grasps the paramount importance of understanding a grounded circuit, especially in their chosen profession. It's not just about knowledge; it's about safety, efficiency, and professional credibility.

Using the Challenge Wheel, Rae Lyn structures her session in a way that electrifies (pun intended) from the get-go. She begins with real-life incidents, some that ended well, and others that... didn't. The air is thick with intrigue. Why did some situations end safely while others ended in sparks and disaster? The answer lies in understanding grounded circuits.

As the hour progresses, she doesn't lecture, she employs multimedia, integrating animations that show the flow of electricity, and hands-on experiments with simple circuits. The visual learners can see the flow, the kinesthetic learners can feel the connections, and the auditory learners can hear the buzz of electricity and Rae Lyn's guiding voice.

As the culmination, the Cognitive 3Rs (Reflect, Revised Thinking, and Report Out) come into play. Within the Report Out, students spoke of how they'd approach certain situations. Their answers would reveal if they've genuinely grasped why understanding a grounded circuit is non-negotiable. She listens intently, feeling the depth of their comprehension, their confidence in articulation, and the nuances of their perspective.

By the time the lights dim again, Rae Lyn's measurement of success becomes evident in the enriched, thoughtful responses echoing in the room. The real victory? She knows she's not only shared knowledge but has also instilled a respect for the unseen dance of electrons, grounding their future in both understanding and safety.

# Step-By-Step: Rae Lyn's Electric Challenge Wheel

## Initial Thoughts

- **Big Idea** - Rae Lyn introduced the concept that understanding a grounded circuit isn't just about preventing a short circuit, but it's akin to the heartbeats of every electronic device. She emphasized, "The grounded circuit is the silent guardian of the electrical world. Ignoring it is like a car without brakes."

- **Analogy of the Big Idea** - She drew a parallel between the grounded circuit and the foundation of a house. "You wouldn't see it, but without it, the entire house, your entire safety is compromised."

- **Disequilibrium** - To introduce disequilibrium, Rae Lyn showcased two devices. One with a proper grounded circuit, and another without. She then displayed what happens when both are overloaded. The difference was stark and alarming, driving home the unpredictability and danger of not understanding grounded circuits.

- **Challenge Question** - Rae Lyn posed: *"How can grounding circuits better protect you?"* Then gave the class 60-seconds to write down their PRIVATE answers. Just their thoughts on personal safety and the class about grounded circuits.

**Multiple Perspectives**

- **Temporal Lobe** - Rae Lyn played two sound bites. One of a smoothly running electric device and another with a noticeable hum and irregularities. The contrast emphasized the auditory difference between devices with and without grounded circuits.

- **Occipital Lobe** - A captivating video was shown, tracing the journey of electricity. Highlighting how grounding plays a pivotal role in safeguarding devices, the visuals detailed the damage that can occur without it, complete with animations of sparks and damaged circuits.

- **Parietal Lobe** - Rae Lyn handed out simple circuit kits. Students got hands-on, building a basic circuit. Half the room was instructed to ground their circuits, and the other half wasn't. They then simulated a short circuit, witnessing firsthand the protective role of grounding.

- **Prefrontal Cortex (PFC)** - To engage the analytical minds, Rae Lyn presented real-world statistics, detailing the number of electrical mishaps that occurred due to a lack of understanding of grounded circuits. She then presented a quick video of a group trying to solve a puzzle: "If 70% of electrical failures can be prevented by grounding, how many out of the 1000 yearly reported incidents could've been avoided?" and the discussion that ensued.

From the beginning of Initial Thoughts until now, the end of Multiple Perspectives, thirty minutes transpired.

### Cognitive 3Rs

**Reflect** - As Rae Lyn transitioned the class into a moment of reflection, she prompted them with the three reflection questions. A digital timer was projected, giving them a structured time of two minutes to ponder. Here's how the students engaged:

- **What was Surprising?** Many wrote they found it startling to realize how often they encounter grounded circuits without noticing them. Some were surprised to learn about the extensive safety mechanisms in place and the consequences of an ungrounded circuit.

- **What did I already know but now see differently?** Several students mentioned they had a basic idea about grounding in circuits, but Rae Lyn's detailed session illuminated the true depth and importance of it in their professional field. They began to grasp the broader implications and the critical role grounding plays in overall safety.

- **What do I still need help with?** A few students expressed uncertainty about specific technical aspects or wanted further clarification on how grounding could fail and the precautions to take.

**Revised Thinking**: Rae Lyn placed the students in 'Breakthrough Groups' for fifteen minutes, encouraging them to discuss their reflections. The room buzzed with energy, and the structured exchange became animated. Some students eagerly explained intricate details, while others listened intently, drawing diagrams on scratch paper or gesturing with their hands to explain their points. Many of them began correcting misconceptions they initially held, while others expanded on their understanding based on their partner's insights. It was evident that through these discussions, they were synthesizing the information, leading to those sought-after "aha" moments.

**Report Out**: Rae Lyn then opened the floor, inviting groups to share their revised thoughts. One group, who named themselves 'The Short Circuits,' described their newfound appreciation for grounded circuits, equating them to a guardian angel for electrical systems. Another group, 'Buzzed Lighthairs,' shared a real-life incident, emphasizing the importance of grounding for safety. Yet another group, 'AC/DC,' showcased a quick diagram, capturing the essence of grounded circuits and its relevance to their profession. As each group shared, the entire class benefited from the cumulative knowledge, reinforcing the Big Idea Rae Lyn had aimed to impart, all while laughing, engaging, learning, and growing.

Through the Cognitive 3Rs, Rae Lyn's students not only absorbed the key concepts but also internalized them, paving the way for genuine understanding and application. The class left feeling more connected to the topic and equipped to recognize and prioritize the significance of grounded circuits in their future endeavors.

Interwoven through the Challenge Wheel, these Surprises act as cognitive stimulants. When you masterfully employ this framework, you leverage the natural curiosity of the human brain, ensuring that the element of Surprise remains a potent tool for engagement throughout the learning process. The Challenge Wheel is a marvel and an intricate dance of predictability and unpredictability, balancing the known with the unknown and constantly propelling the audience forward on a journey of discovery.

# MORE SURPRISATION, LESS NEGOTIATION

While traditional negotiation relies heavily on logical reasoning, strategic persuasion, and transactional dialog, the emerging field of Surprisation represents a paradigm shift, harnessing the power of surprise to captivate attention, engage curiosity, and facilitate deeper understanding. Here's an argument to support the claim that Surprisation might be equally, if not more, impactful than negotiation in today's fast-paced, information-saturated world.

## Cognitive Science and the Power of Surprise

Neuroscientific research has long established the potent influence of surprise on our cognitive processes. According to a study published in the Journal of Experimental Psychology in 2018, surprise intensifies our emotions by about 400%, increasing the emotional impact of the information delivered. Not only does surprise enhance emotional engagement, but it also significantly impacts our memory and recall. In a 2016 study in the journal "Nature," researchers found that surprising events can cause our brains to create robust, lasting memories. In the context of communication, this means that Surprisation has the potential to make messages more memorable, thereby enhancing their impact and influence.

In the era of digital communication, the human attention span has been significantly reduced. A Microsoft study suggested that the average human attention span is now shorter than that of a goldfish, at just eight seconds. This reality underscores the importance of capturing and maintaining attention in any form of communication or persuasion — an area where Surprisation excels. By introducing unexpected elements, Surprisation can instantly grab attention and maintain interest throughout a conversation or presentation, making it an increasingly valuable tool in today's distraction-prone society.

**Real-World Examples**
- **Education** - The flipped classroom model, in which traditional homework and lectures are reversed, provides an example of Surprisation in action. Students are often surprised by the novelty of this approach, which can lead to increased engagement, deeper understanding, and better academic performance.

- **Marketing** - Many successful marketing campaigns employ Surprisation. A notable example is the "Dove Real Beauty Sketches" campaign, which surprised viewers by challenging societal beauty norms and the way women perceive their own beauty. The surprise factor was integral to the campaign's viral success.

- **Politics** - Politicians often use Surprisation to make memorable points during debates or speeches. For instance, during his 1984 presidential campaign, Ronald Reagan famously quipped about not exploiting his opponent's youth and inexperience, a surprising comment that defused concerns about his own age.

While negotiation remains a powerful tool for persuasion and conflict resolution, the emerging practice of Surprisation offers a new avenue for capturing attention, fostering engagement, and enhancing memory retention and reducing the need for negotiation because the communication was delivered and understood as intended.

As we wade through the era where every tick of the clock showers us with information, it's tempting to feel overwhelmed. Like standing in the heart of a bustling city square, surrounded by a cacophony of voices, each trying to tell its story. How do we ensure our voice isn't just another in the crowd but one that genuinely resonates?

Enter Surprisation: a method I've been privileged to delve into and share with you. Drawing upon our discussions of the Challenge Wheel and other cognitive frameworks, Surprisation emerges as our compass in this digital wilderness. It's not just a flashy new term but a beacon, grounded in neuroscience and tailored for our times.

**Surprisation**: The act or process of strategically implementing unexpected feelings or reactions that enhance engagement, awareness, or inspire a shift in perspective, often resulting in deeper connections or insights.

We spoke to the allure of the unexpected with the Challenge Wheel. Surprisation leans heavily into this. By introducing the unexpected, it naturally draws attention, almost like a captivating twist in a gripping novel. This isn't just a stylistic choice; it's a dance with our brain's chemistry. Surprising elements release dopamine, a neurotransmitter linked with pleasure and novelty. This not only makes the learning experience enjoyable but also enhances memory retention. In essence, it's the difference between a fleeting thought and a lasting memory.

Moreover, by consistently challenging the status quo and breaking patterns, Surprisation fosters cognitive flexibility.

**Cognitive Flexibility**: The brain's ability to adapt to new information, switch between tasks, and adjust one's thinking based on changing circumstances and environments. It's foundational for problem-solving, learning, and understanding diverse perspectives.

Cognitive Flexibility encourages us to adapt, think on our feet, and approach problems from fresh angles. It's like taking a familiar route home and suddenly discovering a hidden alleyway filled with art and music – unexpected but undeniably enriching.

I'd be remiss if I didn't address its effect on creativity. Just as the Challenge Wheel nudges us to look at issues from multiple lenses, Surprisation stimulates innovative thinking. By subtly disrupting conventional narratives, it nudges us out of our comfort zones, prompting us to view the world through a myriad of perspectives.

Yet, amidst all its merits, Surprisation stands distinctly apart from techniques like negotiation. While the latter often leans on rewards and repeated practices, Surprisation gracefully bridges gaps in understanding, reducing the tug-of-war of perspectives.

I share this with utmost humility, not as a proclamation but as an invitation. An invitation to journey together, to harness the combined power of personal touch, empirical knowledge, and the magic of Surprisation. In this ever-evolving landscape of communication, may we find our voice, ensure it's heard, and make an impact that echoes through time.

Surprisation operates by invoking an immediate cognitive response to unexpected or novel information. As a cognitive process, it's about structuring and delivering information in a manner that triggers curiosity, engagement, and enhanced understanding in the receiver's mind. It doesn't rely on external rewards or consequences, but rather on the inherent human interest in novelty and the unexpected. This not only makes the information more impactful and memorable but also facilitates a deeper understanding, as the receiver is more likely to be mentally present and engaged.

Navigating this ever-evolving, information-laden landscape of ours, we're continually in search of newer ways to grasp and retain the messages around us. Surprisation is one such innovative approach that not only captures attention but also fosters a shared understanding. I'll explain...

Imagine the delicate dance of a storyteller and their audience. The storyteller, our Surprisator, spins an unforeseen narrative, adding layers of intrigue and novelty. Yet, the story isn't entirely theirs. Each revelation is shaped, in part, by the audience's own experiences, perspectives, and cognitive interpretations. It's a mutual act of creation, where both the teller and the listener play a pivotal role. Such co-creation deepens the bond, leading to a richer, shared comprehension. This is why we love specific authors before publicity...they are our collaborators in the stories they tell. They get us.

But there's more to Surprisation than just the unexpected. It's also a tool to gracefully unveil and address any lurking misconceptions or gaps in knowledge. By presenting information in a manner that gently challenges the receiver's existing beliefs, Surprisation promotes a journey of self-reflection, coaxing individuals to uncover and bridge their understanding chasms organically.

To paint a clearer picture, envision a team leader addressing a delicate performance concern with a colleague. The traditional route might involve laying out the issue and negotiating a path forward. But what if, through Surprisation, the leader introduces the feedback in such an inventive way that the colleague arrives at an insightful realization on their own? This proactive self-awareness not only eliminates the confrontational aspect of negotiation but also encourages genuine ownership and rectification of the issue.

It's this profound intertwining of cognition, engagement, and mutual understanding that sets Surprisation apart. While there will always be scenarios where direct negotiation is required, embracing the elegance of Surprisation might just reshape how we connect, converse, and comprehend in our digital age.

Surprisation that amplifies our experiences as a cognitive dance that awakens our senses, making the ordinary feel extraordinary.

Let's dive into personal growth first. Embracing Surprisation is like shifting the lens through which you view the world. Instead of just accumulating knowledge, you begin to seek the unexpected, the startling, the new. You might find yourself watching a documentary that you'd never have picked before, or studying from flashcards filled with intriguing facts. This isn't just about Surprise for Surprise's sake. It's a strategic step to enhance memory retention and kindle a deeper curiosity.

Now, visualize your professional environment. Imagine you're about to deliver a presentation. Instead of the usual routine, you start with a riveting story or a compelling question related to your topic. Your colleagues' eyebrows raise, their attention piqued. This is Surprisation at play. And when challenges loom, why stick to the tried and true? Surprisation encourages you to look beyond, to consider unexpected solutions, and often, these are the ones that shine brightest. In your daily communications, whether it's a team meeting or a simple chat by the coffee machine, introducing Surprising elements can transform mundane interactions into memorable ones.

Transitioning to relationships, Surprisation weaves its magic here too. Think about the relationships you cherish. How about adding a dash of the unexpected? A Surprise gesture, perhaps an unplanned date or a thoughtful note. It's these unexpected moments that often leave the most lasting impressions. And during disagreements or conflicts, Surprisation can be your ally. Instead of the same predictable arguments, a Surprising response or gesture can pave the way for more productive and understanding conversations.

Incorporating Surprisation into various facets of your life doesn't just enhance your experiences but reshapes them. It's like adding color to a canvas, making everything vivid and vibrant. It's an art, a cognitive process, and as with any art, mastery takes time and practice. But the rewards, from enhanced connections to enriched experiences, are truly unparalleled.

Imagine this Surprisation process as charting an expedition: one begins with maps (theoretical knowledge), joins a seasoned crew (a community of fellow explorers), sets sail and navigates uncharted waters (practical application), and constantly updates the charts with new findings (continuous learning).

First, you immerse yourself in the rich tapestry of theories and cognitive sciences that underpin Surprisation. Consider pursuing a Brain-Centric Instructional Designer (BcID) Certification. Think of this as your compass—guiding you in crafting experiences that resonate with the very rhythm of our brains. But a seasoned explorer isn't confined to maps alone. By stepping into Brain-centric community events, and joining hands with fellow navigators, sharing stories of distant shores, marveling at new discoveries, and refining your understanding of the world of cognitive science. Here, in this melting pot of ideas and insights, Surprisation comes alive.

Next, armed with knowledge and community insights, you set sail. In your daily dialogues, presentations, or personal quests, the techniques of Surprisation find their voice. Like any seasoned sailor, experimentation becomes second nature—sometimes the winds are favorable, sometimes they challenge, but with each iteration, you learn, refine, and grow.

Yet, the ocean of cognitive science is vast and ever-evolving. So, as you gain proficiency, anchor yourself in continuous learning. Keep an ear to the ground for the latest in cognitive research—allowing it to refine your understanding and techniques of Surprisation. Consider further courses or certifications; they're like discovering new navigation tools that can unveil even more of this vast sea.

As we conclude this chapter, know that mastering Surprisation is akin to becoming a master navigator of the cognitive seas. With theory as your compass, community as your crew, practice as your journey, and continuous learning as your guiding star, you're well-equipped to chart a course that profoundly engages, communicates, and influences.

## APPLICATION BEGINS NOW

As you stand on the precipice of this enlightening voyage into Surprise, you're ready to mold it into a powerful tool of action. We're about to transition into a pragmatic guide that presents actionable strategies, integrating elements of Surprise into your dialogues and personal tales.

Place this into action immediately, inviting preludes, reminiscent of the joy in uttering phrases from a freshly learned language. See these iterations of Surprise as rituals, much like the gentle warm-ups before a rigorous exercise regimen. Always remember, Surprise isn't just an act—it's an art that demands nurture and refinement.

To unleash the power of Surprise, consider for a moment the art of storytelling. Quentin Tarantino, the renowned filmmaker, excels in weaving tales like no other. His stories, laden with unforeseen twists and riveting plots, captivate his viewers, perpetually subverting their expectations and ensuring they're perpetually engaged.

Narrowing our focus to personal relationships, even the slightest gestures infused with Surprise can forge deeper bonds. Maybe it's an impromptu date night, a heartfelt note sneakily tucked into a favorite novel, or an unexpected gift arriving just because. These acts, sprinkled with the magic of Surprise, carry an amplified emotional depth.

Continual discovery is at the heart of surprise. By constantly immersing yourself in fresh knowledge, you're bound to stumble upon revelations that both amaze and inspire. Think about delving into a hobby you've never considered before, reading a book that's not your usual pick, or simply choosing an unfamiliar path on your morning walk.

Routine has its place, but there's undeniable allure in the unexpected. Take a chance on a dish you've never tasted, spontaneously invite friends over for an evening chat, or arrange an unplanned weekend escape. These moments of spontaneity add zest to your days.

Then there are those thoughtful moments that leave a lasting impact—those quiet gestures of care. A handwritten note left on the breakfast table, a Surprise coffee for a colleague, or an out-of-the-blue appreciation message can tighten bonds and inject joy into everyday interactions.

Furthermore, don't let your beliefs go unchallenged. Consistently reflect on your values and understandings. In doing so, you're opening doors to a world of newfound insights, not only about the vast universe but also about the intricate maze that is you.

And, as life inevitably tosses its curveballs, catch them with grace. Surprise, be they pleasant or challenging, are stepping stones, carving out a journey of growth and tenacity. Consciously weaving Surprise into your narrative to magnify your personal evolution, adaptability, and sheer delight in the dance of life.

Crafting a Surprise doesn't necessitate elaborate schemes. It's a game of fill-in-the-blanks. Each of the items in the following schema have been covered, outlined, and templated within this book and there is both free and advanced training for you online. Clear your working memory and get the thoughts out and onto a schema as simple as the following:

- Identify the recipient(s)
- Understand their expectations
- Devise a Surprise to deviate from these expectations
- Implement your Surprise
- Observe and learn from the reaction

# FINISH

With countless words, messages and opinions exchanged every second, the quest to be heard, understood, and remembered has never been more critical. Whether you're a coach, educator, business executive, or simply someone yearning for more profound connections, understanding what initiates and sustains engagement offers a beacon, guiding you towards more meaningful interactions.

In "SURPRISED: The Science & Art of Engagement," I embarked on an exploration into the heart of what keeps our minds alert, eager, and receptive. And in that very brain, pulsing with all that is us, was the element of Surprise—nature's own formula to capture attention, stir emotion, and etch memories.

Every professional communicator's dream is to create moments that leave an indelible mark, to craft messages that resonate long after they're delivered. And now, equipped with a blend of scientific understanding and artistic intuition, you're poised to do just that. With the essence of Surprise as your compass, your communication will not just be heard, but it will echo in the corridors of your audience's minds.

Like every art form, the mastery of engagement is not a destination—it's an ongoing journey. A journey filled with continuous learning, experimentation, and above all, a perpetual sense of wonder. Embrace this journey with an open heart and mind, savoring every moment of discovery.

To the communicators, coaches, educators—and each one of you who opened these pages—you hold a remarkable force within your grasp. It's the might to ignite wonder, to kindle inspiration, and to catalyze transformation. By intertwining elements of Surprise in your tales, you have the capability to turn an audience of one or many into active contributors, and passive spectators into passionate champions.

As you close this chapter and return to your world, remember the potency of Surprise. Keep your eyes wide open to the endless opportunities around you—to learn, to connect, to Surprise, and to be Surprised. For in every Surprise, lies a story waiting to be told, a lesson yearning to be shared, and an experience eager to be felt.

Stay curious. Stay engaged. And above all, always stay **Surprised**.

# GLOSSARY

**Active Listening**: Fully concentrating, understanding, and responding to spoken communication.

**Adaptive Learning**: Personalizing learning experiences based on learner needs.

**Affective Neuroscience**: Study of neural mechanisms of emotion and their interactions with cognitive processes.

**Aha Moment**: Sudden comprehension or clarity.

**Anchoring**: Relying heavily on an initial piece of information when making decisions.

**Attentional Spotlight**: The brain's ability to focus on a particular stimulus while filtering out a range of other stimuli.

**Behavioral Engagement**: Participation in tasks reflecting a learner's behavior.

**Brain Architecture**: Structural composition and connectivity in the brain.

**Brain Mapping**: Technique used to study the brain's functional activity.

**Brain-Brain Synchrony**: Phenomenon where two people's brain activity aligns during interaction.

**Brain-centric Design** (BcD): A teaching model rooted in neuroscience principles, focusing on how the brain processes and retains information.

**Brainwave Modulation**: Adjusting the brain's wave frequencies.

**Cognitive Bias**: Systematic patterns of deviation from norm or rationality in judgment, where individuals create their own subjective reality from their perception.

**Cognitive Dissonance**: Mental stress experienced when holding contradictory beliefs.

**Cognitive Empathy**: Ability to comprehend another person's feelings.

**Cognitive Engagement**: Mental investment in learning, tied to intrinsic motivation and interest.

**Cognitive Load**: Mental effort required to learn a new concept.

**Cognitive Resonance**: Alignment of thought patterns or beliefs with new information.

**Curiosity Loop**: Psychological process where a gap in knowledge creates an emotional and cognitive response.

**Dopaminergic Pathways**: Neural pathways influenced by dopamine, affecting reward-motivated behavior.

**Emotion Regulation**: Ability to manage and respond to emotional experiences.

**Emotional Contagion**: Phenomenon of having one's emotions and related behaviors influenced by another's emotions.

**Emotional Valence**: Intrinsic attractiveness (positive) or averseness (negative) of an event or situation.

**Engagement Metrics**: Tools and indicators measuring the level of engagement.

**Episodic Memory**: Memory of autobiographical events.

**Eudaimonic Motivation**: Actions driven by one's purpose or profound values.

**Eustress**: Positive, beneficial stress that can boost performance.

**Explicit Memory**: Information that's consciously stored and recalled.

**Extrinsic Motivation**: Engaging in behavior due to external rewards or pressures.

**Flow State**: Optimal state of intrinsic motivation, where the person is fully immersed in an activity.

**Greenhousing**: A BcD concept; creating an optimal environment conducive for learning.

**Growth Mindset**: Belief that abilities can be developed through dedication and effort.

**Heuristic Learning**: Gaining knowledge or problem-solving through self-discovery and experimentation.

**Hippocampal Circuitry**: Refers to the intricate network of neurons in the hippocampus, a region of the brain crucial for memory formation.

**Implicit Memory**: Memory of which we're not consciously aware.

**Information Encoding**: Transformation of perceived information into memory.

**Interleaved Practice**: Mixing different topics or subjects to improve learning.

**Intrinsic Motivation**: Internal drive to engage in behavior out of personal interest.

**Knowledge Acquisition**: Process of obtaining, assimilating, and storing information.

**Limbic System**: Brain system supporting emotions, behavior, motivation, and long-term memory.

**Metacognition**: Awareness and understanding of one's thought processes.

**Mirror Neurons**: Neurons that fire both when performing an action and witnessing another perform that action.

**Mood Congruence**: Memory process where an individual's current mood determines the mood of memories recalled.

**Multisensory Learning**: Engaging multiple senses in the learning process.

**Neural Correlate**: Specific brain activity patterns tied to a particular experience.

**Neural Efficiency**: Brain's capacity to use resources effectively during task performance.

**Neural Integration**: Linking differentiated parts of the nervous system.

**Neural Network**: Groups of interconnected neurons.

**Neural Oscillation**: Rhythmic neural activity in the brain.

**Neural Plasticity**: The ability of neural networks in the brain to change their connections and behavior in response to new information, sensory stimulation, development, damage, or dysfunction.

**Neural Scaffolding**: Temporary mental structures supporting learning and cognitive development.

**Neurodiversity**: Variation in neurocognitive functioning in humans.

**Neurogenesis**: Formation of new neurons.

**Neuroplasticity**: Ability of neural networks to change through growth and reorganization.

**Neurotransmitters**: Chemicals that transmit signals across nerve endings.

**Nootropic**: Substance enhancing cognitive function.

**Plasticity**: The brain's adaptability and growth capacity based on learning and experience.

**Retrieval Cue**: Stimulus that aids recall or recognition of information from memory.

**Reward System**: Neural structures associated with pleasure, reinforcement, and motivation.

**Semantic Memory**: Memory of general world knowledge.

**Serotonin Pathways**: Pathways influenced by serotonin, affecting mood, emotion, and sleep.

**Somatic Marker**: Bodily sensations impacting decision-making.

**Spatial Memory**: Memory governing a person's knowledge of their environment.

**State-Dependent Memory**: Information learned in a particular state is easily recalled when in the same state.

**Stress Modulation**: Adjusting the stress response.

**SURPRISE**: An unexpected event that temporarily halts cognitive processes as the brain processes new information.

**Synaptic Pruning**: Removal of unnecessary neural structures, optimizing brain functions.

**Top-Down Processing**: Perception driven by cognition, where the brain applies what it knows and expects to help make sense of incoming sensory information.

**Working Memory**: System controlling temporary holding of information.

# REFERENCES

1.  Schultz, W. (1998). Predictive reward signal of dopamine neurons. *Journal of Neurophysiology, 80*(1), 1-27.

2.  LaBar, K. S., & Cabeza, R. (2006). Cognitive neuroscience of emotional memory. *Nature Reviews Neuroscience, 7*(1), 54-64.

3.  Loewenstein, G. (1994). The psychology of curiosity: A review and reinterpretation. *Psychological Bulletin, 116*(1), 75.

4.  Meyer, W. U., Reisenzein, R., & Schützwohl, A. (1997). Toward a process analysis of emotions: The case of Surprise. *Motivation and Emotion, 21*(3), 251-274.

5.  Noë, A., Pessoa, L., & Thompson, E. (2000). Beyond the grand illusion: What change blindness really teaches us about vision. *Visual Cognition, 7*(1-3), 93-106.

6.  Bear, M., Connors, B., & Paradiso, M. (2020). *Neuroscience: Exploring the Brain* (5th ed.). Lippincott Williams & Wilkins.

7.  Amedi, A., von Kriegstein, K., van Atteveldt, N., Beauchamp, M., & Naumer, M. (2005). Functional Imaging of Human Crossmodal Identification and Object Recognition. *Experimental Brain Research*, 166(3-4), 559–571.

8.  Zatorre, R. J., & Salimpoor, V. N. (2013). From Perception to Pleasure: Music and Its Neural Substrates. *Proceedings of the National Academy of Sciences, 110(Supplement_2)*, 10430–10437.

9.   Ullsperger, M., Fischer, A., Nigbur, R., & Endrass, T. (2014). Neural Mechanisms and Temporal Dynamics of Performance Monitoring. *Trends in Cognitive Sciences*, 18(5), 259-267.

10. Garrett, N., & Schultz, W. (2008). Prediction, Surprise, and Adaptation in the Prediction Error Paradigm. *Philosophical Transactions of the Royal Society B: Biological Sciences*, 364(1521), 1127–1136.

11. Mack, A., & Rock, I. (1998). *Inattentional Blindness*. MIT Press.

12. Aston-Jones, G., Rajkowski, J., & Cohen, J. (2000). Locus coeruleus and regulation of behavioral flexibility and attention. Progress in Brain Research, 126, 165-182.

13. Mcewen, B. S. (2007). Physiology and neurobiology of stress and adaptation: Central role of the brain. Physiological Reviews, 87(3), 873-904.

14. Tamir, D. I., & LaBar, K. S. (2022). Surprise enhances memory for unexpected events. Nature Human Behaviour, 6(2), 272-279.

# INDEX

## A

ability
10, 14, 21, 31, 62, 63, 68, 99, 116, 128, 141, 147, 155, 157, 171, 206, 236, 241, 247, 261, 288, 289, 296, 331, 341, 342, 345, 349

absorb
21, 100, 240, 245, 282, 315, 349

academic
137, 244, 261, 281, 330, 349

achieve
24, 49, 67, 137, 159, 178, 182, 187, 214, 215, 306, 349

acknowledged
37, 57, 206, 220, 308, 349

acknowledging
63, 64, 140, 157, 230, 301, 349

action
10, 21, 25, 27, 34, 36, 38, 53, 73, 74, 84, 85, 112, 129, 149, 171, 176, 177, 187, 200, 212, 228, 239, 241, 257, 268, 272, 277, 278, 280, 289, 291, 318, 330, 337, 344, 349

activities
119, 150, 157, 158, 166, 174, 175, 188, 216, 248, 305, 349

adapt
6, 10, 31, 42, 47, 59, 62, 81, 85, 99, 129, 157, 169, 175, 177, 179, 185, 233, 289, 293, 317, 331, 332, 349

adaptability
17, 41, 83, 85, 86, 89, 119, 140, 152, 157, 159, 162, 170, 179, 186, 205, 215, 317, 338, 345, 349

adaptable
22, 84, 86, 148, 170, 175, 215, 296, 308, 314, 316, 349

adjustment
4, 182, 183, 185, 197, 209, 224, 235, 254, 266, 276, 284–92, 310, 312, 349

adrenaline
34, 36, 38, 39, 87, 349

align
22, 27, 38, 47, 62, 78, 101, 109, 117, 187, 248, 259, 349

amplifies
6, 16, 183, 185, 197, 209, 211, 224, 235, 254, 266, 276, 285, 334, 349

amplify
51, 78, 79, 93, 95, 115, 116, 121, 268, 299, 350

**clarity**

34, 93, 99, 100, 177, 183, 185, 191, 197, 209, 224, 235, 247, 254, 266, 276, 278, 280, 285, 288, 297, 298, 341, 353

**coach**

10, 22, 25, 26, 28, 200, 215, 218, 228, 310, 312, 339, 353

**cognition**

142, 333, 346, 347, 353

**cognitive**

4, 8, 14, 18, 19, 37, 43, 47, 57, 61–65, 101, 103, 108–11, 128, 150–52, 155, 157, 166, 173, 212, 217, 230, 235–37, 242, 245, 250, 261, 288, 296, 308, 314, 316, 318, 321–24, 327–29, 331–36, 341, 342, 345–48, 353

**collaborate**

83, 85, 112, 164, 309, 353

**collaboration**

49, 64, 82, 126, 220, 251, 303, 317, 353

**collaborative**

12, 13, 49, 60, 82, 122, 201, 305, 353

**communicate**

10, 29, 41, 69, 84, 86, 143, 163, 164, 169, 181, 203, 245, 288, 299, 300, 303, 308, 353

**communicating**

8, 20, 22, 65, 162, 181, 187, 188, 300, 305, 353

**communication**

8, 10, 11, 14, 16, 18, 21, 28, 30, 45, 46, 50, 53, 57, 65, 69, 71, 72, 74, 79, 84, 86–88, 91, 103, 113, 117, 126, 142, 144, 145, 147, 162, 179, 181–83, 187, 200, 203, 212, 215, 257, 258, 270, 298, 300–303, 305–8, 311, 312, 318, 329, 330, 332, 339, 341, 353

**communications**

11, 14, 21, 46, 57, 71–73, 103, 181, 212, 217, 255, 299, 313, 317, 334, 353

**communicator**

11, 181, 187, 215, 239, 257, 268, 311, 353

**communicators**

181, 200, 215, 239, 312, 339, 353

**compelling**

11, 17, 55, 60, 78, 81, 98, 116, 121, 146, 171, 193, 229, 297, 313, 318, 322, 334, 354

**complacency**

9, 51, 81, 171, 354

**complex**

11, 12, 37, 49, 108, 110, 119, 121, 142, 144, 146, 150, 166, 175, 242, 269, 282, 314

**concept**

12, 22, 42, 43, 49, 78, 108–11, 114, 115, 121, 127, 131, 133, 138, 151, 163–67, 178, 197, 213, 216, 228, 299, 300, 303, 305, 307, 310, 311, 313–15, 318, 320–22, 325, 342, 343, 354

# F

# G

## J

**Jake**
249, 250, 361
**Jennifer**
89, 90, 361
**Jesse**
96, 97, 192–95, 206, 219–21, 232, 272, 273, 361
**journey**
9, 14, 40, 44, 48, 50, 71, 76, 93, 94, 110, 111, 120, 129, 153, 154, 161, 162, 166, 167, 170, 175, 183, 191, 198, 205, 216, 221, 228, 236, 240, 246, 250, 252, 256, 262, 278, 281, 289, 290, 293, 294, 299, 301, 302, 306, 312, 320, 321, 326, 328, 332, 333, 336, 338, 339, 361
**judgment**
53, 342, 361

## K

**Kinesiology**
155, 361
**kinesthetic**
322, 324, 361
**knowing**
19, 29, 43, 72, 103, 129, 182, 260, 276, 282, 302, 316, 323, 361
**knowledge**
10, 17, 18, 43, 44, 47–50, 58, 61–64, 72, 78, 85, 103, 107–9, 120, 128, 130, 172, 175, 178, 187, 188, 198, 213, 261, 287, 304, 306, 316, 324, 328, 332–35, 337, 342–46, 361

## L

**landscape**
6–8, 36, 57, 94, 110, 332, 333, 361
**layers**
3, 12, 13, 87, 138, 198, 333, 361
**learning**
3, 9, 12, 18, 19, 41, 42, 47–50, 57–59, 62–65, 77–79, 81, 83, 84, 86, 89, 100, 105, 108–11, 120, 121, 125, 129, 130, 142–44, 151, 152, 154, 158, 159, 161, 162, 164, 166, 167, 170, 175, 178, 179, 183, 188, 199, 212, 213, 216, 217, 236, 238, 240, 241, 245, 259, 269, 286, 297, 298, 305, 312–17, 319, 320, 322, 328, 331, 335, 336, 339, 341–45, 361
**levels**
11, 31, 37, 76, 149, 152, 286, 361

## S

www.ingramcontent.com/pod-product-compliance
Lightning Source LLC
Chambersburg PA
CBHW061041110426
42740CB00050B/2525